DISCOVERING TURKEY

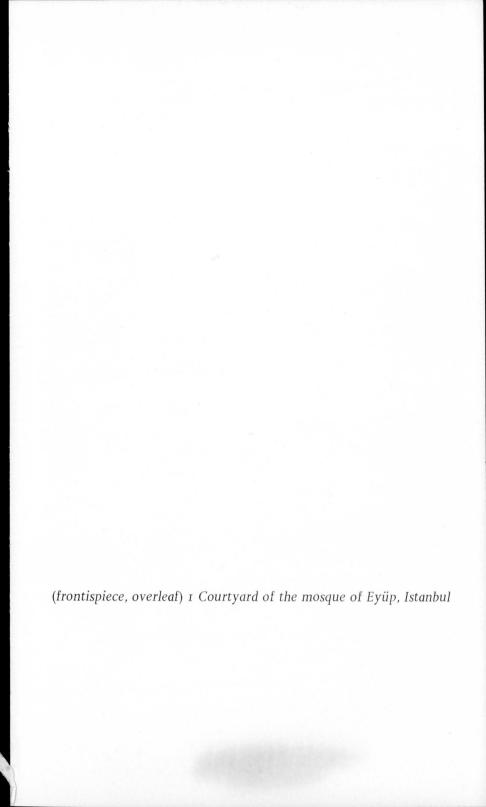

(frontispiece, overleaf) 1 Courtyard of the mosque of Eyüp, Istanbul

Andrew Mango

DISCOVERING TURKEY

Hastings House, Publishers
New York, New York 10016

First published 1971
Reprinted 1973
© Andrew Mango 1971. All rights reserved,
including the right to reproduce this book or portions thereof
in any form or by any means, electronic or mechanical, including
photocopying, recording or by any information storage
and retrieval system, without permission in writing from
the publisher. All inquiries should be addressed to Hastings
House, Publishers, 10 E. 40th St., New York, N.Y. 10016.
Library of Congress Catalog Card Number : 75-165460
ISBN : 8038 7111 2

Text printed in Great Britain by Fletcher & Son Ltd.
Plates printed and books bound by Richard Clay
(The Chaucer Press) Ltd., Bungay, Suffolk

B + T
9.95

Contents

The Plates

Acknowledgments

The Author and Publishers wish to thank the following for
supplying photographs reproduced in this book: Mr A. F.
Kersting for plates 1, 8-12, 14-16, 20, 22 and 25-28; and Mr
Nejat Sönmez, Turkish Press Counsellor, London and the Direc-
torate general of the Press, Ankara for the rest. Mr Münci Giz
and the Turkish Ministry of Tourism have repeatedly helped the
Author by providing transport and facilities during his travels
in Turkey. The Author's thanks are due to them and also to Dr
G. L. Lewis of St Anthony's College, Oxford, for reading the
typescript and making useful suggestions.

Turkish pronunciation, spelling and terms

Turkish is written in the Latin alphabet, supplemented by diacritical marks. Consonants are pronounced as in English, except for the following:

c=j in joy
ç=ch in chair
ğ is silent, but lengthens the preceding vowel
j as in French or s in measure
ş=sh in ship
y is always a consonant as in yellow

Double consonants are pronounced separately, as in Italian.

Vowels have 'continental' (non-diphthongised) values. ö and ü are pronounced as in German. The undotted ı, is a back, unrounded vowel, resembling the phantom vowel between the b and l in 'table'. It should never be pronounced as an ordinary i (as in 'pin'), lest confusion ensue, e.g. *kıl* means hair, while *kil* means clay.

Modern Turkish phonetic spelling has been followed for all Turkish proper nouns, or common Muslim terms (of Arabic or Persian origin) when used in Turkey, except that (a) accepted English spellings have been kept, as in Coran, and (b) the dot on the capital I has been omitted. In accordance with modern Turkish usage, Mehmed, Ahmed, Murad, etc., have been spelled Mehmet, Ahmet, Murat, etc.

The meaning of many Turkish place names and of all such terms as occur is given in the text, but to summarise:

şehir=city, town

köy = village
hisar, kale = castle, fortress
kule = tower
köprü = bridge
ılıca, kaplıca = hot springs, baths using them
pınar = spring
çeşme = fountain
mahalle = neighbourhood, district, quarter
hane (alone or in combinations) = house
tepe = hill
dağ = mountain
çay, su, ırmak = stream, river
dere = narrow valley or stream flowing in it
ova = plain
yaylâ = plateau
boğaz, geçit = pass
kum = sand
baş = top, chief, head
orta = middle
çukur = hollow
yeni = new
eski = old
kara = black
ak = white
sarı = yellow
kızıl = red
gök = blue
altın = gold
gümüş = silver
cami = mosque
mescit = oratory
medrese = Coranic college, seminary
şeriat = the shari'a or canon law of Islam

Nouns qualified by other nouns take the ending -i/-si (with

variations in accordance with the rule of vowel harmony), thus cami, Yeni Cami but Yeni Valide Camii; dağ, Uludağ but Ağrı Dağı. The suffix is sometimes omitted when the two words are written together, i.e. become one.

The spelling given in *Türkiye Istatistik Yıllığı 1968* (1968 Statistical Yearbook of Turkey), Ankara 1969, has been followed wherever possible.

Introduction

We live in an age when jet aircraft transport not only ourselves but our surroundings, spreading a sameness over the face of the globe. But the sameness is only skin-deep. The apartment blocks of Beirut may reflect the towers of Manhattan, but they mark the old trading frontier of the Levant and not the technological frontier of the New World. Feeling and then living the difference is one of the pleasures open to the observant traveller, and nowhere can that subtle pleasure be savoured more fully than in Turkey.

There it is added to the more obvious pleasures afforded by a sunny climate, natural beauty, the intimations of a great history, a friendly and hospitable people, and, more prosaically, a profusion of bargains in travel, food, drink and at least in some of the goods offered for sale. However, 'added' is perhaps the wrong word, for without the appreciation of the Turkishness of Turkey, enjoyment of the many other good things that the country has to offer can be marred by an incomprehension which all too easily turns to irritation. There are, it is true, travellers who succeed in shutting out Turks from Turkey, and many classical itineraries have been written in which the country has been treated as a museum, with the Turks receiving an occasional and often unfavourable notice as keepers of a vast treasure-house. But this approach will not commend itself to the sensitive traveller who will rightly see in it the sign of intellectual blindness, transforming living gold into dead dross. He will seek to connect with the reality of Turkey and will be

mortified if he fails. True, not every traveller will be as tren-
chant as Simone de Beauvoir, the *doyenne* of French Mandarins,
who wrote off an unsuccessful visit to Istanbul with the words:
'Annoyed at not being able to get beneath the décor of the place,
we left after three days.' Most others would stay on in spite of
a feeling that they were missing something essential. But it is
easier to identify the missing element as the Turkishness of
Turkey than to define it. One difficulty is that many Turks with
whom the traveller comes into contact resent the implication
that they are in any way different from Europeans, while many,
if not most, others feel that as Muslims they are obviously and
completely different. The truth is more subtle than either of
these extremes.

To a European traveller, Turkey is, of course, a mixture of the
familiar and the unfamiliar. The familiar comprises the
classical heritage, the pre-Turkish Christian past, the modern
European importations – from French bureaucracy, nine-
teenth- and then twentieth-century European architecture, to
the Latin alphabet, elements of modern technology and the beginnings of consumer society. To the familiar we could also
add the obviously European physical type of most Turks, and
the physical aspect of Mediterranean coastal Turkey. The unfamiliar includes the Turkish language, the Muslim religion
and way of life, the Turkish frontier tradition, the hard, bare
Asiatic table-land of Anatolia, the hard, lined faces of Anatolian peasants, the almost mediaeval variety of human types –
products of widely differing conditions of nurture, descent,
accident or disease, the pre-technological core of Turkish life,
the underdeveloped or Third World aspect of Turkey. But
while in much of the Third World European elements are ex-
traneous, superimposed, in Turkey they are woven into the
fabric of life, for Turkey has been both within and outside
Europe throughout its history.

Geographically and historically, Turkey is a frontier country
and the Turks of Turkey are a frontier people, influenced by

and influencing their neighbours to the east and west. Life on a frontier affords both advantages and disadvantages, advantages because a firmly held frontier is a barrier behind which human energy accumulates, fructifying the country, and this disadvantage that when the barrier is broken, not only can the land be devastated, but, more seriously, centres of creative endeavour may be permanently shifted elsewhere. In the uncertain conditions of a frontier, prosperity is perforce fitful. So, achievement and decline have succeeded each other in Turkey. In comparison, the history of Western Europe with all its vicissitudes, seems to trace a course of steady and cumulative progress. There are parts of Turkey which are now being developed after some fifty years of neglect; in others the trough of decline has lasted more dramatically since the fourteenth century or even the seventh century. Today, it is true, there are few places in Turkey which economic development has not touched, but fewer still where it has obliterated the historical configuration.

Geography and history, the two co-ordinates of the development of any human society, stand out in Turkey, establishing the place and the moment with a unique clarity, and the imaginative traveller can see not only a land and a people, part strange, part familiar, but also a living past and thus himself in history.

1. Geography and History

On a map, Turkey looks a natural unit. It has the shape of a long rectangle, covering an area roughly three times that of the United Kingdom (301,000 square miles as against 94,000 square miles), its eastern end firmly embedded in the land mass of Asia, while the north-western corner extends into Europe, not accidentally, but in order to complete the rectangle and carry westwards its physical features. Turkey forms a long bridge between Europe and Asia, 981 miles long to be exact, and 425 miles across at its widest point, separating the Black Sea in the north from the Mediterranean in the south. The Black Sea extends farther east than the Mediterranean, and so the rectangle of Turkey which is bounded by the Black Sea along almost the whole of its northern edge, has both a sea and a land frontier in the south. The southern frontier follows the Mediterranean coast for some 940 miles, and then extends inland, for approximately 560 miles along the borders of Syria and for another 200 miles along those of Iraq.

As important as the geographical position of the country as a whole, is the location and general direction of the mountain chains within it. These run from west to east, bordering the northern and southern coasts, rising as they extend eastwards, and meeting in the east in a maze of high peaks and plateaus. Thus Turkey has both a sea and a mountain barrier along its northern and southern frontiers, and a third mountain barrier covering its eastern approaches. But once this eastern barrier is crossed, there is no important north-south obstacle within

2   *Roman Statue of Aphrodite, Philadelphia (Alaşehir)*

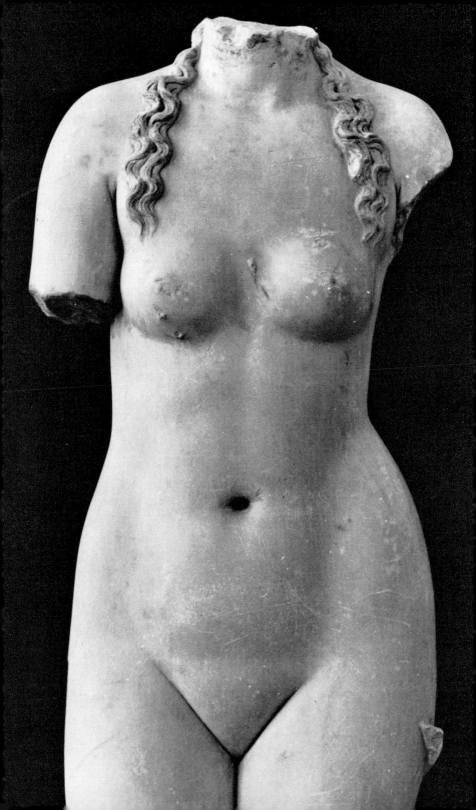

3 *Roman head of a boy, Izmir Archaeological Museum*

4 *Hellenistic head of Zeus, Ephesus (Selçuk)*

5 *Head of Hermes, Istanbul Archaeological Museum*

6 *Roman relief, Istanbul Archaeological Museum*

the rectangle until one reaches the Mediterranean and its northern extension, the sea of Marmara and the Straits. The comparison with a bridge once again comes to mind: railings along the two edges, a turnstile at one end, and a clear passage in the middle.

This physical configuration explains the ease with which invaders have moved from east to west and from west to east, the ease also with which, even in primitive times, the political and cultural influence of a capital lying on the eastern or western periphery of the rectangle could spread throughout its whole area. The word Asia, after all, was given by the Romans to the province of Ephesus which covered only the south-western corner of modern Turkey, but which was open-ended to the east. And the whole rectangle, or at least that portion of it which sticks out between the northern and southern seas is known as Asia Minor, or Little Asia, leading ineluctably to Asia proper. The Greeks, incidentally, often referred to it simply as the East, Anatole, hence the Turkish Anadolu and the English Anatolia. Today the European traveller speeding to Ankara and points farther east follows the footsteps of Alexander, of the Celtic Gauls, the Romans and the Crusaders, and, as he turns home he retraces the westward advance of Hittites, Persians, Arabs, Turks and Mongols.

The predominantly east-west orientation of the mountains, concentrated along the northern and southern shores and in the eastern part of the country, dictates the pattern of river valleys in which much of the population has always been concentrated. In western Anatolia rivers flow from east to west between parallel ranges of mountains, and their valleys – the valleys of the Gediz (Hermus), the Greater and the Lesser Menderes (Maeander and Cayster) – provide easy access to the central Anatolian plateau. In the north and south, rivers are either short, swift streams finding a quick way from the mountains to the sea (as is the case with all the rivers that have their headwaters in the southern Taurus mountains, from the Dalaman river in the west to the Tarsus river in the east, and also with many streams flowing from the eastern Pontic Alps, like, for example, the Herşit river) or, if they rise in inland parallel ranges, they have to meander this way and that, before finding a weak spot in the coastal mountain barrier, through which they can pound their way to the sea. To the second category belong most of the main rivers of northern Turkey, from west to east, the Sakarya (Sangarios), Kızıl Irmak or Red River (Halys), Yeşil Irmak or Green River and the Çoruh river. Southeastern Anatolia (south of Mount Ararat (Turkish, Ağrı Dağı) and of the Palandöken, Monzur and Antitaurus chains) is part of the Mesopotamian basin. Here rise the Euphrates (Turkish Fırat) and the Tigris (Turkish Dicle), with their many tributaries. Finally, there are isolated basins in inland Anatolia. On the central plateau, a number of small streams drain into lakes, the largest of which, Tuz Gölü or Salt Lake, is little more than a vast marsh. Central as well as eastern Anatolia is dotted with isolated mountains, many of them extinct volcanoes which attract a certain amount of rain. Draining down, this rain irrigates part of the surrounding plateau, thus allowing the establishment of important centres of population. Kayseri (Caesarea) owes its existence to the presence nearby of the 12,800-foot high Mount Erciyeş (Argaeus). In eastern Anatolia, besides the Black Sea, Caspian and Mesopotamian river basins, there is the virtually independent basin of Lake Van. Lake Van covers over 1,400 square miles, but its waters have a very high salt content and are useless for irrigation.

Asia Minor is a unit, but one that has many natural subdivisions, formed by mountain, sea or river. Across the sea of Marmara from Turkey-in-Europe or Thrace (properly speaking Eastern Thrace, in Turkish Trakya or Paşaeli) lies the old province of Bithynia, centred on the fertile plain, stretching from its capital Bursa (classical Prusa, Levantine Broussa) to the sea. Bithynia is bounded inland (in the south) by the Uludağ range of mountains (classical Bithynian or Mysian Olympus, rising to 8,000 feet), in the north by the Black Sea, and in the west by the more hilly district of Mysia (roughly between Balı-kesir and the sea of Marmara, and forming the core of the thirteenth-century Turkish principality of Karasi). Still farther west, between the sea of Marmara and the Aegean is the penin-sula of Troad (now the *vilayet* or province of Çanakkale). The Aegean coast, south of the Troad, was divided into the districts of Aeolis (round Bergama, classical Pergamum), the fertile coastal plain of Ionia (the country round Izmir, classical Smyrna) between the Gediz river in the north and the Carian mountains in the south; and finally Caria (corresponding roughly to the present-day *vilayet* of Muğla and forming the south-western corner of Asia Minor). Turning the corner, one comes to the classical districts of Lycia, where the western Taurus meets the sea, the rich plain of Pamphylia (centred round Antalya, classical Attaleia, Levantine Adalia), and Cilicia, first 'Rough Cilicia', inland from Anamur, then, farther east, 'Smooth Cilicia', (today the plain of Çukurova, whose chief city is Adana). The coastal province of Hatay (until 1939, the dis-trict or *sandjak* of Alexandretta, Turkish Iskenderun) was trad-itionally considered to be part of Syria, its chief city, Antakya (classical Antioch) being the Syrian metropolis. As for the north, the Black Sea coast east of Bithynia was divided between Paphla-gonia (which was thought of more commonly as an inland wooded province, centred on the present *vilayets* of Kastamonu and Çankırı) in the west, and Pontus in the east, leading on to Colchis (known until recently as Lazistan or Land of the Lazes).

As against a dozen or so coastal provinces, corresponding to the swift alternation of enclosed plain and divisive mountain, the inland divisions were simpler. South and east of Bithynia lay Phrygia (capital Gordium), corresponding roughly to the *vilayets* of Eskişehir (classical Dorylaeum) and Kütahya (classi-cal Cotyaeum). Aeolis and Ionia were bounded on the east by Lydia (capital Sardis); Lycia and Pamphylia were overlooked by the mountain countries of Pisidia and Lycaonia (roughly the present *vilayets* of Burdur, Isparta and Konya, classical Iconium), while the Taurus mountain country north of Cilicia was known as Isauria (today the *vilayet* of Niğde). At the centre of Asia Minor lay the districts of Galatia (centred on Ankara, classical Ancyra, Levantine Angora), and, to east of it, Cappadocia (capital Caesarea, Turkish Kayseri). The mountain country farther east was, throughout most of history, known as Armenia, while the south-eastern corner of modern Turkey was in recent times often referred to as Kurdistan or Land of the Kurds. Finally, the inland southern *vilayets* of Urfa (classical Edessa) and Mardin and Diyarbakır were usually considered part of Mesopotamia.

The frontiers of these antique districts, provinces and kingdoms were often vague, but the divisions which they represented were rooted in the geography of Turkey, so that even today geographers and travellers find it convenient to speak of the Bithynian, Cilician, Pamphylian or Ionian plains, of the Cappadocian plateau or of the Pontic or Lycian mountains. In any case, these provinces had more reality than the 67 modern *vilayets*, modelled on the post-revolutionary French *départements*, into which the country is today divided for administrative purposes. Turkish planners group these provinces into eight regions (Thrace, Black Sea coast, Marmara and Aegean coasts, Mediterranean coasts, West (inland) Anatolia, Central Anatolia, South-eastern Anatolia and East Anatolia) which have more geographical reality.

The classical districts represented not only geographical, but also to some degree national, tribal, linguistic or cultural entities. Their inhabitants were often known by national stereotypes: Isaurians were savages, Rough Cilicians pirates, Ionians wily Greeks, Cappadocians homosexuals, etc. To understand these human divisions we must turn to the history of Turkey.

The prehistory of Turkey goes back to about 7000 B.C.; history starts five thousand years later, at about 2000 B.C. The main prehistoric sites excavated so far are in the west and south of the country. This is partly due to accident, since excavations have unearthed only a small part of the treasures that lie buried in Turkey, and partly to the fact that northern Turkey was covered with dense forest which extended across the Straits into the Balkans. The forests on the mountains of Bolu, which can be seen today from the Istanbul-Ankara road, may give some idea of the wilderness that stretched over much of Turkey throughout prehistory and most of recorded history, explaining for example why the country of Paphlagonia, between Ankara and the Black Sea has always remained on the edges of Turkish history.

The main prehistoric sites which have been excavated are – from the north-west to the south-east – Troy, Hacılar (near Burdur, north-west of Antalya), cave and rock dwellings near Antalya, Çatalhöyük (literally the Forked Mound) near Konya, a mound near the south-coast port of Mersin, mounds near the Syrian frontier, and the surroundings of Diyarbakır in upper Mesopotamia. The oldest settlements – in the Antalya caves and at the lowest levels of Hacılar – were established by Stone Age people who had not yet learnt to make pottery, domesticate animals or grow crops. Agriculture seems to have started at Hacılar at about 7000 B.C., pottery at the Antalya caves and Çatalhöyük goes back to approximately 6500 B.C., while agriculture, the domestication of animals and the art of making primitive copper tools were probably all mastered in Upper Mesopotamia between 7000 and 6000 B.C. Arguments put forward by some archaeologists, including, of course, patriotic Turkish ones, to show that all these arts were first invented in Turkey, are, in the nature of things, incapable of proof. However, the great variety of geographical conditions found in Turkey, the presence within a relatively small compass of mountains, river valleys and alluvial plains, of forests and savannahs, of metal ores and clay, and the consequent richness of fauna and flora, naturally favoured the acquisition of new skills – of farming as a supplement to hunting, of pottery and then of

metal-working to supplement stone-carving. Cilicia is a miniature Nile Delta, upper Mesopotamia could well have been a
testing ground for techniques later applied on a much larger
scale lower along the course of the Tigris and the Euphrates, in
what is now Iraq. Geographically a frontier country, Turkey
was uniquely suited to be also at the frontier of human knowledge. But when the arts learnt in the microcosm of Anatolian
valleys found a large-scale application in the macrocosm of the
fertile lowlands of Mesopotamia, Egypt and Syria, Turkey was
for a time overtaken. However, it had two advantages which
showed themselves time and again. Climatic conditions – life on
a high plateau with its extremes of heat and cold, life on the
mountains, life in the forests or the need to enter forests to
hunt and forage for food – bred physical fitness into its people.
Secondly, the geographical fragmentation of Turkey, particularly on the periphery of the central Anatolian plateau, favoured a plurality of political units. The oppressive weight of
the despotisms which dominated the larger and more homo-
geneous geographical units of the Middle East, was never felt
to the same extent in Turkey, being at worst mediated through
small local political structures. The need to adapt to a wide
range of climatic conditions produced a supply of fit men; con-
flicts between fragmented societies led to a demand for them,
so that Turkey became naturally a breeding place of warriors
who, when not employed at home, could easily turn to conquest abroad.

Of the origins of the Palaeolithic, Neolithic and Chalcolithic
inhabitants of Turkey we know nothing; of their arts a great
deal. Excavations at Çatalhöyük have uncovered multi-coloured
wall paintings, including one of an erupting volcano, which has
been described as the oldest existing landscape painting. There
are also hunting scenes and pictures of dancers. Religious pictures and clay figures point to the existence of a fertility cult,
with a male Bull God and a female Great Mother, the precursor
of the Phrygian Cybele, the typical and dominant goddess of

7   *Roman theatre in the Aesculapium of Pergamum (Bergama)*

Anatolia. The inventors of agriculture and animal husbandry could easily have been also the inventors of fertility religions. At the same time, Anatolia was in the vanguard of the arts of pottery and metal-working, as witness the beautifully painted pottery and the metal implements found in Hacılar and dated to 5500-5000 B.C.

These pioneering achievements were apparently followed by a long period of stagnation, although one must be careful not to draw hasty conclusions which the discovery of new sites may well revise. While Anatolia marked time, the Near East and then Aegean Greece moved ahead, and new arts – writing, Cyclopean building in stone – seem to have been imported into Anatolia from these neighbouring regions. With writing, we come to the dawn of history and to the reappearance of Anatolia on the civilised scene.

Cappadocia was conquered or came under the influence of the Akkadian dynasty from Mesopotamia at the end of the third millennium B.C. Then, true history began in Anatolia with the arrival on the plateau of Assyrian traders about 1900 B.C. The records which they left, on clay tablets inscribed in cuneiform script, have been found at the important site of Kültepe (the ancient city of Kanesh, which is probably identical with the Hittite Nesa) near Kayseri, and elsewhere. Some names on the tablets suggest that Indo-Europeans were already then established in the country. The destruction of the second citadel at Troy between 2200 and 2100 B.C. provides another pointer to the date when Indo-European tribes first reached Asia Minor.

The best known of the inhabitants of Anatolia before the arrival of the Indo-Europeans are the people of the district of Hatti (north-central Anatolia), whose name has been given in error to their Indo-European conquerors, the Hittites. The Hatti may have spread well beyond the confines of Anatolia. It has been suggested, for example, that some at least of the pre-Indo-Europeans and pre-Semitic inhabitants of Syria and Palestine may also have been Hatti, and that the Hittites mentioned

8   *Temple of Hadrian in the Marble Street of Ephesus*

in Genesis as selling a cave to Abraham and providing wives for Esau belonged to this original ethnic substratum, rather than to the Indo-European Hittite people.

Hatti power in Anatolia radiated from the fortress of Hattusas (Turkish Boğazköy) near Yozgat, east of Ankara. Hattusas, situated on the northern escarpment of the Anatolian plateau, dominated the crossing of the two main Anatolian routes, the route from west to east (today the Istanbul-Ankara-Yozgat-Sıvas-Erzurum road) and the route from north to south (which can be traced from Sinop on the Black Sea through Çorum, Yozgat and Kayseri to the Cilician Gates and then on the Mediterranean). We know a few words of Hatti language, although not its origin nor its affiliations. It provided much of the vocabulary of the Indo-European Hittite, just as Hittite art developed round and out of the earlier Hatti art. Beautifully designed pottery and intricate metalwork which can be seen at the Archaeological Museum in Ankara (such as the disc chosen for its emblem by the Turkish Ministry of Tourism) testify to the development of the Hatti foundations of Hittite art.

With the Indo-European Hittites in control of the old Hatti city states of the Anatolian plateau, the map of Asia Minor begins to assume a recognisable pattern. Indo-Europeans provided the ruling class, but not the majority of the population, although their numbers and their influence increased as one travelled west. In the east, in upper Mesopotamia, the Hurrians, from whom the Hittites seem to have derived much of their religion, including their chief Storm or Thunder God, were possibly of Caucasian origin. However, at one stage many of them were ruled by an Indo-European tribe of horsemen, the Mitanni. The kingdom of Urartu (Ararat), round Lake Van, a kingdom which emerged later in history, is considered by patriotic Armenians to be the first political creation of their people. Whatever the truth of this assertion, the Urartians were probably the successors of the Hurrians. The eastern Black Sea coast and its hinterland were probably inhabited by wild Caucasian tribes. In south-western Anatolia, on the other hand, the Luwan tongue was a dialect of Hittite, and the inhabitants of the mountain country of Lycia also spoke an Indo-European language. In the west, the Hittites were almost certainly in contact with the Achaean Greeks. It is probable, although not certain, that it is the Achaean country which is designated in Hittite texts by the word *Ahhiyawa*. In the north-west the Hittites were probably in touch with the Achaeans' Indo-European kinsmen and political enemies, the Trojans. However, the main direction of Hittite political endeavour and artistic influence seems to have been south-eastwards, possibly because these were precisely the lands inhabited by the original Hatti people. Cilicia, upper Mesopotamia, Syria and, possibly, Palestine figured at one time or another among Hittite conquests. Apart from Boğazköy and its environs, the main Hittite sites are in the south-east: Karkamış (Carchemish), Karatepe, Sakçagözü, Zincirli and Malatya, as well as over the border in Syria (Aleppo, Hama and elsewhere). The main influences also on the Hittites, apart from that exerted by the indigenous Hatti, came from the south-east, from the Hurrians, Sumerians (the pre-Semitic inhabitants of Mesopotamia, whose language gave many ideograms to Hittite) and Assyrians. However, the resulting amalgam was a local Anatolian product like the later Seljuk and Ottoman civilisations.

The Hittites established a civilised society, under the rule of written law, developed agriculture and animal husbandry, were adept at making pottery and metal objects, including the originally rare ironwork, used silver for currency and built strong fortifications. The facial characteristics of the figures represented in their carvings are recognisably Anatolian, while the pointed hats worn by their gods presage the later Phrygian bonnet. Many Anatolian and Near Eastern place names date from their time: Adana, Niğde, Maraş, Malatya, Aleppo and others.

The Hittite kingdom lasted throughout most of the second millennium. In the south it eventually succumbed to the Assyrians, while the core of the Hittite lands on the Anatolian plateau, including the capital Hattusas, fell to Indo-European Thracian tribes who crossed from the Balkans into Asia Minor, established themselves in Troy at about 1200 B.C., and pressed east as far as the frontiers of Assyria by about 1170 B.C. Between these dates and the eighth century B.C. most of present-day Turkey, outside the south-east where Hittite civilisation survived and gradually fused with that of the Semitic Assyrians, Aramaeans and Phoenicians, seems to have reverted to primitive conditions. Indo-Europeans who had come from the east and proved a fertilising influence at their first contact with indigenous Anatolians, now came back as wild westerners. It took several centuries to civilise them.

As the Thracians invaded Anatolia, another Indo-European tribe, the Dorians, moved south into Greece, squeezing some of the Greeks eastward across the Aegean into Asia Minor. About a century later they were followed by the Dorians themselves who established settlements on the coast of Caria, south of the Maeander (Menderes). So, in the dark centuries that followed the Thracian invasion, the classical divisions of Anatolia took shape. The Thracian invaders settled along the southern coast of the sea of Marmara, in Bithynia, Mysia and the Troad, as well as inland in Phrygia and Lydia and they probably formed the ruling class in Armenia. Aeolians from Thessaly gave their name to Aeolis, Ionians from Athens and elsewhere to Anatolian Ionia; there were Dorians, as well as indigenous Anatolians, in Caria, and a mixed bag of refugee Greek tribes in Pamphylia (literally All-Tribes). Then, there were secondary settlements, like the inhabitants of Megara in Greece founding Byzantium in Thracian country. The population of Anatolia came to include Greeks of various tribal affiliations, non-Greek western Indo-Europeans, like the Thracians, possibly the remnants of the Hittites and other eastern Indo-Europeans, (especially in the Taurus region), peoples known to the Greeks as being of eastern origin, but in fact deriving probably from the Hatti substratum (in Cappadocia and Paphlagonia), peoples of Caucasian origin in Pontus and Armenia, and finally Semites in the south-east.

Soon another group of eastern Indo-Europeans was added — the Medes, precursors of the Persians and, almost certainly, ancestors of the Kurds, who have thus been part of the eastern Anatolian scene for some two and a half thousand years. But before Persian domination began, western Anatolia saw the brief flowering of two local cultures.

The Phrygian state (approximately 725-675 B.C.) was established on the north-western edges of the Anatolian plateau, its capital Gordium (today Yassıhöyük or The Flat Mound), lying just off the Ankara-Eskişehir road, near the small town of Polatlı. Phrygia is remembered by the legend of King Midas, the worship of Cybele and the ruins of Gordium and of the City of Midas (Yazılıkaya or Inscribed Rock), east of Kütahya. Phrygian power was destroyed by raiding Cimmerians, barbarians from the northern shores of the Black Sea. (Unlike the east, south-east and west, the north was a secondary source of danger to the territory of Turkey, at least until the rise of Russian power, but one to which the comparatively open country of north-western Anatolia has always been vulnerable.)

Farther south, the Lydians, and other people probably of Thracian origin, closely connected with, but distinct from, the Greeks, briefly established their supremacy over western Anatolia, until their king Croesus was defeated by the Persian Xerxes, and their capital Sardis (near Salihli, on the Izmir-Uşak road) was sacked in 546 B.C. The fact that both Midas and Croesus were remembered by the Greeks for their wealth shows that the economic potential of inland western Anatolia was finally beginning to be realised after the long interval of Thracian barbarism. In the coastal lands also, the Greek settlers had become temptingly prosperous. This new wealth acted as a magnet to the Medes and Persians, warrior peoples established in the mountain country on the eastern edges of Asia Minor and

Mesopotamia. Long-range raiding across the Anatolian plateau had always been possible, as witness the appearance of the Thracians on the edges of Mesopotamia. Now the Persians achieved a great advance in social organisation by making long-range government possible. This government was exercised through the satraps, autonomous military governors, who in turn relied on local city tyrants. But central authority subsisted in spite of the delegation of some powers. It achieved a first unification of Asia Minor and the Near East, and established a large area of peace which survived for some two centuries.

The coasts of Asia Minor, and particularly its western and southern shores, are subject to a dual pull. They are most easily reached by sea and have, therefore, often derived their inhabitants and their culture from western lands overseas. On the other hand, they are not only vulnerable to attack from the Anatolian plateau, but their economic well-being depends on unimpeded contact with the interior. In spite of their wars with the Greeks, the Persians allowed this contact to be maintained. Under their rule the Anatolian Greek city states could usually keep up relations both with the west and the east. Thus, for example, Herodotus, a native of Halicarnassus (Bodrum) in Caria, could travel not only to Greece and southern Italy, but also through the Persian dominions in Asia Minor, Egypt and Persia itself.

The Persian domination of Asia Minor gave birth to a new concept, the concept of the rivalry between Asia and Europe and to the association of despotism with the former and of democracy with the latter. Personal rule, whether by the Great King or by persons designated by him, was in fact the bond that held the Persian Empire together, and this explains why the Persian party in the Greek city states was usually represented by tyrants or, as we might prefer to call them, dictators. The fragmented Greeks, on the other hand, could maintain the primitive institution of a council of elders, which lies at the beginnings of human society, and develop it into the wider oligarchy which we call democracy.

Persian supremacy in Anatolia lasted for two centuries, from 546 B.C. to 334 B.C., when Alexander crossed the Hellespont (Dardanelles) and defeated the Persians at the river Granicus (on the southern shore of the sea of Marmara, between Çanakkale and Bandırma). Although relations between Anatolian Greeks and their Persian overlords were often strained, with some Greeks emigrating westward in search of a freer life, Greek culture in Anatolia continued to develop under Persian rule. The creative age of Ionian Greek cities – Miletus, Ephesus, Priene and the other nine – had started, it is true, just prior to the advent of the Persians. The sages – Thales of Miletus, Bias of Priene and Heracleitus of Ephesus – were contemporaries of Croesus. But the prosperity of the Greek coast lands of western Anatolia continued undiminished under the first period of indirect Persian rule, until the Ionian revolt of 500 B.C. and its defeat by the Persians. Flourishing Greek culture survived the Persian wars of the fifth century B.C. and the reimposition of Persian rule under the King's Peace of 386 B.C. So that when Alexander arrived on the scene some fifty years later, he found the Anatolian coast studded with Greek cities, whose reserves of vitality could finally come into play in the more unified, larger world which his conquests had created.

The Hellenistic period of the history of Turkey, which started with Alexander and ended with the direct imposition of Roman rule in Asia Minor in 133 B.C., was politically eventful. The struggles between Alexander's generals, which in most of Asia Minor ended in the victory of the dynasty of Seleucus, ruling from Antioch; the rise of the kingdoms of Pergamum in western, Bithynia in north-western and Pontus in eastern Asia Minor; the invasion of the Celtic Galations or Gauls in 278 B.C.; the activities of pirates along the southern coast – all these events constituted the political surface of a process whose content was the Hellenisation of much of Asia Minor, with Lydians, Carians, Lycians, Bithynians and even the newly-arrived Celts becoming gradually absorbed by the Greeks. It is in the Hellenistic age that the territory of Asia Minor came to be dominated by the two 'historical nationalities' – the Greeks and the Armenians, who remained in possession of most of the country for over a thousand years, until the Seljuk Turks finally broke through the eastern mountain ramparts at the end of the eleventh century A.D. The simplification of the ethnic picture was accompanied by a large increase in population, in prosperity and by a vast building activity. All these processes gathered strength under the Romans. The Roman provinces of Asia, ruled from Ephesus, of Bithynia, and Pontus saw several centuries of peace and prosperity, a prosperity that in much of Asia Minor remained unequalled until the Seljuks or even until our own days. The overwhelming majority of the great classical ruins in Turkey is of Hellenistic or, more often, Roman origin. The temples, theatres and civic buildings in the show places of Turkish classical tourism – Pergamum, Ephesus, Priene, Didyma, Hierapolis, Perge, Side, Aspendus and the rest – date back in most cases to these two ages. And even where, as in Troy, a city had decreased in importance in late classical times, it is still the Roman theatre which usually constitutes the most complete surviving monument.

Roman rule unified the territory of the present Turkish Republic and attached it to what we would call today the western world. The political frontier with Asia moved east, to Mesopotamia, where Roman progress was halted by the Parthian rulers of Persia. Much of Turkey is fertile, the country is reasonably well endowed with natural resources, its inhabitants have often been in the vanguard of human progress. But the prosperity of the country has repeatedly been destroyed when Anatolia found itself astride an embattled frontier, when government was too fragmented or too weak to control malefactors to whom the broken terrain of Turkey can so easily give shelter, or when the land was used solely as a reservoir of human and material resources, abused by distant rulers. By

9 *St Peter's grotto in Antioch (Antakya)*

10 *(overleaf) St Sophia, Istanbul—interior with Ottoman pulpit and shield*

guaranteeing the external security of the country and by imposing on it an effective central administration, the Romans removed two of the main obstacles to the realisation of its potential. As for the third, some of the wealth of Anatolia was, it is true, syphoned off to the capital, particularly in the early stages of Roman rule. But as the centre of gravity of the Roman Empire shifted to the east, and as great metropolitan centres – Ephesus, Antioch, Nicomedia (Izmit), Nicaea (Iznik) and finally Constantinople – developed locally, wealth, the 'plus-value' beloved of the Marxists, came to be consumed largely within the confines of the country.

It took the Romans a long time – from the battle of Magnesia (Manisa) in 190 B.C. to the defeat of King Mithridates of Pontus in 66 B.C. – to unify the whole of Asia Minor under their rule. From then on, until the plundering expeditions of the Goths in the middle of the third century A.D., Anatolia was a safe land. Then enemies moved in, usually to plunder: the Goths, the Scythians, the Persians, the Arabs, a whole range of Turkish tribes, the Slavs, the Normans, the Latins. Subsequently parts of Turkey were to enjoy great prosperity – Constantinople and its environs in Byzantine times and then, as Istanbul, under the Ottomans; central Anatolia under the Seljuks. But the achievement of the Romans in ensuring the prosperity of the country as a whole has not been equalled. True, fitfully under the Byzantines and then for longer stretches under the Ottomans, the country was reunified, but only to have its resources and its energy used up in ceaseless wars on or beyond its frontiers.

Roman rule, so important in the history of Turkey, left a mass of monuments, statues and inscriptions. The largest surviving Roman inscription is at the temple of Augustus in Ankara, the so-called Monumentum Ancyranum. The most complete surviving Roman theatre is at Aspendus near Antalya. For a long time, the Romans also gave their name to the country and to its inhabitants. Constantinople was the New Rome, the Byzantine emperors were officially Roman emperors, their

Christian subjects were Romans, *Romaioi*. In the late Middle Ages, the surviving fragments of the Byzantine empire in the Balkans, the Aegean islands and Constantinople with its environs were known in the west as Romanie, a designation that was only in modern times restricted to the old Roman border province of Dacia, between the Carpathians and the Black Sea. To the Arabs, the Byzantine empire was the land of Rum, its inhabitants and the adherents of its official Eastern Orthodox faith were known as Rumis. Since Byzantine provinces south of the Taurus were quickly overrun by Muslim Arabs, the term Rum came to mean, in the first place Anatolia, and also territory to the west of it. After the Seljuk Sultan Alpaslan had defeated the king of Rum, i.e. the Byzantine Emperor Romanos Diogenes, at the battle of Malazgirt in 1071, the Seljuk kings who established their capital in Konya became known as Sultans of Rum. One of their most illustrious subjects, the great Muslim mystic poet Mawlana Jalal al-Din (in Turkish spelling, Mevlâna Celalettin), was surnamed Rumi. Later, roughly from the end of the twelfth century, western writers began to call Asia Minor Turkey (Turchia); later still, the Turks took over from the Greeks the word *Anatole* (the East) and Turkicised it Anadolu, restricting to the Balkans the designation of land of Rum, in Turkish Rum-ili, later Rumeli. As a national description Rum continued to be used by the Turks to designate their Eastern Orthodox subjects, Greek or Slav, but mainly the former, both in Anatolia and in the Balkans. The Greeks called themselves *Romaioi* until they were told by Greek nationalists that they were really Hellenes. Today Rome survives in Turkey in 'Rum' the name given by the Turks to the 20,000 or so Greeks left in Istanbul, and in the Arab Levant in 'Rumi', the designation of Arabs belonging to the Eastern Orthodox church.

What the Romans did not leave behind was their language. For centuries, under Roman as well as Byzantine rule, Latin was used in the territory of Turkey alongside Greek as one of the two official languages. Masses of bilingual inscriptions in Latin

and Greek, the Latin usually preceding the Greek, have survived
from this period in all the major classical sites. Then Latin disappeared from official use while among the people it had never
caught on. But words of Latin origin are legion (or should one
say in Turkish *lejyon*?) in modern Turkish : early borrowings
through Arabic or Greek (like the Turkish word for table, *masa*,
from *mensa*) then loan words from Italian (mainly shipping,
military and commercial terms) and French, and finally a flood
of international technical, and generally, 'modern' terms.

Christianity, which of course came under the Romans, has
also more or less disappeared from Turkey, the last important
local Christian communities leaving the country in the exchange
of minorities after the First World War. Before the advent of
Christianity, Anatolian religion – with the possible exception
of that of the Hittites, whose main gods were male – was marked
by a predilection for goddesses, a worship of fertility being perhaps natural in one of the main agricultural areas of the civilised world. In north-western Anatolia the principal local deity
was the Phrygian Great Goddess Cybele; in the south-east, with
its mountainous hinterland, she merged into the hunter goddess
Artemis/Diana, whose main temple was in Ephesus; in the east,
among the Armenians, it was Anahita/Aphrodite/Venus who
had pride of place. Zoroastrianism and its offshoots Mithraism
and, after the birth of Christianity, Manichaeanism, also had
their followers. The sun god Mithras was represented in Anatolian Phrygian dress, and his cult is said to have been introduced into Rome by captive Anatolian Cilician pirates in the
first century B.C.

Anatolia was inevitably one of the first areas of Christian
missionary endeavour. Among the languages which Christ's
disciples miraculously learned to speak at Pentecost (Acts 2,
9-10) were those of Cappadocia (probably Armenian), Pontus
(the Laz tongue), Asia (Anatolian vernacular Greek), Phrygia
(did Phrygian survive, or was the Celtic language of the Gala-
tians meant?) and Pamphylian (possibly the local language

which, we know, survived into classical times at least in Side).

Christianity spread to Anatolia, first to its great cities, with their important Jewish communities, and then to the country-side – almost immediately after the crucifixion. Tradition – or at least one tradition – reports that the Virgin Mary and St John the Apostle (identified with St John the Divine) migrated to and died in Ephesus, where the ruins of the great basilica of St John and the restored house of the Virgin Mary are to be seen today. Tradition has also St Peter worshipping with the first group of Christian converts in a cave outside Antioch (Antakya), the site today of the Grotto Church of St Peter. St Paul, born in Tarsus in Cilicia, certainly travelled through the length and breadth of Anatolia, staying in Myra (Demre) and Patara in Lycia, Perge in Pamphylia, Pessinus and Ancyra (Ankara) in Galatia, Iconium (Konya) in Lycaonia, and in Miletus, Ephesus, Adramyttion (Edremit) and Assos in the western Anatolian Roman province of Asia. Three of his epistles were written to Christian congregations in Anatolia – in Ephesus, in Galatia and in Colossae (near Denizli); Timothy, who had an epistle addressed to him, was the first Christian bishop of Ephesus. St Peter's first epistle was addressed to all Christians in Anatolia, 'to the strangers scattered throughout Pontus, Galatia, Cappadocia, Asia and Bithynia'.

The earliest known separate written account of a Christian martyrdom, the genuineness of which is unquestionable, also comes from Anatolia, in the shape of a letter from the Church of Smyrna relating the burning of its Bishop St Polycarp (c. A.D. 155, in the reign of Marcus Aurelius). The letter states that St Polycarp was 'together with those from Philadelphia (Alaşehir), the twelfth martyr in Smyrna'. He was condemned to death by the Roman Proconsul for refusing to swear 'by the genius of Caesar', i.e. for refusing to deify the state.

After the Emperor Diocletian had fixed his seat of government in Nicomedia and effected the first division of the Roman Empire (A.D. 292), its centre of gravity moved to the eastern

11 *Byzantine Cisterna Basilica (Yerebatan Saray), Istanbul*

12 *The land walls of Istanbul near Adrianople Gate (Edirnekapı)*

13 *The walls of Heracleia ad Latmum on Bafa Lake, western Turkey*

half, of which Anatolia was the core. Between A.D. 292 and the loss to the Muslims of what are now the Arab countries of the Near East and North Africa (A.D. 633-709), the territory of Turkey was the centre of the civilised world. Diocletian is remembered for his persecution of the Christians, who were numerous throughout his dominion. But one of his protégés, the Armenian king Tiridates (Tirdad) was converted to Christianity by an Armenian from Caesarea (Kayseri), St Gregory the Illuminator, and anticipated Constantine by being the first king to make Christianity an official religion.

The complete conversion of Anatolia took, of course, more than Constantine's decision in A.D. 311 to give Christianity official recognition on an equal footing with paganism, more even than the efforts of Emperor Theodosius 1 from A.D. 380 onwards to make Christianity the only permitted religion in the state. There were certainly pagans in Anatolia in the reign of Justinian (A.D. 527-565), so that we can assume that the disappearance of paganism from the territory of Turkey did not antedate by much the emergence of Islam. In fact, in Harran, (near Urfa, in south eastern Turkey), which the Fathers of the Church called 'the heathen city', paganism survived the Muslim conquest and was not extirpated until the eleventh century. However, from Constantine to the irruption of Seljuk Turks in the eleventh century, the territory of Turkey was predominantly a Christian country. Thus the history of Turkey as a whole counts at least eight Christian centuries. But since the history of the country is often synonymous with that of its capital, the Christian period can be extended from A.D. 330 when Constantine fixed his capital in Byzantium, to 1453 when Constantine's city was conquered by the Turks.

The importance of the territory of Turkey in the history of Christianity has been immense. The first seven Councils of the Church, recognised by Catholics and Eastern Orthodox alike, were all held within it; two, including the first, in Nicaea (Iznik), three in Constantinople, one in the capital's Asiatic suburb of Chalcedon (Kadıköy), and one in Ephesus. It was at these Councils that the Catholic faith was gradually defined. It was also Christians from Anatolia, Greek Fathers like St Basil the Great (born in Caesarea in 329), his contemporary and fellow-Cappadocian St Gregory Nazianzene (born in Antioch in 347), who helped to put down the brief pagan revival under the Emperor Julian, and developed Christian forms of worship, spirituality and philosophy. Certainly from the time of St Paul, Christianity, whatever its appeal to the underprivileged, was never without its intellectuals. But in fourth-century Anatolia, it was Greek intellectual thought that became the dominant influence in it, and, to borrow a term from the vocabulary of modern Greek nationalists, Hellenic-Christian civilisation took shape.

The thought of these early Anatolian Fathers of the Church was defined in opposition to heresies which were also often centred in Anatolia. Arius wrote his heretical works in Nicomedia and was repudiated by the Church in the neighbouring Bithynian city of Nicaea, in spite of which his followers were briefly in control of Constantinople. Nestorius started his heretical career in Antioch, was for a short time Patriarch of Constantinople and was condemned at the Council of Ephesus in 431. His last remaining followers, the so called Assyrians, survived in the south-east Anatolian mountains of Hakkâri until the First World War, when they sided with the Allies and had to flee the country. The rival sect of Monophysites, condemned at Chalcedon in 451, still has a few adherents in Turkey, who are known in the west as Jacobites and call themselves Syrians of the Old Rite (Süryani-yi Kadim). They speak, or spoke, Arabic among themselves, used Syriac in their liturgy, and have an archbishop residing in a monastery near Mardin, in southeastern Turkey.

It has been claimed that the special reverence paid to the Virgin Mary in the Catholic and Eastern Orthodox churches derives from the Anatolian cult of the Great Mother/Cybele/

Artemis/Anahita/Aphrodite, and much is made of the fact that the divine maternity of Mary was defined in Ephesus, the site of the Great Temple of Artemis. This disregards the fact that the Council of Ephesus, like those of Nicaea before and Chalcedon after it, was concerned with defending the integrity of Christ and that the honour paid to the Virgin Mary by the Fathers in Ephesus was a logical consequence of this defence. In fact, Anatolian Christians were, if anything, more careful than Catholics in the west to honour the Virgin Mary always within the context of the worship of Christ, while their resolute opposition to statues in churches, as distinct from two-dimensional images, sprang from a conscious repudiation of the pagan heritage.

The virtual disappearance of Christianity from Turkey tends inevitably to produce a foreshortening of history and false perspectives. Outside Istanbul, the traveller today sees few memorials of the Christian centuries – the church of St Sophia in Trebizond (Trabzon), turned today into a museum like its famous namesake in Istanbul; a few ruined churches and monasteries, as at Ephesus, Alahan in the Taurus mountains, Göreme near Ürgüp, at Sumela, near Trabzon and elsewhere; Armenian ruins at Ani and Ahtamar; less conspicuous Byzantine structures preserved as mosques, or as bridges and fortifications, where they are usually overlaid by Seljuk and Ottoman Turkish repairs and extensions. It adds up to little in comparison with the acres of Hellenistic and Roman antiquities, and outside the tourist showplaces and scheduled archaeological sites, time and the building activity accompanying economic development are completing the destruction of buildings which to the local inhabitants are the products of an alien and irrelevant culture. As for the smaller works of art, such as icons, carved ivories and manuscripts, they have all but disappeared from Turkey, where the Christian art departments of museums have to content themselves largely with cemetery sculpture.

Nevertheless, the few surviving monuments of Christian art

are impressive by anyone's standards. St Sophia in Istanbul alone is an unequalled museum of Byzantine art from A.D. 537, when the fabric of the church was completed, to the reigns of the Palaeologi (thirteenth-fifteenth centuries), when the church was decorated with some new mosaics. In fact, every phase of the great tradition is represented in Turkey by its most striking work – from the ruins of the fifth century basilica in Ephesus to the fourteenth century frescoes in Kaariye Cami in Istanbul. But perhaps nothing illustrates more vividly the continuity of Roman Byzantium up to the time of Turkish conquest and beyond, than the great land walls of Istanbul. Built largely under Theodosius II (A.D. 408-450), they protected the seat of an immensely centralised government which had its apex in the Byzantine imperial court. Unbreached until 1453, they remind us of the military function of the Byzantine empire as a frontier state of Christendom. From Constantinople eastwards to Theodosiopolis (Erzurum, its Turkish name still preserving that of Rome), the empire stretched over most of the territory of Turkey. However, the frontier was everywhere: round the impregnable walls of Constantinople, no less than outside the walls of every important Anatolian city, most of which changed hands repeatedly during the history of the Empire. Many of the assaults which Constantinople withstood devastated large portions of Anatolia. The prosperity of the capital was, however, more or less continuous until 1204, when the accumulated treasure of centuries was pillaged by the Latins.

We can distinguish several phases in the history of the Byzantine empire. There was, first of all, the late Roman period, which reached its apogee with the reconstruction of a universal Roman Empire under Justinian the Great, and ended in the seventh century with the Slav breakthrough in the Balkans and the Arab breakthrough in the east. At this point the Empire nearly came to an end. But it was saved by the great Iconoclast, or image-breaking Emperors (716-787; 814-843), the first of whom, Leo III (the Isaurian, i.e. a native of the Taurus country north of Silifke, a country which was later to be known as Karamania), repulsed the Arabs from Constantinople in the decisive siege of 717. While the survival of the Empire was thus assured, wars with the Arabs continued. The country south of the Taurus was ruled and largely peopled by Muslims. The influence of the Caliphs and Muslim emirs was strong in the frontier kingdom and principalities of Armenia. Much of Cappadocia was devastated. It was western Anatolia that had now become the anchor of the Byzantine empire and, as the Arab Abbasid Caliphate in Baghdad gradually fell prey to dissension and decay, it was from western Anatolia that the Byzantine emperors with their motley armies of mercenaries, many of them recruited from tribesmen in the steppes of southern Russia, moved east again. In the tenth century, most of what is now eastern and south-eastern Turkey was reconquered by the Byzantines. But the character of these lands had changed. Devastated eastern Cappadocia was repeopled by Armenians. Armenians in the east and Slavs in the Balkans had, in any case, become the two dominant nationalities of the Byzantine empire. The Byzantine reconquest of Cilicia, northern Syria and western Mesopotamia (corresponding roughly to the modern *vilayets* of Adana, Hatay, Gaziantep and Urfa) was also followed by an expansion of Armenian settlement in the region. At the same time Byzantine rule was reimposed on Armenia proper, the capital Ani (lying today just inside Turkey, on the Soviet frontier) passing into Byzantine hands in 1045 and Kars in 1064.

The great Arab expansion of the seventh century had taken place just as the Byzantine reconquest of the Near East from the Persians had been completed by the Emperor Heraclius the Great. So too, no sooner had the Byzantine emperors recovered their southern and eastern marches, becoming once again masters of roughly the whole of the present territory of Turkey, than the Seljuk Turks appeared on the scene and the final elimination of Roman-Byzantine-Christian rule began. In 1064 the Byzantines were masters of Kars, as well as of Cilicia, Antioch, Edessa (Urfa) and Melitene (Malatya). True, Seljuk raids against Byzantine territory had started in 1045, but after each raid the Turcomans, led by their Seljuk chiefs, had withdrawn to their bases in northern Persia. All this was changed by the victory won by the Seljuk Sultan Alparslan over the Byzantine Emperor Romanos Diogenes in Malazgirt (north of Lake Van, in the present *vilayet* of Muş) in 1071. As Claude Cahen, the historian of Seljuk Turks, puts it 'henceforward there would no longer be any need to return'. By 1073 the Turks had raided as far west as Miletus on the Aegean. They acted either on their own or as supporters of Byzantine factions in the internal feuds which tore the Empire apart. It was in fact the Byzantine, Nicephorus Botaniates who established the Seljuk Süleyman, son of Kutlumuş, in Nicaea in 1078. It was equally Byzantine faction which in 1084 allowed Süleyman to occupy Antioch without a fight. At first, the Seljuk Sultans Alpaslan and Melikşah do not seem to have contemplated the permanent annexation of Anatolia. But Byzantine rule there had broken down permanently, the frontier had moved west and with it the Turcomans, the new frontiersmen of Islam. Moving unruly tribes to the frontier and beyond was, in any case, a measure essential alike for the self-aggrandisement and the self-preservation of rulers of settled lands.

Byzantine rule in Constantinople was to survive the loss of upland Anatolia by almost four centuries. But long before 1453 the Byzantines had ceased to be the champions of Christendom in the frontier conflict. That role fell to the Latins – Catholics from western and southern Europe – whom the Byzantine Emperor Alexius Comnenus called to the rescue. Only 24 years separate Malazgirt from the preaching of the first Crusade in 1095. However, although the crusaders crossed Asia Minor, they did not stay there. They caused confusion among the Muslims and killed a certain number of them, but over the greater part of the country they did not prevent the Turks, who were still semi-nomadic, from returning when the crusaders had left. What the Crusades did was to delay by some two centuries the establishment of Turkish rule and of Turkish settlement on the edges of the plateau. Nicaea, which the Turks had captured in 1097, did not revert to them until 1330. The Black Sea coast, the Aegean coast, Pamphylia, Cilicia, Antioch, Edessa, all had an extra bonus of Christian rule.

In the north and west of the Anatolian lowlands, the rulers were Greek, although Italian influence gradually grew. In the south-east, the Byzantines were replaced by Armenians or Latins. Thus Adana, the chief city of Cilicia, which the Crusaders occupied in 1097, passed into the hands of the Armenians, who kept it, with brief intervals, until finally overwhelmed by the Turkish Mamluks of Egypt in 1359. Antioch was ruled by Latin princes from 1098 to 1268 when, likewise, it passed to the Mamluks. But in central Anatolia, Konya, which the crusaders had captured, quickly reverted to the Turks, becoming after the loss of Nicaea the principal place of residence of the Seljuk Sultan Kılıç Arslan, the son of Süleyman. Thereafter, Konya remained the main centre of the Seljuk Sultanate of Rum.

Although the Turcomans were thus driven back from the Anatolian coast, the Sultanate of Rum did not long remain land-locked. At the beginning of the thirteenth century the Seljuk Sultans established themselves firmly at Sinop on the Black Sea, and from Antalya to Anamur on the Mediterranean. Sinop and Antalya both became centres of overseas trade, while in the Mediterranean seaport of Alanya the surviving ruins of a Seljuk shipyard show that the transition from overland raiding to seafaring did not take long to accomplish. Indeed, even earlier, Çaka, one of the first Turcoman chiefs to penetrate to the Aegean coast at the end of the eleventh century, had established himself as a redoubtable pirate.

On land as on sea, razzias were separated by intervals of peaceful intercourse. The Turcomans had after all been drawn west by Byzantine intriguers, used to buying the support of

warlike nomads. The fact that from temporary allies the Turcomans had become the permanent successors of the Byzantines
in much of Anatolia, did not prevent intercourse between Rum
and Byzantium. Seljuk princes worsted at home, spent their
exile in Constantinople, while Byzantine exiles found refuge
in Konya. Turcoman princes forged dynastic alliances with
Greek ruling families from Constantinople and Trebizond. Nor
were the Turks' relations with the Latins invariably warlike.
From the eleventh to the fifteenth centuries, Byzantine, Turcoman, Armenian, Latin, Arab and Kurdish princes – and later
the Mongol overlords of some of them – all fitted into a feudal
pattern in which alliances and wars, trade and raids succeeded
each other with great rapidity. These kaleidoscopic changes
signalled the transition from one great Empire, that of the
Byzantine successors of Rome, to another, that of the Ottomans.
During these four centuries the ethnic makeup of Anatolia
underwent a gradual, but profound transformation, which can
best be described as the birth of Turkey in the north-eastern
corner of the Mediterranean world. The Crusaders, who first
impeded the process, may have accelerated it later by their
capture and sack of Constantinople and the subsequent dismemberment of the Byzantine Empire, although the transfer of
the Byzantine capital to Nicaea did briefly consolidate the
Greek presence in the north-western corner of Asia Minor. After
the enthusiasm of the Crusaders had died down, and until the
Ottomans began to threaten Catholic Europe, the Latins were
more concerned with trade and with containment than with
the expulsion of the Turks from Anatolia.

Today the main surviving monuments of Latin endeavour
remind us of these two purposes. The tower of Galata in Istanbul overlooked a Genoese merchant colony which grew up as
a self-governing suburb of Byzantine Constantinople across the
Golden Horn. The castle of St Peter at Bodrum (the ancient
Halicarnassus) on the Aegean, was built by the Knights Hospitallers at the end of the fourteenth century to defend the

approaches to Rhodes. The older Kızkalesi (Maiden's Castle) on
a small off-shore island near Silifke, served the same purpose
with regard to the defence of the Crusader kingdom in Cyprus,
as well as providing a link with the Armenians of the hinterland.

However, it was not on the periphery but in the heartland of
Anatolia that the seeds of the future were being sown. The
Turcoman breakthrough after 1071 had led to two developments: the creation of a basically Turkish Turkey and a re-
markable growth in the prosperity of the Anatolian uplands.
Both developments were surprisingly rapid. Until the Mongol
invasion in the middle of the thirteenth century, the Turks
probably formed a minority of the population of the country.
One source puts them at as little as one tenth of a population
still largely made up of Anatolian Greeks, Armenians and, in
the south east, Jacobite Syrian Christians. But it was the Turks
who set the tone, and their numbers grew constantly as a result of intermarriage and conversions, as well as of new arrivals.
The towns, in particular, quickly took on a traditional Islamic
aspect, and because the Seljuks had come to Turkey through
Persia and had been formed by Islamic Persian culture, it was
Persia rather than Greece or Rome which gave its civilisation
to the renewed and expanded towns of inner Anatolia. Two
of these towns – Erzincan and Erzurum – probably had at first
more Armenian than Turkish inhabitants, but the rest (and
there were many of them, even if not quite one hundred, as
one thirteenth-century traveller related) were predominantly
Muslim, and one – Aksaray – purely so. The building activity
of the Seljuks was prodigious: in all places of importance they,
of course, built or rebuilt castles and other fortifications, while
most towns were dotted with new mosques, Coranic colleges
(*medreses*), hospitals, mausolea, dervish monasteries, bath-
houses, markets and inns. Anatolia became an important centre
of Islamic learning and literature. On the main roads, fortified

caravanserais were provided for the comfort and safety of travellers.

At the time of the First Crusade, central Anatolia was largely a devastated country. A hundred to a hundred and fifty years later, it was flourishing, in spite of the Second Crusade, of the existence of roaming Turcomans in the countryside and of lively struggles among Seljuk princes in which the Turcomans took part. Several factors accounted for the sudden prosperity of the country, which was reflected in the flowering of urban life. In Byzantine times most of the land had been divided into large estates and farmed inefficiently on behalf of absentee landlords, the revenue being creamed off to Constantinople. In the more settled conditions introduced by the Seljuks, husbandry improved and the proceeds were consumed locally. The arrival of the Turcomans led to an extension of stockbreeding in a country eminently suited to it, while also increasing the labour force in what had been an under-populated area. Contemporary travellers mention the abundance of fruit trees, and a lively export trade in timber and minerals. The Seljuk conquest linked Anatolia with the Muslim world, without severing its links with the west. The country was visited by merchants from Persia and the Arab lands, as well as from Italy, southern France and Russia. The Seljuks themselves traded across the Black Sea and had a commercial settlement in the Crimea. The economic potential of Anatolia was so large that a little peace and stability and the absence of outside exploitation sufficed to create a golden age, which has left more monuments than the preceding era and more impressive ones than the one which succeeded it.

A close reading of political happenings in the twelfth and thirteenth centuries could in fact lead us to doubt that there was any peace at all in Asia Minor. But most of the dynastic struggles, the Second and Third Crusades, the intermittent fighting on the marches with Byzantium, Trebizond and the Armenians of the Taurus, did not impede the economic development of inner Anatolia. However, the absence of outside exploitation, which followed this development, was brief. In 1243 the Mongol hordes defeated the army of the Seljuk Sultan Keyhüsrev II at the battle of Kösedağ (in the province of Erzincan), sacked Erzurum and Kayseri, and occupied Sivas which was, after Konya, the second city of the kingdom. The power of the Seljuks was broken and Anatolia was constrained to pay heavy tribute to the Mongol Great Khan. At first Mongol rule was indirect, but the emergence of the Mamluks in Egypt as the Mongols' main adversaries in the Near East forced the latter to consolidate their rear. From 1278 onwards Mongol control was tightened. Nor was that control either uniform or stabilising. For the Ilkhanid Mongol dynasty, now established in north-western Persia, on the edges of Anatolia, was riven by faction which naturally spilled over into the former Seljukid dominions. To fighting between Mongols and Mamluks, much of which took place in the territory of Turkey, and to the struggles among the Mongols, was added a new and crucial factor – the rising power of the Turcomans.

It was the Turcomans who had conquered the Anatolian plateau for their chiefs, the Seljuks. But in the Seljuk Sultanate these warlike nomads were generally kept under control. Soon a split appeared between the prosperous Seljuk cities, centres of classical Persian-Islamic civilisation, and the countryside where the Turcomans could always be stirred up by wild preachers either to raids against the infidels or to revolt against their urban masters. Although the Turcomans' raids against Byzantine possessions were the lesser evil, they often embarrassed the foreign policy of the Seljuk Sultans. After the Mongol conquest, not only was urban control over the Turcoman largely lost, but their numbers were considerably swollen by new arrivals displaced by the Mongols from central Asia and Persia. The Mongols themselves had to fight the power which they had unleashed, but they failed to subdue it, and as the

Ilkhanid State broke up it was the Turcomans who inherited the debris.

The Turcomans who were at first best placed to profit from the confusion were those established on the Cilician march, centred on Ermenak in the Taurus country, a castle which they had captured from the Armenians. Troublesome even before the arrival of the Mongols, these Turcomans, who were led by the Karaman dynasty, briefly occupied Konya in 1277. When the Armenians of Cilicia and the Latins of Antioch were reduced by the Mamluks, the Karamanians found themselves in a profitable position between the Mongols and the Mamluks, and when Mongol power finally disintegrated they established themselves firmly in Konya (some time after 1327). They remained in occupation of that city in the first place until 1397 when they were driven out of it by their western rivals, the Ottomans. Karamanian power was, however, restored after Tamerlane's victory over the Ottomans in 1402, and it was not until 1466 that Konya was finally added to the Ottoman dominions.

The Karamanians were survived by their eastern rivals, the Turcoman dynasty of Dülgadır (1337-1522), centred on Elbistan and ruling over Maraş, Malatya and, briefly, Kayseri. The Dülgadır were usually in alliance with the Mamluks of Egypt. Still farther east, Diyarbakır was the centre of a federation of Turcoman tribes, known as the Men of the White Sheep (Akkoyunlu). Their power began to be felt in the middle of the fourteenth century, when they repeatedly attacked Byzantine Trebizond, and it reached its peak under Uzun Hasan (Hasan the Tall) (1466-1478). Hasan failed to stop the eastern advance of the Ottomans, but became master of Persia and Mesopotamia, where his descendants were to be supplanted by yet another Turcoman dynasty, the Shiah Safavids, based on Persian Azarbayjan. Less successful than the Men of the White Sheep were their northerly Turcoman neighbours, the Men of the Black Sheep (Karakoyunlu).

However, it was not on the eastern confines of the former Seljuk dominions, which were after all an internal Islamic frontier, but on the western marches, where Islam and Christianity met, that the future of Turkey was to be decided. In the second half of the thirteenth century, as Seljuk rule disintegrated, the western Turcomans pushed forward into Byzantine territory where they established new principalities. By releasing them from central control, by linking also Anatolia directly with central Asia and thus allowing the westward movement of Turkish tribes, the Mongols were in fact responsible for a new wave of Turkish conquests. It was in the century that followed the defeat of the Seljuks at Kösedağ that the Aegean coast was irretrievably lost to Byzantium and that the foundations of Ottoman power were laid.

Osman, from whom the Ottoman dynasty derives its name, appears on the scene as the master of a small principality near Söğüt on the Bithynian march, i.e. on the north-western edge of the Anatolian plateau, nearest Constantinople. The Turcoman principalities in the west differed significantly from their eastern neighbours. Poised as they were for fresh conquests, the western Turcomans could hope for greater riches as the results of their endeavours, and consequently attracted more recruits. Religious enthusiasm was added to material incentive. The frontiersmen of the west were warriors for the faith, *ghazis*, who could draw on the Muslim tradition of Holy War or *jihad*, whose arm was strengthened by the certainty of heavenly reward. So it was not a Turkish march, but the western march of Islam that was again set in motion after the impetus of the early Arab conquest had died down. The tribal origin of the leaders of the western Turcomans quickly lost its importance, and their principalities became peopled not by tribal kinsmen but by brothers in religion, of all tribal affiliations and none.

In the closing years of the thirteenth and the first half of the fourteenth centuries, the Turcomans reduced the whole western seaboard of Asia Minor. Tralles (Aydın) fell in 1280 to the Turcoman Lord of the Coast (Sahil Beyi), the Emir Menteşe. His son-in-law, Sasa, captured Ephesus, only to be supplanted by Mehmet Bey, the founder of the Aydın dynasty, who added Izmir (Smyrna) to his possessions. Mehmet's son, Umur Bey, not content with holding the coast, raided across the sea into the Balkans and had the distinction of becoming the personal object of a crusade. The Latin crusaders' recapture of Smyrna was of brief duration, but they did for a time stop Turkish expansion in the Mediterranean.

Farther north, in about 1300 the Karasi dynasty established themselves in Balıkesir, acquiring a port in Edremit, which like Smyrna had been in Genoese hands before passing into those of the Muslims. But the most important conquests were the last ones which were effected by Osman's son Orhan in the northwest. He captured Prusa (Bursa) the chief city of Bithynia, in 1326 and made it his capital. Soon afterwards he conquered Nicaea (Iznik) and Nicomedia (Izmit), pushing the Byzantines to the Straits. He then turned against his Turkish fellow-princes and thus began the unification of Asia Minor under Ottoman control, which was about to be completed when Tamerlane, the last great invader from central Asia, arose to claim the inheritance of the Mongol Great Khans and checked the process by defeating the Ottoman Sultan Beyazit 1 near Ankara in 1402. By that time the Ottomans, always fighting on two fronts – against the Christians in the west and fellow-Muslims in the east – had already been in Europe for some fifty years. Crossing over in 1352 as allies of a Byzantine faction, and thus repeating the history of the first Seljuk penetration to the west, they occupied the great fortress of Gallipoli in 1354, after its walls had been laid low by an earthquake. In 1362 Orhan's successor Murat 1 captured Adrianople (Edirne), made it his capital in place of Bursa, and reached the western frontier to which Turkey was to revert after 1913.

The conquest of Edirne can be considered a watershed in the

history of Turkey and as the end of the fruitful independence of Anatolia inaugurated by the Seljuks and enjoyed fitfully until the centre of gravity moved over the Straits to Europe. True, the Ottomans preserved some sort of balance between their dominions in Asia and Europe, between Anadolu and Rumeli. True also, they at first visited quite often their Asiatic dominions to extend them at the expense of local dynasties and to fight their interminable wars with Persia. But it was Europe which attracted the attention of the Ottomans as *ghazis*, and after 1453 Anatolia was progressively exploited, neglected and finally feared as a wild, primitive land.

In spite of the dislocation and the loss of life which it produced, the Mongol invasion of 1243 had not done irreparable harm to Anatolia. There was, of course, economic change. Stock-breeding probably increased at the expense of agriculture. But foreign trade continued and may even have been favoured by the incorporation of Anatolia in the vast Mongol empire. Fortified caravanserais were still built on the main roads, testifying to the existence of a lively caravan traffic. Konya, the old capital, declined, but urban centres further east, such as Sivas, Erzurum, and Erzincan, did well. Intellectual life too benefited from closer links with Persia. There were noted Muslim jurists in Konya and other Anatolian cities. But the greatest figure spanning pre-Mongol and post-Mongol Anatolia was the mystic poet Rumi (*c.* 1207-1273), the founder of the Whirling Dervishes, whose headquarters remained fixed in Konya. Rumi was a native of Balkh in Afghanistan. He wrote in Persian. Whatever his exact national origin, he was the product of that Persian-Muslim civilisation which he and his companions planted on Anatolian soil. Seljuk architecture, strongly influenced by northern Persian and Caucasian forms, continued to flourish under the Mongols. In the Seljuk mosques, colleges, caravanserais and fortifications, the Mongol invasion did not produce any significant change of style, and the same tradition was continued by the Turcoman princes once they had settled

in the cities. As central authority weakened and until the Turcoman princes and finally the Ottomans established their direct
control, semi-religious tradesmen's guilds known as *akhis* (from
the Turkish *akı*, generous, but assimilated to the Arabic *akh*,
brother) developed a form of autonomous urban government.
In the countryside the Turcomans also developed their specific
religious and literary forms of life largely after the Mongol
invasion. One can discern the beginnings of this individual culture just before the invasion, for example in the revolt of the
Turcomans of the Cilician march led by the dervish Baba Ishak.
His tradition was continued by the main popular saint of Anatolia, Hacı Bektaş, who was active in the second half of the
thirteenth century. The Bektashi order of dervishes (whose
mother house lies on the Kırşehir-Nevşehir road) is noteworthy
because it absorbed many Christian practices and was consequently thought to be lax in the observance of Muslim laws,
particularly the prohibition of wine. The order's importance
was, however, due mainly to its special link with the janissary
corps, a body of soldiers formed from forcibly recruited and
converted Christians who were considered the personal military slaves of the Ottoman Sultans.

The best and best-known poems written in simple Turkish
until modern times were the work of an Anatolian dervish,
Yunus Emre, who also probably lived in the second half of the
thirteenth century. Many towns dispute for the honour of
being his birthplace, Karaman among them, but he probably
lived in north-western Anatolia. Another figure who shaped
Turkish imagination, Nasrettin Hoca (Khodja in European spelling), the jester, whose stories are endlessly quoted by Turks, is
popularly supposed to have lived through the invasion of
Tamerlane, and local tradition names Akşehir (between Konya
and Afyon) as his birthplace. (His mausoleum in that town is
largely a modern building.)

After the Mongol invasion new prosperous cities developed
in the western *ghazi* principalities – in Aydın, Balıkesir and

14   *The Southern gate in the Byzantine walls of Nicaea (Iznik)*
15   *The two mediaeval castles of Corycus near Silifke, south-
      ern Turkey*

above all in Ottoman Bursa, which was described by an Arab traveller as a great and flourishing city as early as 1333, i.e. seven years after its conquest.

The two centuries which separate the Mongol invasion from the final consolidation of the Ottoman Empire as the predominant power in the Near East saw a large increase in the number of Turks and of other Muslims in Asia Minor. At what precise stage the peninsula acquired a Muslim majority it is impossible to say, but the thirteenth century seems to have been the turning point. The Mongols were preceded by the Khwarizmians (Turks from the present region of Khiva in Soviet central Asia, south of the sea of Aral). They were accompanied and followed by migrations of large numbers of Turcomans. Some Mongols settled in Anatolia. More influential were the Persians or Persianised Turks, both from Central Asia and from Persia, who chose to live in Anatolian cities either to flee the Mongols or to benefit from the opportunities for educated Muslims in a newly established Islamic realm. With the freedom of travel which characterised the Islamic world through most of its history, Arab scholars and merchants also moved in. At the same time many Anatolian Christians were converted to Islam. Muslims are allowed by their canon law, the *sharia* (in Turkish spelling *şeriat*), to take Christian or Jewish wives, and in Anatolia this permission was used to the full. In addition, many Christian men – Greeks, Armenians, Georgians and Syrians – chose Islam for reasons of self-advancement in order to join the governing institution. History records many famous converts, from the Byzantine prince John Comnenus in the twelfth century, through the Ottoman warriors of Christian origin like Mihaloğulları in the fourteenth century, to Ibrahim Müteferrika, a Hungarian convert to Islam who set up the first Arabic printing press in the Ottoman Empire in the eighteenth century, and beyond him to a number of European advisers and adventurers in the nineteenth century. Conversions were so numerous that in Seljuk times there was a specially designated

16 *Anamur castle, southern Turkey*

group of mixed breeding, the *ikdish*, who in time formed an urban aristocracy and supplied a military corps, thus becoming the precursors of the Ottoman janissaries. Whole indigenous national groups went over to Islam, like the Georgian Lazes along the eastern Black Sea coast, and later the Bulgarian Pomaks, Serbian Bosnians and the majority of the Albanians in the Balkans. The process of Islamisation which started in Asia Minor under the Seljuks spread to the Balkans in Ottoman times. But unlike Asia Minor, Ottoman possessions in Europe, taken as a whole, never acquired a Muslim majority.

Muslim canon law does not require the forcible conversion of subject peoples. Provided they are 'People of the Scriptures' (Christians, Jews, Sabaeans and Zoroastrians), they are allowed to retain their religion and choose the status of protected citizens or *dhimmis* (in Turkish spelling *zimmi*), subject to the capitation tax, *jizya* (*cizye*) and certain restrictions, such as a ban, more or less strictly enforced, on the construction of new religious buildings, occasional differentiation in dress etc. Otherwise each community of *dhimmis*, which in Ottoman times became known as *millet* (a word that gradually acquired the connotation of nation), retained its own laws, customs and leaders. They even occasionally supplied troops to their Muslim overlords (like the Greek *armatoloi* and the Slav *voynuks* in the Balkans), although more usually non-Muslims were not called to military service. Certainly in the age of conquests, whether Seljuk, Turcoman or Ottoman, there was no genocide of non-Muslims and massacres were rare. As for deportations, they were as a rule limited to the non-Muslim inhabitants living within the walls of captured fortresses. Walled cities were largely peopled by Muslims, the main church in the citadel being usually converted into a mosque (as at Antalya, Iznik, Trabzon and, the most famous instance of all, St Sophia in Istanbul). Non-Muslims then withdrew into the suburbs, which in the years of Ottoman decline were often more prosperous than the old walled cities. The pattern of Muslim walled cities and Christian suburbs survived until modern times, hence the former concentration of Greeks at Fener in Istanbul, Çekirge in Bursa, Şarampol in Antalya etc. It can still be seen in Cyprus, where the old towns of Nicosia and Famagusta remain to this day Turkish enclaves surrounded by Greek suburbs.

It was during the Ottoman phase of Turkish history that Turkey entered Europe and Europe Turkey. The Turkish advance into Europe was remarkably quick. The first crossing was made in 1352, Adrianople captured ten years later, the power of the Bulgarians broken in 1371 and that of the Serbs at the Plain of Blackbirds, Kosovo, in 1389, by which time the Ottomans were already in occupation of Albania. In 1396 a Catholic counter-offensive led by the king of Hungary was defeated at Nicopolis on the Danube. Tamerlane's victory over the Ottoman Sultan Beyazit I Yıldırım (the Thunderbolt) in 1402 brought a brief respite to the Latin west and above all to the Byzantine Empire, now largely limited to an enclave round Constantinople. However, Ottoman power soon revived. Another Catholic attempt to halt the Ottomans and relieve Constantinople – an attempt made primarily by Hungarians and Poles – came to grief at Varna in Bulgaria in 1444.

Varna sealed the fate of Constantinople, which fell to Mehmet II, the Conqueror, on 29 May 1453. Soon afterwards the Ottoman Sultan rounded off his conquests by occupying the Peloponnese (Morea) in Greece and Trebizond (Trabzon) in Asia Minor. Thus the Byzantine Empire and all its successor states were incorporated within the Ottoman Empire, whose adversaries in the west were now Poland, Hungary, Austria and Venice. In 1480 Ottoman troops seized Otranto in southern Italy.

However, the Ottomans failed to establish themselves in the Italian peninsula either then or in their second great advance under Süleyman the Magnificent, known in Turkish as *Kanunî*, the Lawgiver (1520-1556). Süleyman's troops also briefly held Otranto in 1537, but his lasting conquests were elsewhere: Belgrade (1521), Rhodes, the headquarters of the Knights of St John (1522), and Hungary (1526). Only two important provinces remained to be added to the Empire – Cyprus, where the Venetian stronghold of Famagusta fell to the Turks in 1571, and Crete whose conquest was not completed until 1669.

As these last conquests were being made the tide was already turning. The Ottomans had failed to take Vienna in 1529 and Malta in 1565, while 1571, the year that saw them conquer Cyprus, also witnessed the defeat of their fleet at Lepanto. In 1683 the failure of the second Ottoman attempt to capture Vienna turned into a rout which ended in the permanent loss of Hungary. In 1699 the Ottomans signed at Carlowitz their first peace treaty as a defeated power. Significantly, Tsarist Russia figured for the first time among the victors. Thus ended the Ottoman advance into Europe, which had lasted from 1352 to 1699. The withdrawal to the present frontiers of Turkey was to occupy more than two centuries, until 1913.

The Turkish advance into Europe has affected deeply the history of the Balkan countries, of Hungary and of Europe in general. Thus the establishment of Lutheranism in the territories of the Holy Roman Empire would not have been easy or even possible if the Habsburg Emperors had not been mainly preoccupied with the defence of their eastern frontiers against the Ottomans. Similarly, the toleration of Protestants and Unitarians in the Ottoman vassal principality of Transylvania (Erdel in Turkish) was an example that had important consequences in the internal policies of western countries. Even the Spanish endeavour in the New World was partly the result of a diversion of energy which could not find an outlet in the east where, for example, the Catalan Company had formerly found a fruitful field of gainful activity. The Ottoman Empire also became an important factor in the European balance of power. As early as the end of the fourteenth century, the Milanese played the Ottoman card in their rivalry with Venice; in the sixteenth century the Ottomans were allied with France against the House of Austria, in the nineteenth with Britain against Russia and finally in the twentieth with Germany against the Allies.

But what did Turkey derive from the centuries of Ottoman concentration on conquest in Europe? Obviously, Istanbul, Eastern Thrace up to the Meriç (Maritza) river and the offshore islands of Imroz (now Gökçeada, Greek Imbros) and Bozcaada (Greek Tenedos) remain a permanent gain. Another gain was the immense enrichment of Turkish stock by the presence in the territory of Turkey of converted Greeks, Bulgarians, Serbs, Hungarians and of other national groups such as the Jews and even some Andalusian Moors expelled from Spain. Just as the Anatolian mixture of Turcoman, Greek, Armenian, Caucasian and, to a lesser extent, Persian and Arab easily absorbed these newcomers, so too the Turkish language, already enriched by Persian and Arabic borrowings, acquired a host of new loan words – Greek for fish and vegetables, Italian for shipping and banking and, later, French to express new objects and, above all, new ideas. The economy of Turkey was of course deeply affected and with it the structure of Turkish society and, therefore, the social conditioning of the Turkish people.

Conquests brought spoils, tribute and slaves on a vast scale which maintained an equally extensive power structure. The capital, Istanbul, but also some other important cities of present-day Turkey, became prosperous and populous on the proceeds both of war and of trade with Europe. They owe to the European adventure their flowering, just as some of them owe their decline to subsequent defeats in Europe. Today it may be difficult to determine the part played by revenue from the lost provinces in the construction of the great Sultans' mosques in Istanbul or Edirne, but the Balkan or Middle Eastern origin of some of the best works of art in the Archeological Museum in Istanbul is a small reminder of the spoils of the Empire which had enriched Turkey permanently, counter-balancing to some extent European spoils from Turkey such as the carvings from

Pergamum in Berlin or the statues from Cnidus in the British Museum.

However, the European adventure had a profoundly unfavourable effect in the prolonged abuse of the human and material resources of Anatolia, from which Turkey, now more or less reduced to this region, is only slowly recovering today. Conquests in Europe benefited Istanbul, whose inhabitants were exempt from military service, and European trade in Anatolian cities, such as Bursa and later Izmir. But the rest of Asia Minor was used largely as a reservoir of men, money and materials, into which the Sultans dipped deeply and repeatedly. True, the Ottoman period has bequeathed to Anatolia a large number of monuments, of mosques, other public buildings and castles, which form the the major part of its architectural heritage. But these monuments conceal the losses suffered by the land from war and exploitation.

The massacres of Shiah Turcomans (known in Turkish as *Kızılbaş* or Redheads, from the red felt hats which they wore), in the reign of Selim I Yavuz (the Grim) (1512-1520) may have been a by-product of a policy of settling nomads, but they certainly impoverished the economy of southern and south-eastern rural Anatolia, just as the nomads themselves had earlier brought devastation to a number of cities. More seriously, the cessation of conquests flooded Anatolia with thousands of irregular soldiers (*sekban*), who had earlier been profitably employed fighting the Christians. These irregulars formed the nucleus of the *celâli* bands which roamed and plundered Anatolia at the beginning of the seventeenth century, in opposition to the licensed exploiters of the land, the holders of military fiefs (*timar*), their feudal cavalry and the Sultans' slave troops (*kapıkulu* or Slaves of the Porte). The power of the predatory *sekbans* in Anatolia was checked for a time by the Grand Viziers of the Köprülü family (mid-seventeenth century) to re-emerge after the failure of the second siege of Vienna. In 1688 the Sultan's government issued a proclamation ordering the

people of Anatolia to rise and kill 'roaming braves and Turcoman and Kurdish bands who have ruined and devastated the
whole country of Anatolia, leaving no village or hamlet standing, let alone any large town, so that no one dares travel from
one village to the next'. But order was not re-established in
Anatolia. In the eighteenth century most of the peninsula was
in the hands of local feuding lords (*derebeys* i.e. Lords of the
Valley) and of usurping pashas (military governors originally
appointed by the Sultan). Since the *derebeys* had a stake in the
land, they did at least attend to the security of their fiefs and
to the welfare of their subjects, but they warred constantly
among themselves and with the central government, while the
exactions of the pashas were often merciless. The hinterland of
Izmir was in the hands of the Karaosmanoğlu family, inland
northern Anatolia was ruled by the Çapanoğlu, Trabzon by the
Canikli, the Cilician Taurus by the Menemencioğlu etc. Their
power was not broken until the beginning of the nineteenth
century, but banditry and the depredations of Kurdish and
Turcoman tribesmen and, to a lesser extent, of Lazes from the
Black sea continued, becoming particularly extensive when-
ever the state was weakened by defeat in foreign wars as in
1878 and 1918.

The decline of the Ottoman Empire is usually dated from the
Treaty of Carlowitz in 1699, and as the decline progressed so
European penetration of Turkey increased. European tradesmen – originally Genoese, because they were the rivals of the
Ottomans' enemies, the Venetians, and then French, Dutch,
English and others – who had been granted privileges and safe-
conducts necessary for the pursuit of their activities, grew in
importance, displacing local merchants. Their official protectors, the foreign envoys and consuls, tried to create for their
nationals enclaves of order in the chaos of decaying oriental
despotism, and in so doing began to play an important part in
affairs of state. At the same time the Ottoman rulers themselves decided to acquire the learning or magic of their victors.

In the brief period of equilibrium at the beginning of the eighteenth century, European inventions and tastes began to appear in Istanbul. A first printing press was established for Turkish books. French design began to influence the palaces of the rich, which also contained some items of European furniture. Tulips, which had originally come from Asia, were reimported from Holland. A taste for tobacco spread from the west. Turkish envoys were sent to European countries and Europeans began to visit Turkey in greater numbers. In 1720 a Turkish ambassador went to France instructed 'to visit fortresses, factories and the works of French civilisation generally and to report on those which might be applicable' in Turkey. At the same time Europeans began to turn up in Turkey with projects of reforms in their pockets. These reforms were at first of a military character, some of the advisers following an old tradition and turning Muslim. Such was the case of the Frenchman Comte de Bonneval (1675-1747) who became known as Humbaracı (Bombardier) Ahmet Pasha. A first western-type institution of learning, a school of military engineering, was opened in 1734 in the Istanbul suburb of Üsküdar (Scutari). Other schools of engineering followed in 1769 and 1776. The prime movers of these first reforms were the French, whose main interest lay in strengthening Turkey's resistance to the encroachment of Russia. Russia acquired nevertheless control of the Black Sea and a privileged position in the Ottoman Empire by the Treaty of Küçük Kaynarca in 1774. After losing yet another war with Russia, the Ottoman Sultan Selim III launched the most ambitious reforms attempted until then. Under the New Order (Nizam-ı Cedit) promulgated in 1792, taxation and administration were to be modernised, and with the proceeds an effort was made to set up a European-type corps of infantry. However, traditional forces – provincial warlords, the janissaries and the city guilds to which they were allied – put an end to the reforms, and overthrew the Sultan in 1807. The delay which this caused in the spread of European influence was brief. The new Sultan Mahmut II (1808-1839), who benefited from the support of Britain rather than France, destroyed and massacred the janissaries in 1826, subdued the warlords and provincial notables, formed a new army and started to build a western façade for the administration of the Empire.

While European ideas were thus being put into practice to save the Ottoman Empire, nationalism, also an idea originating in Europe, had already begun its break-up. The Ottoman Empire, like the Seljuk Sultanate of Rum and the Byzantine Empire before it, was a multi-national state, but the criterion of differentiation among its subjects was religion and not nationality. *Millet*, a word of Arabic origin which in modern Turkish means 'nation', was until recently used to describe a religious community. The ruling *millet* was, of course, made up of Muslims regardless of their ethnic origin. But apart from Muslims, the Empire numbered among its subjects many Greeks, Slavs, Roumanians, Christian Albanians, Christian Semites and Jews.

As long as the Byzantine Empire was the enemy, the Muslim rulers of Turkey favoured disaffected Christian communities – Monophysites, Nestorians and Gregorian Armenians – against the Greek Orthodox. Later, Latin Christendom became the main adversary, and the rift between Latin and Greek was an advantage which the Ottomans did not fail to exploit in their march westwards. Soon after the conquest of Constantinople, Mehmet II appointed to the vacant Greek Patriarchal See of the capital, Gennadius Scholarius, the main opponent of the Union of Western and Eastern Churches which had been effected at the Council of Florence (1438-42), but which had met with widespread criticism among the Greeks. In accordance with existing Muslim precedent, the Greek and Armenian Patriarchs and the Jewish Chief Rabbi were given considerable secular as well as religious authority over members of their communities, for whose loyal behaviour they became answerable to the Sultan. Subsequently, Greeks in the Peloponnese, Cyprus, Crete and elsewhere benefited from the ending of Latin rule. This policy reduced the danger of a large-scale collaboration between the Christian subjects of the Ottoman Empire and its Catholic foes. Nevertheless, attempts at subversion were made and were sometimes successful: Albanians, some of whom were in any case Catholics, as well as Orthodox Greeks, did occasionally rise at the instigation of Venice, and there was a rebellion of Christians in Greece at the time of the victory won by Don John of Austria in the great naval battle of Lepanto (1571). A more dangerous situation developed when an Eastern Orthodox outside power, Russia, began to threaten the Ottoman Empire. As early as 1657, the Greek Patriarch Parthenius III was hanged by the Turks, apparently for engaging in treasonable correspondence with the Czar in Moscow. In 1711 Peter the Great issued a proclamation to the Eastern Orthodox subjects of the Ottoman Empire, inviting them to join his forces and promising them the same privileges that they enjoyed under the Turks. The Russian Empress Catherine II sent agents to stir up the Greeks, and in 1770 the appearance of a Russian fleet off the Peloponnese sparked off a rebellion which was brutally put down by local Muslims, mostly Albanians. However, although subversion based on religious ties continued, the 'Greek project' of Catherine the Great and her successors, aiming at the establishment of a Greek kingdom under Russian protection, was thwarted by other European powers.

The French Revolution, and the ideal of national liberation and of nation states which it engendered, proved more destructive. The new secularist nationalist philosophy, while making use of religious passions and affiliations, could transcend, or pretend to transcend, at least for a time, divisions between Christian churches, and even, as in Syria and Albania at the beginning of this century, the rift between Christians and Muslims.

The Greek revolution (1821-1830) was not purely nationalist in inspiration. It was the product of various discontents, among which the rivalry between Christian and Muslim Albanians was perhaps the least appreciated and one of the most important. However, through the intervention of Europe, it ended in the creation of the first nationalist state carved out of the Ottoman Empire. After the Greeks, the Serbs (who had anticipated the Greeks by rising in 1804, but whose independence was not consummated until 1878), the Roumanians (who as Wallachs and Moldavians had always enjoyed considerable autonomy, but who likewise did not become fully independent until 1878), and the Bulgarians (for whom Russian arms created in 1878 a principality which proclaimed itself independent in 1908) – all formed their own national states.

The rise of nationalism, which both incited and was incited by the Great Powers of Europe to work against the unity and integrity of the Ottoman Empire, and the steady encroachment of Russia, frustrated the efforts of Ottoman reformers. Yet the westernising reforms from 1826 onwards, which culminated in the enactment of the first Ottoman Constitution in 1876, did effect many important changes in the territory of Turkey. The traditional checks on the authority of the Sultan were removed one by one. The janissaries, provincial warlords and notables, tribal units and the representatives of organised Islam, were either destroyed or bribed, tamed and pressed into the service of the new bureaucracy. A new élite was created of Muslim Turks, educated in western learning as taught in new schools for officers and civil servants. Even more important was the rising prosperity and power of non-Muslims. The creation of the Greek Kingdom had, it is true, produced an alternative focus of allegiance for the Sultan's Greek subjects. But conditions in the Ottoman Empire became more attractive for them when the reforming Sultan Mahmut II, responding to western criticism of Muslim oppression, affirmed in 1837 his wish to see harmony reign among his subjects, without distinction of origin or religion. Greeks, Armenians and Jews set themselves with a will to the task of self-promotion in the new 'civilised' Ottoman state. Helped by the spread of secularism, by the abolition

of distinctive traditional forms of dress, by the gradual accept-
ance of the idea of equality, the Sultan's non-Muslim subjects
could also benefit from their ties with co-religionists in Europe
and from the protection which European powers extended to
them. This protection was the product of sentiment or interest,
and sometimes amounted to a concession to blackmail, since
non-Muslims were as adept as the Sultan himself in playing off
European powers against each other. The first charter of re-
form, published in 1839, guaranteed the inviolability of the
life, property and honour of all Ottoman citizens. Non-Muslim
merchants profited also from the Anglo-Turkish commercial
agreement made in 1838, which threw the Ottoman Empire
wide open to European manufactures. The Crimean War (1854-
6), in which the Sultan's armies fought alongside those of
Britain, France and Piedmont, brought new concessions to
Ottoman non-Muslims, such as the abolition of the old capitation tax. True, personal and commercial freedom was greatest
in the cities, while in the countryside traditional restraints
sometimes reduced the non-Muslims' opportunities. But in the
great cities – Istanbul, Izmir, Salonica – conditions were so
favourable that they even attracted Greeks from the new independent kingdom. In 1897, when the armies of the Ottoman
Sultan Abdülhamit II (1876-1909) came into conflict with
Greece, over the support given by the latter to the rebels in
Crete, some prominent Ottoman Greeks sided with the Sultan
against Athens.

So the rise of a modern bureaucracy and officer caste among
the Muslims was, under the reforming Sultans, paralleled by
the rise of a commercial middle class among the non-Muslims.
In Istanbul, Izmir, Trabzon, Adana and elsewhere, dilapidated
Turkish districts (*mahalle*) contrasted sadly with the new prosperity of their Greek and Armenian neighbours. The nineteenth century was a golden age of the Levantines (called in
Turkish 'Sweet-water Franks') – westernised local Christians
and Jews or easternised westerners – very few of whose descen-

dants have survived in Turkey. Their homes have either been destroyed in war (as in the great fire of Izmir in 1922) or in the course of redevelopment, or they have degenerated into slums (as in the Beyoğlu district of Istanbul). However, the Levantine age has left a few relics, such as the villas on the Princes Islands, and these might perhaps be classed among the monuments of past civilisations, not in the same class, of course, as temples, churches and mosques, but nostalgic nevertheless.

The economic advancement of non-Muslims (usually referred to as the minorities, which they were in Asia Minor, but not in the Balkans) increased their pretensions to national emancipation, while Ottoman reforms allowed them to organise for its attainment. The stage was thus set for the final dismemberment of the Ottoman Empire. Until 1878 the Sultans had tried to safeguard their realm by reforms and by alliances with European powers (first France, then England), and at times by a combination of internal reforms and external alliances. After 1878 and the loss of Bulgaria, Thessaly, Cyprus and the border provinces of eastern Anatolia, Abdülhamit II tried another way. While continuing to play skilfully on the rivalry of European powers, he turned away from the novel concept of constitutional rule, which he saw as a factor of disruption, and sought to foster a religious Muslim nationalism, buttressed by a great expansion of education. The Sultan has been much abused both for the massacres of Armenians which occurred in his reign and for his reactionary politics. Yet he did less harm to the Armenians than his successors, the progressive Young Turks, while the schools and public buildings put up in his reign were until recently unrivalled throughout Turkey. In the end, the new schools, and above all the military schools, proved his undoing. The revolutionaries which they bred professed to see imminent catastrophe everywhere, and argued that only a return to the Constitution, granted in 1876 and suspended two years later, could arrest the centrifugal nationalism of Armenians, Greeks and Slavs in Macedonia and the more traditional tribal troubles

in Albania and Arabia. The standard of revolt was raised by
the army engaged in combating nationalist bands in Macedonia.
In 1908 Abdülhamit was forced to reintroduce constitutional
government, while in 1909 a popular mutiny against the new
régime, served as a pretext for the Sultan's deposition.

The Young Turkish revolution of 1908 appears in retrospect
a typical military coup, preceded by the agitation of progressive intellectuals, who, however, were neither concerned in its
execution nor, by and large, benefited from its consequences.
These were almost uniformly disastrous. Although the Young
Turks marched under the banner of liberalism – the progressive
ideology of their age – their slogan of freedom, justice, equality
and fraternity translated itself into an attempt at imposing
uniformity and centralisation. The Ottoman Empire was shaped
too individually to fit into this Procrustean bed. Arab and
Albanian tribesmen revolted against the new concept of a
modern state; Greek, Slav and Armenian nationalists against
the new Ottoman nationalism in which they saw the beginnings
of a Turkish nationalism. A less supple foreign policy united,
instead of dividing, the enemies of the state. In 1908 Austria-
Hungary formally annexed Bosnia and Herzegovina, and Bulgaria proclaimed its complete independence. These were purely
formal losses, but real ones were to follow. In 1911 Italy invaded Tripolitania (Libya); in 1912 Greece, Serbia, Montenegro,
Bulgaria and Roumania joined forces and all the Ottoman possessions in the Balkans, up to and including Edirne, were lost.
A quarrel among the Balkan allies allowed the Young Turks to
recapture Edirne, but an attempt to benefit from European dissension by establishing an alliance with the Central Powers led
to final disaster.

The Ottoman Empire entered the Great War in 1914 as a
result of German intrigues and in a spirit of irresponsible adventure. It had nothing to gain, since Bulgaria was an ally and
Greece started by being neutral. It could not thus hope to regain
its lost possessions in Europe, while the bait of a Great Turan,

of lands inhabited by Turkic peoples in the Caucusus and Central Asia, lay outside the historic frontiers of the Ottoman Empire and did not quicken the sentiment of its Muslim inhabitants. In the event, defeat in the Great War completed the sorting out of the constituent nationalities of the Empire and thus led to the creation of a Turkish nation state. Both the stupidity of the Young Turks in entering the war and the stupidity of the Allies in victory contributed to this result. But while, in an age of nationalism, the emergence of a national Turkish state may now seem inevitable, its actual realisation in 1923 and the ample boundaries which it won for itself were achieved by the intelligence of one man, Mustafa Kemal Atatürk.

The traveller in Turkey will see portraits, photographs and statues of Atatürk everywhere – in public buildings and shops, in streets and city squares, on coins, banknotes and stamps. He will hear Atatürk praised everywhere as the saviour of the country, the founder of the republic, the great reformer. Of these titles the first is the least controversial, for it was Atatürk who gained recognition for the Turks' right to their own country.

Mustafa Kemal (the surname Atatürk or Father of the Turks dates only from 1935, when surnames became obligatory as the result of one of his innovations), was born in Ottoman Salonica in 1881, the son of a junior civil servant.

He had a military upbringing, engaged in mild conspiratorial activities against the absolutist régime while still a cadet and in more serious plotting as a young officer. The Young Turks' military coup of 1908, with which he was only marginally connected, opened new opportunities before him. In 1909 he was actively concerned in the suppression of the Istanbul mutiny against the Young Turks, but thereafter disagreed with the leading lights of the new régime and concentrated on his military career, which took him to Libya in the war against Italy in 1911, to Sofia as a military attaché before the outbreak of the Great War, and to a command in the Dardanelles in 1915.

It was in the Gallipoli campaign that Mustafa Kemal made his name. He played the major part in the defeat of the Allied attempt to break through to Istanbul, became a popular hero, and kept his reputation intact in his subsequent commands in the east against the Russians and in Palestine against the British.

In October 1918 when the Ottoman Empire capitulated, Mustafa Kemal was holding a new line of defence roughly along Turkey's present southern frontier with Syria. As the Young Turkish leaders had fled from the capital, the Sultan Vahdettin was looking for new advisers and for a new policy to salvage the remnant of his Empire. There were two possible courses of action: to go along with the demands of the Allies or to resist them as far as possible. Mustafa Kemal advised the latter, the Sultan chose the former. At first, the intentions of the Allies with regard to Turkey were not clear. Resisters and compliers both waited and plotted in Istanbul, with the Allies in occupation of all the strategic centres of the country and the Ottoman Army in process of disarmament and demobilisation. Then, as it became clear that the Allies, divided as they were among themselves, had agreed on dismembering Turkey, Mustafa Kemal moved to unoccupied Anatolia to organise resistance. The landings which the Greeks made in Izmir with Allied blessing had proved the Sultan and his advisers wrong in their assessment. However, it took time, a minor civil war between the Sultan's supporters and those of Kemal, and a Greek advance almost to the outskirts of Kemal's base in Ankara, before Kemal was proved right in his view that resistance was not only necessary, but also possible. It proved possible because of Kemal's leadership and of the impossibility of disposing of some 9,000,000 Anatolian Turks, but also because the Allies were half-hearted in their absurd plan to defeat Turkish nationalism indirectly by supporting against it Greek nationalism in the west and Armenian nationalism in the east. A direct clash with the Allied Great Powers was avoided, since Kemal

17   *Mosque of Alaettin, Konya*

18 *Stable of royal caravanserai (Sultan Hanı) on the Kayseri–Sıvas road*

19 *Main portal of caravanserai of Karatay, Kayseri*

had limited his aims to the liberation of lands inhabited by a Turkish majority and had made it clear that once this was achieved he had no quarrel with anyone, least of all with Britain and France. The point was taken. The Turkish War of Independence (1919-1922) was fought and won against Armenians and Greeks, while Britain, France and Italy withdrew peacefully from the Turkish territory which they had occupied.

The Great War, the War of Independence and the Peace Treaty of Lausanne in 1923 completed the sorting out of the nationalities which were to be found on the territory of Turkey. In the Great War large numbers of Armenians, whose sympathies with Russia were well known, were deported from the north-east and east of the country, many perishing on the way. In the extreme south-east, the small, but historically interesting community of Nestorians fled from the mountain province of Hakkâri to the Mesopotamian lowlands. During the War of Independence the Armenians remaining in Anatolia – in the eastern provinces which they sought to incorporate in the new Armenian republic, in the south-east where they had sided with the French occupation forces, and everywhere else in Turkey outside Istanbul – were similarly ejected. With them went a number of Arabic-speaking Christian Syrians. Finally, the Greeks, having failed in their objective of annexing large tracts of Anatolia, also left, again except for a small and decreasing community in Istanbul. Some fled with the retreating Greek armies, the rest were exchanged against Muslims stranded in the kingdom of Greece. Anatolia and eastern Thrace (outside Istanbul), became purely Muslim for the first time in their history. True, the Turks were not the only remaining inhabitants, since there were also many Kurds and some Arabs. But as Muslims these had never been treated as minorities or felt themselves in any way alien.

It was this purely Muslim country that Mustafa Kemal sought to modernise, first of all by disestablishing Islam. The last Sultan, Vahdettin, had fled from Istanbul in November 1922, preceding by a few months the departure of the Allied occupation forces. On 29 October 1923 Mustafa Kemal proclaimed a Turkish Republic and had himself elected President. In 1924 he abolished the institution of the Caliphate, which, for all its vagueness, gave Islam an official standing. He also closed down all religious schools, expelled from Turkey all members of the Ottoman dynasty and took over religious foundations. In 1925 dervish orders were dissolved. In 1926 the last vestiges of Muslim canon law were swept away with the adoption of the Swiss civil code, which incidentally ended polygamy and emancipated women, at least on paper. In April 1928 Islam ceased to be the official religion of the state, while in November of the same year the Latin alphabet was introduced and the use of the Arabic alphabet banned. In 1934 women were admitted to parliament. It is true that parliament had no power, since, except for brief intervals, only Mustafa Kemal's Republican People's Party was allowed to exist and its handpicked deputies dutifully endorsed all the decisions of the President and of his ministers.

Between 1919 and 1923, as commander of the forces of Turkish national resistance, Atatürk had won a country; between 1923 and 1938, as President of the Republic, he endowed it with new institutions. The development of the people and of the economy which they operated was, of course, a much slower process. Visually, the new capital Ankara is the main monument of the Atatürk era. It was planned as a small and orderly European town, with adequate services, tree-lined avenues and imposing public buildings. It has developed into a large and ungainly city, new certainly, but one that mirrors Turkish society rather than that of western Europe. Another achievement with which the traveller may come into contact is the railway system which Atatürk extended at great cost from the original German-built single line across the country (the Baghdad Railway), with its spur to Ankara, and the British-built line from Izmir. Atatürk's extensions, reaching out to the Soviet frontier and to the Black Sea and linking Ankara with Izmir, absorbed a great part of the Turkish revenue between the wars, but helped to open up large tracts of Anatolia. Such money as was left over was used on education and on first projects of industrialisation. But least discussed and most important of Atatürk's achievements was the establishment of security of life and property within stable frontiers. By securing peaceful, stable and safe conditions for the first time in centuries, Atatürk allowed the Turkish nation to replenish its human resources which had been depleted by constant wars. Anatolian Muslims and large numbers of Muslim refugees from surrounding countries, and even from as far afield as Chinese Turkistan, grew and multiplied from an estimated 9,000,000 or 10,000,000 at the end of the Great War to some 17,000,000 at the time of Atatürk's death in 1938 and to 36,000,000 today.

Atatürk died on 10 November 1938 just as his last project, the return to Turkey of the province of Hatay (the sandjak of Alexandretta), which had been within the frontiers originally claimed in 1919, but was lost to French-mandated Syria, was about to be realised. As Hatay became Turkish, Turkey joined Britain and France in an alliance, which formalised Atatürk's preference for and reliance on the western democracies, both as exemplars of civilisation and as defenders of international order. Atatürk had benefited from Soviet help in the War of Independence, but he repressed communism internally and, after he had achieved Turkey's independence and constructed his régime, he naturally sided with the western defenders of the status quo.

Atatürk was succeeded by his Prime Minister Ismet Inönü, who will probably be remembered for two major achievements: keeping Turkey out of the Second World War and allowing and then fostering and defending genuine parliamentary government after it. Turkish neutrality during the war was due both to a desire to avoid a repetition of the sufferings which the country had endured from 1911 to 1922, and to the conviction that the main threat came not from Germany but from Soviet Russia. From 1945 to 1947 Turkey did not have the benefit of secure western backing as it resisted Soviet claims for territory and for the control of the Straits. However, the Truman Doctrine, leading to the Marshall Plan and then to Turkey's accession to NATO, ended the country's isolation. America and its western allies guaranteed Turkey's integrity and aided its development, while Turkey did its duty by its allies in participating in the defence of South Korea against Communist aggression.

In 1950 the Republican People's Party, whose leadership Inönü had inherited from Atatürk, was defeated in the first free elections held under the Republic. In 1960 its successor in power, the Democratic Party, led by another of Atatürk's Prime Ministers, Celal Bayar, was overthrown by a military coup. The coup of 1960, like that of 1908, was carried out under the banner of liberal democracy, which the Democrats were accused of having violated, and much to the surprise of the outside world free elections were in fact allowed in 1961. Inönü re-emerged this time as Prime Minister and held on to power until 1965. He was then succeeded by Süleyman Demirel, leader of the new Justice Party, which had inherited the votes of the dissolved Democratic Party. Demirel was re-elected to office in 1969, only to be ousted by the armed forces in 1971.

But these political changes were only the surface manifestations of a profound transformation of Turkish society, a transformation which had been triggered off by Atatürk and gathered force after his death. The traveller interested not only in the landscape with its monuments, but also in the figures moving across it, will want to know something of this new Turkish society and of the individuals who make it up.

2. The Turks

No matter by what route and at what point the traveller enters Turkey, even if he first sets foot in it in the drab surrounds of the international airport of Istanbul, the individuality of the country soon makes an impression. The language is utterly different and to most Europeans incomprehensible, its peculiarity only emphasised by the international Latin alphabet in which it is clothed. The officials, dour, unhurried, usually unsmiling, often unshaven, are clearly not excitable foreigners, even although most of them look indistinguishable from other and more volatile inhabitants of the Mediterranean. The crowds behind the barrier divide by their clothes into well-off middle class and poor, but the latter do not bow and scrape before the former. Organisation seems indifferent: there are taxis in the way of coaches, touting taxi-drivers in everybody else's way, porters falling over each other as they fight for the travellers' luggage. But some individuals or groups extricate themselves quickly from the disorder, are recognised by their friends or relatives and hurried to waiting cars. Clearly there is a network of influence at work, but not one solely related to wealth.

Then, as one drives from the airport to Istanbul, impressions and, inevitably, quick judgements succeed each other: the traffic is disorderly, the style of driving adventurous. So is the style of the pedestrians trying to cross the road. There are quite a few peasants by the roadside, distinguishable by their gait rather than by their nondescript clothes. As one enters the city the crowds look proletarian, but do not behave submissively. Drivers and pedestrians hurl insults at each other, everyone talks in a loud voice, oriental music blares everywhere – from car wirelesses, loudspeakers in cafés and restaurants or windows of private houses. Most of the buildings look undistinguished – badly-built blocks of flats, shops with crowded but messy windows. Now and then, however, the display of a greengrocer or a fishmonger stands out by its colourful and elegant harmony. And the sprawl of the city is dominated by monuments which immediately impress by their greatness: mediaeval walls, a classical aqueduct and, on all sides, mosques with their attendant tall, thin minarets. Even if the traveller stays at an international hotel in what used to be the European quarter of the city, he will remain within earshot of the muezzin's five daily calls to prayer, the first just before sunrise.

The call to prayer remains a distinguishing sound of home to a Turk even if he himself never darkens the door of a mosque. Islam was the basis of the identity of his ancestors, and is still embodied in his consciousness, however much he may wish to eradicate it. Turks conquered Turkey as Muslims for Islam, and Islam remained the official religion of the state up till 1928. What is its role today?

The obligations of Islam are observed in varying degrees. Almost everyone outside out-and-out intellectual atheists, assents to the profession of faith: 'There is no God but God, and Muhammad is His Prophet.' The majority disregard the injunction to pray five times a day in the prescribed canonical manner: first ablutions, then prostrations, the recitation of Arabic prayers etc. But many do so once a week on Friday, and most go to Friday prayers during the month of fasting or Ramazan, a lunar month which consequently moves gradually through the four seasons. Again – and this is a point which the traveller who comes into contact only with the middle classes will easily fail to notice – most Turks keep the fast. Of the other obligations of Islam, that of performing the pilgrimage to

Mecca at least once in a life-time, remains the ambition of most Turks and the achievement of many. In 1970 there were almost 50,000 Turkish pilgrims. So far as dietary laws are concerned, the ban on alcohol is widely disregarded. Rakı, a drier version of pernod, anisette or Greek ouzo, is the national hard drink; beer is universally popular, but religious scruples still limit the consumption of wine. On the other hand, the idea of eating pork nauseates most Turks, however irreligious. Tradition which may have its origin in the Mosaic prohibitions, but which does not have the force of law in Islam, makes many Turks refuse or dislike shellfish or snails. Finally, Shiahs – Muslims who lay special emphasis on the Prophet's son-in-law Ali and restrict the supreme leadership of the community to his descendants, hence the name Alevî, by which they are known in Turkey – do not eat hare.

But these are outward manifestations of religion. The spirit and traditions of universal Islam have survived in other ways. There is a generalised feeling of kinship for all Muslims everywhere, although for historical purposes this remains largely platonic, except when a foreign Muslim comes to Turkey where, if he wishes, he is easily assimilated. If a Turk marries a foreign girl and she is converted to Islam, she becomes a Turk not only in popular estimation, but paradoxically in the eyes of the secular authorities, and her husband thus escapes the ban on officials and officers marrying foreigners. On the other hand, marriages of Turkish women with non-Muslims, which were forbidden by canon law, are still rare and meet with strong disapproval.

Islam, like all great religions, is unitive within the community of the faithful, all of whom are equal before God. To this extent it is democratic, and, through the accidental almost total absence of a genuine aristocracy among the Turks, it is more democratic than many religious communities elsewhere. It has no clergy, spiritual leadership devolving on laymen who are learned in its law and traditions. In many cases these are, of course, full-time religious officials, although they may combine private pursuits with spiritual service to the community. From the general equality of the faithful, Islam distinguishes its actual leaders both in spiritual and temporal affairs, and therefore pays particular respect to learning, law and authority. Although all three have been secularised in republican Turkey, they retain something of their supernatural aura, partly through the conscious manipulation of authority. Turks are traditionally law-abiding, even in foreign lands where they find themselves under alien laws. They are also almost always legalistic. Legalism breeds its own subterfuges and corruption, but both are preferred to lawlessness and anarchy. The Muslim tradition thus reinforces the Turks' natural human preference for order, which often translates itself into an elusive search for an ideal tranquillity. Until the nineteenth century Turkish critics of society sought the restoration of the good old order, based on the canon law of Islam; from then on they have been searching for a new order – a reformed Muslim, western liberal, nationalist, Marxist or 'scientific' social order.

Islam is a fairly tolerant religion, although of course it insists on its superiority. On that condition it has always tolerated diversity, more so than the modern secular state. Even today the Turk will not be shocked at the sight of a foreigner eating pork, swilling wine and making a pig of himself during the Ramazan. He will not be surprised if foreign women behave immodestly, although he may seek to take advantage of it.

In spite of secularisation, the position of women has changed slowly. In Muslim, as in other traditional societies, they were subject to a strict code of morals, which stressed modesty as the highest feminine virtue. In addition, Islam reserved for women a distinct and unequal function in the world. Women were required to be submissive to men in authority over them – their fathers, of course, but also brothers and, later, husbands, or in their absence, to any male relatives acting as their protectors. However, within their unequal, protected status women always exercised considerable influence over the family or even the state. On the other hand, their labour was exploited to the full. Today laws proclaim feminine equality, and society is gradually and painfully adapting itself to the new edict. Nevertheless, outside the cities, or rather middle-class areas in them, women are rarely seen in public places – restaurants, cafés or beaches – and never unaccompanied. Most Turks prefer their womenfolk at home and remain uncomfortable in feminine company in public.

A traditional society is obsessed by what it forbids, and in Turkey there are many signs of sex obsession: of voyeurism, bottom-pinching, occasional molestation of unaccompanied women (on the assumption that no respectable woman is unaccompanied), girly pictures everywhere, and an insatiable curiosity about foreign sexual practices. Certainly any Turk returned from abroad, or a foreign male visitor with whom a Turk strikes up a friendship, is questioned minutely on the subject. Is virginity not valued abroad? Are women easy? Are husbands complaisant? Whether the jealous guard kept over women encourages homosexuality and other unorthodox sexual practices, as many foreigners and Turkish modernists allege, it is impossible to say. Many Turks believe that conservative cities in Anatolia are centres of pederasty. However that may be, foreigners should not be misled by the sight of Turkish men holding hands or kissing each other in public. These are social and not sexual acts.

Sexual curiosity and frustration are one side of the coin. Hospitality, reticence, respect and generosity are the other. Foreigners, irrespective of sex or creed, benefit from all these Turkish qualities. For a member of a traditional society, the Turk is remarkably ready to welcome a foreigner into his home, provided he is convinced of his guest's respectability. Men will invite foreign men or families, women invite other women. The host becomes the protector, a position which does credit to him in the community, and the guest's benefactor through his protection, gifts and advice. Sometimes the protection can become irksome, since the guest is never left alone. Individualists have to negotiate many pitfalls in their dealings with traditional societies.

Some of the traits described so far are specifically Muslim, others are common to all traditional societies, while others again can be attributed to the Turkish experience. In the Ottoman Empire the Turks were peasants, soldiers, scholars and administrators. The virtues corresponding to these occupations are patience, courage, loyalty, perseverance and dignity. The main corresponding vice is harshness to the enemy in moments of danger. On the other hand the alien with whom there was a compact could always expect fair treatment from the Turk. Children too benefit from their protected status, provided the protectors' authority is respected.

One result of the military background of Turkish society is the tendency to management by capricious order easily changed ('an Ottoman ban lasts for three days', as the Turkish proverb has it), only to be superseded by some equally arbitrary dispensation. In the past arbitrariness was circumscribed by an unchanging canon law. Secular law has been a less solid guarantee.

Since most Turks have until recently been strangers to trade, commercial virtues – thrift, a regard for money, for the conservation of resources, business efficiency – are rare. Traditionally, tradesmen from other faiths were allowed to grow fat, often at the expense of their Muslim customers, but were made to disgorge all or part of their gains in times of crisis. Today, the Marxist theory of plus-value – of the portion, that is, of the fruit of labour which is denied to the labourer – appeals to the strong Turkish instinctive feeling that there is somewhere a reservoir of ill-gotten gains, amassed through the excessive tolerance of the community, and therefore properly revertible to it. Thus Marxism, like other alien ideas, can adapt itself to local traditions, in this case to the habit of substituting expropriation for good management as a principle of economic policy.

A frontier people, the Turks have learnt the value of solidarity in defence and attack. Foreigners find it difficult to divide them from their leaders. They criticise themselves endlessly, but resent foreign criticism.

These national archetypes are, of course, wide generalisations applicable to the traditional core of Muslim Turkish society. But that society is changing and change has brought both division and a crisis of identity. Change started under the reforming sultans and it led gradually to the alienation of the élite from the mass of the people. Turkish society always had its leaders, but until the westernising reforms these shared the common Muslim faith and way of life. The bureaucratic and military élite, which grew in power as traditional forces were destroyed, was first the servant and then the successor of the sultans. At the same time it changed its culture and lost much of its religious faith. True, the change is by no means complete: the westernised Turk is not, except in rare instances, a westerner, since he operates in a different society, enjoys a different position and is subject to different pressures. But neither is he an oriental. As the common bond of Islam was disowned under the Republic, the division of society into rulers and ruled, people learned in and ignorant of the new western knowledge, hardened. This division forms today the main factor in Turkish politics, which have been a struggle not so much between social classes, definable in economic terms, as between the secularist establishment and the rest of the people. Since the establishment has lost every single free election held in Turkey, the more militant members of it have come to despair of parliamentary government and have put their faith in authoritarianism, modishly disguised as socialism. In Turkey, socialists are largely to be found among the sons, and now the more strident daughters, of the upper classes, conservatives among the outsiders.

But change imposed from above in the shape of western laws and institutions has not been the only factor in the transformation of Turkish society. Internal social change has gathered strength, particularly since 1950. Atatürk's railways had opened up some isolated areas of Anatolia; the roads constructed with American help and advice after the last war have extended the progress. Secure, peaceful conditions and preventive medicine – above all the virtual elimination of malaria through the use of the now discarded DDT and the success achieved in controlling tuberculosis by a campaign of preventive inoculation – have lowered the death-rate. At the same time the high birth rate has continued to reflect the instincts of a pre-industrial society, making provision against losses of manpower through war, drought and disease. This has led to a doubling of the population since the death of Atatürk. Modern roads have helped to transport some of the excess manpower to the cities, whose growth has exceeded by far that of the population as a whole. Roads, the wireless and newspapers have allowed the mass of the people to make contact with the outside world and to learn of the existence of more prosperous communities. Popular expectations have increased dramatically. The introduction of parliamentary government, with inter-party rivalry for electoral support, has turned these expectations into political problems to which governments of whatever complexion have had to address themselves. Modern services – medicine, transport, water supply, irrigation and drainage, housing – have been extended and new factories have been built, dwarfing the beginnings of industrialisation under Atatürk. However, the degree of development which has been achieved has fallen far short of the aims which the mass of the people had set themselves. Western Europe, above all Germany, had attracted by 1970 over a third of a million of Turkish workers, with another million queuing up to join them. Atatürk's stated ideal of achieving the standards of contemporary civilisation had been visualised by the old republican élite as a state of affairs where they, the educated, would be permanently in power. To the workers who have been to the west or have heard reports of it, the ideal had become a concrete image, the image of a democratic, industrial European society.

Although development has not matched popular expectations, it has changed some aspects of society. Turks have shown increasing willingness to change settled habits for the sake of material advancement: villagers have migrated to the cities or to foreign countries, they have sought education as the key to advancement, have experimented in various degrees with trade, gambling, thrift and investment. As some, but not all, have achieved their object, made money, made good, social jealousy has increased. Trade unions have appeared on the scene, social insurance has been introduced to cover some 1,000,000 workers in industry and services. Nevertheless, not only has poverty not been banished, but it has become more evident in the new urban setting, while, as elsewhere, advertising and the better distribution of consumer goods have stimulated appetites. Contrasts – between cities and villages, as well as within cities – and generally all the physical and spiritual discomforts of change have bred militancy of the left and a conservative backlash. Both extremes often find a convenient scapegoat in the alleged misdeeds of foreigners, above all of Americans, although the worst that is likely to befall a tourist is to be lectured on the subject by some passionate revolutionary. Otherwise, both traditional hospitality and the belief, propagated by the government and by now widely held, that tourism is indispensable to economic development, guarantee the traveller's welcome provided that he displays a modicum of common sense. Political and religious arguments are, however, best avoided. Above all, the traveller should remember that Turks have been criticised far too often in the past as Asiatic fanatics by people ignorant of their civilisation, their involvement in Europe and the injustices which they have suffered at the hands of civilised Europeans, to accept criticism with equanimity. Moreover, change brings a crisis of identity, which in turn leads to over-reaction both to praise and to blame. The traveller may find that one careless remark is enough to turn him from 'a friend of the Turks' into an 'enemy of the Turks'.

The traveller in Turkey will not fail to notice that he is not in a uniformly backward society, nor yet in a highly developed one. He will see shops well stocked, largely with home-produced goods. He will find food cheap, although not by the standards of local earnings. Manufactured goods, particularly when they are imported are, on the other hand, expensive, since local industry is young and not very efficient. But there are exceptions: textiles, leather goods and medicines are on the whole cheap. In any case, the foreign traveller will not lack any of his modern necessities, whether patent medicines or detergents. Services, above all transport, are cheap. So is labour. But the traveller will notice that many services are indifferent and skilled labour scarce. One obvious reason is that modern technology is new to the Turks. Another is that not only trade, but also many arts and crafts, were carried on largely by non-Muslims, who left the country after the Great War. Finally, while individual skills can be and are being gradually acquired, organisational ability and the kind of team work that the provision of modern services requires are more difficult to attain. Both will grow with industrial experience. For the moment, improvisation is more common than good organisation.

The persistence of traditional attitudes is not surprising in a society, some 40 per cent of whose members remain illiterate and whose level of economic activity (as reflected in a gross national product of some $375 per person per year) is roughly one sixth of that obtaining in western Europe. However, the statistical average conceals wide variations: townsmen are better off than villagers, employed workers often do better than civil servants, the coast lands are more prosperous than the plateau, the west richer than the east. But although Atatürk did not revolutionise society, carry out a land reform or introduce other radical social measures, the contrast between rich and poor is less striking in Turkey than in most countries to the east and south of it. Moreover wealth as such still attracts little respect, but much jealousy, respect going rather to age, position, authority, learning and gentlemanly manners.

To its members Turkish society can often be repressive; to individual foreigners who respect it, it is usually friendly, however much foreigners in the abstract may be blamed for the country's difficulties. And friendship once extended, is usually lasting. 'An old friend never becomes an enemy' is one of the most quoted of the many proverbs with which Turkish conversation is replete.

3. Culture, Art and Crafts

To the traveller, architecture is the most easily accessible of the arts of a country. Before the advent of the box as the universal container of flats, hotels and public offices, Turkish architecture had an immediately perceptible individuality in its two main phases, Seljuk and Ottoman. Public architecture was represented, above all, by mosques (*cami*, i.e. places of congregational worship), but also by Coranic colleges (*medrese*), mausolea (*türbe*), dervish monasteries (*tekke*), almshouses (*imaret*), inns and caravanserais (*han, kervansaray*), Turkish baths (*hamam*), palaces (*köşk, saray*), fountains (*çeşme, şadırvan, sebil*) and bridges (*köprü*).

The religious requirements which mosque architects have to meet are simple. There must be sufficient room for the worshippers, who stand in rows, behind the *imam* or prayer-leader, facing the direction of Mecca (*kıble*). The wall which they face has a central niche or recess (*mihrap*), serving to focus the eyes of the congregation on a point which seems to transcend the spatial limitations of the building. A pulpit (*mimber*), usually surmounted by a conical hat, and often elaborately carved in wood or marble, completes the essential internal structures. More elaborate buildings have galleries, enclosures (*maksure*) and raised platforms (*mahfil*). Circular shields on the walls are inscribed in Arabic with the names of Allah, Muhammad and his first four successors or caliphs, Ebu Bekir, Osman, Ömer and Ali, as well as the latter's sons Hasan and Hüseyin. Since worshippers touch the ground with their foreheads as

20 *The Fluted Minaret (Yivli Minare) in Antalya, looking across the bay to the Bey mountains*

21 *Mosque in Mardin, south-eastern Turkey*

they prostrate themselves in prayer, the floor is kept scrupul- ously clean and is covered with mats, woven rugs (*kilim*) or tufted carpets (*halı*). There are low X-shaped desks or lecterns (*rahle*) for use by squatting cantors.

Outside the mosque there is always a fountain, sometimes very elaborate, for the ritual ablutions which must precede prayer. Attached to a congregational mosque (but not to a chapel or *mescit*, used for prayers on days other than Friday or holy days, *bayram*), there is at least one minaret (*minare*), from which the call to prayer (*ezan*) is recited five times a day by the *müezzin*. Minarets have one or more balconies (*şerefe*) set at different levels. The internal decoration of a mosque is a mat- ter of taste, which varies with time and place. The whitewashed walls of village mosques are often left completely plain. Usu- ally, however, verses from the Coran, prayers or invocations, are inscribed on the walls or hung up in frames. Arabic in- scriptions, usually of verses from the Coran, are often carved in wood or stone, and woven into patterns of leaves and tendrils. Since human representation is forbidden and animal representa- tion has disappeared from the external surface of gates, more or less with the passing of the Seljuks, calligraphy in ink, paint, stucco and stone, and floral and abstract designs in wood, stone and above all tiles, have been developed into a major art form.

In Turkey, unlike some other Muslim countries, mosques may be visited by followers of other faiths, although these visits are usually restricted to times when prayers are not in pro- gress. Both visitors and worshippers have to remove their shoes on entering the mosque and are sometimes supplied with slip- pers for which a small gratuity is expected. Women are ad- vised to cover their hair, and both men and women should be dressed and behave as in any other place of worship.

Essentially any square or rectangular building can meet the simple liturgical requirements of Islam. The actual shape which mosques took derived from the traditions, influences and tastes of the time. Much of Seljuk architecture presents a complete contrast between simplicity of structure and extravagance of decoration, which is often compared to baroque. Internally many Seljuk mosques are built on the pattern of a basilica with the roof supported by parallel rows of columns, often taken from earlier Christian structures. The arches, however, tend to be pointed, oriental. (Pointed arches are also a hallmark of the elegant Seljuk stone bridges, many of which are preserved in Anatolia.) The decoration is particularly elaborate on the gates or portals, which had a symbolical significance since they gave access to a place dedicated to God, and were thus comparable to the gates of Paradise. Arabic inscriptions, arabesques, abstract shapes, flowers, leaves, tendrils, and occasionally animal shapes, carved in stone or stucco, were elaborately interwoven in carpet-like patterns. Within the arch of the gate there is often an external equivalent of the *mihrap* or prayer niche, drawing the eye towards the mystery of faith. Seljuk mausolea are easily distinguishable by their round or polygonal shapes, surmounted by pointed domes. Influenced by and later influencing Armenian churches, these *kümbets*, as they are called, sometimes incorporate columns, pilasters, or the tall blind arches which Armenian architects developed in advance of western Gothic. In addition to stone, brick was used more widely than in later times.

Ottoman mosques are squarer, more compact than their Seljuk predecessors. A narthex, for which Muslim worship has no use, reappears. The elevation is higher, the minarets thinner, taller and plainer than before, with fluting usually the only kind of decoration, and instead of being incorporated in the façade or loosely attached to the building, become part of a three-dimensional composition, grouped round the central dome. It is the dome, above all, which is different. From the one small dome on a basilica-like structure, to a multiplicity of small domes of equal size, as in the early Ottoman Ulu Cami in Bursa, Ottoman architecture developed finally the dominant dome, often surrounded at a lower level by small domes or supported by half-domes in a pyramidal composition. Arches are rounder, windows more numerous, in order to reduce the weight of essentially heavy buildings. Extensive porticos serve the same purpose. The courtyard wall, often rising to a considerable height broken by barred windows, and outbuildings to house schools, almshouses or mausolea are worked into the general plan. Mausolea are also surmounted by round domes instead of conical or other pointed roofs. Decoration, particularly in the portals and the *mihrap*, although still rich, stands out less than in Seljuk buildings. Coloured tiles are used extensively, brick much less so. The quality of stonemasonry is superb, thus continuing the local tradition of craftsmanship which had earlier found striking expression in the ashlar-built Armenian churches of the late middle ages.

The development of other public buildings, while being in line with the general evolution of taste, was also affected by functional considerations. The fortified caravanserai or *han* in the countryside gradually disappeared, *hans* in the cities becoming larger. In addition to a courtyard, stables, guest rooms, communal halls and an oratory, they also contained store-houses, offices and shops where merchants transacted their business, so that the word *han* has come to mean an office block in modern Turkish.

The Turkish or steam bath (*hamam*), without which no Muslim settlement was conceivable, since it served for the general ablution (*gusul*), obligatory after sexual intercourse, developed into a building of the utmost technical perfection. The four main rooms of the Roman bath were usually reduced to two: a changing room and the steam room, the latter, as in so many Muslim buildings, surmounted by a large dome with apertures covered with thick bottle glass to let in light. The same bath house was used by men and women at alternate times, or different sets of buildings were allocated to the two sexes, often within the same architectural complex.

Turkish palace architecture grew away from the castle used

as a royal residence (*kasr*) and came to favour a multiplicity of pavilions (*köşk* or kiosks) within a palace wall, which also enclosed barracks, council chambers (*divan-hane*), oratories, offices, stables, store rooms etc. Later, with the spread of European ideas, there was a return to the monumental, as seen in the nineteenth-century Dolmabahçe palace in Istanbul.

Public buildings were usually built of stone throughout, although the Byzantine technique of sandwiching two courses of brick between courses of stone survived, particularly in the outbuildings of some mosques. In domestic architecture, Turks outside central and eastern Anatolia used wood even for wealthy mansions, where the Byzantines had preferred brick. This strange aversion to brick continues to the present day when, according to a recent survey, Turkish architects use much more concrete and structural steel and much less brick than their West European counterparts. It is as if Turks reserved permanence for public and, above all, religious building and considered it natural that private houses should not long outlive their occupants. Significantly the Turkish word for mansion (*konak*) means basically a resting place on a journey. These wooden houses, often squeezed into a narrow space in walled cities, were regularly destroyed by fires which left vast stretches of devastated ground (*yangın yeri*). The season of aubergines, which Turks like to eat sliced and fried, was traditionally the season of great fires, starting in kitchens as cooking oil caught fire and spreading quickly through tinder-dry buildings. The scars of these fires were until recently visible in most Turkish cities.

These Turkish houses were wooden from the foundations up, half timbered with clay packed between beams as along the Black Sea or made of rubble packed between laths hammered on to wooden posts (*bağdadi* or Baghdad-style houses). All these structures are elastic enough to withstand earthquakes, which are notoriously common in Turkey, particularly along the so-called Anatolian fault, running eastwards from the Aegean

along a line more or less parallel to the Black Sea. More suscept-
ible to earthquakes were houses built of stone or with a wooden
upper storey rising above the ground floor built of stones
covered with clay or mud mixed with chopped straw (*kâgir*, a
word which also designated brick or stone houses). Most dangerous of all, not only in earthquakes but also in cases of flood
or even heavy rain are the typical houses of the central Anatolian poor. These are square structures built of mud brick
(adobe, in Turkish, *kerpiç*) and surmounted by a heavy earth
roof on which more mud is piled and rolled flat after every
heavy fall of rain. In the colder climate of eastern Anatolia
stone takes the place of this unfired mud brick.

Turkish houses usually had projecting upper storeys with
windows covered in wooden lattice work. In large houses
women's apartments (*harem dairesi*) were separated from men's
which visitors were allowed to enter (hence the name *selâmlık*,
or place where one presents one's greetings). Furniture was
extremely simple and consisted basically of raised platforms
(*sedir*), covered with hard cushions (*minder*), and of carpets or
matting on the floor. Rolls of bedding (*yatak*, a word now
meaning bed) were spread on the floor and then tidied away
into chests. Food was eaten off trays (*tepsi*) placed on the
ground or on low legs, with the diners sitting cross-legged or
squatting round them. Spoons (*kaşık*), usually wooden and
brightly decorated, were the universal tool for eating. Water
was kept cool in large porous earthenware jugs (*testi*).

With a minimum of furniture and a maximum of surface,
carpets, mats, lace and hangings were widely used and the taste
for them has survived the introduction of modern furniture.
Carpet-making is a traditional Turkish art, which Anatolian
Turks brought with them from Central Asia, and the best
carpets always came from the inland areas of Anatolia which
the Turks had made their special home. The carpets and rugs
of Gördes (in eastern Anatolia), Kırşehir and villages near Kayseri (in central Anatolia) and of Uşak, Milâs and Bergama in the

west were particularly prized. The Turks distinguish between the hard-wearing, thick tufted carpet (*halı*) and the more ephemeral and cheaper woven rug (*kilim*). The latter are produced in large quantities by villagers and particularly by Kurdish and Turcoman tribesmen from wool, mohair and, cheapest of all, ordinary goat hair (*keçi*), and tend to have simple, attractive designs in bright primary colours contrasting with black stripes. Gaziantep in the south-east is today the main centre producing cheap *kilims*. With antique carpets and *kilims* rarer and more expensive in Turkey than in England, and with modern carpets also both more expensive and much less attractive in their combination of traditional designs and hard modern industrial dyes, the traveller who is not a connoisseur is well advised to stick to cheap *kilims*. In these too, industrial dyes are exclusively used, vegetable dyes having more or less disappeared at the turn of the century, but their simpler designs, not to mention their ridiculously low price, makes the substitution tolerable.

Craftsmanship is generally on the decline in Turkey as elsewhere, the position in Turkey being made worse by the sudden switch to industrial techniques often applied haphazardly by half-trained peasants, and also by the departure of the Armenians whose traditional skills (in silver and other metal work, pottery, some carpets etc.) are sorely missed.

Turkish pottery and glassware used to be much sought after in Europe, Iznik and, later, Kütahya pottery and *Çeşm-i bülbül* (literally 'eye of the nightingale') and Beykoz glass being particularly famous. Today pottery of traditional design is still turned out in Kütahya, but the workmanship is often poor, the plates chip easily and the product tends to be thick and clumsy. On the other hand, glass produced at the modern factory at Beykoz in Istanbul is of good quality and often elegant in the modern manner.

Most travellers will be offered and many will buy pipes and other objects made of meerschaum (*lületaşı* or Eskişehir stone,

from the town in western Anatolia whose neighbourhood sup-
plies this material to the whole world). The pipes have the advantage of being cheap, but the disadvantage of being so badly
designed as to be virtually unsmokable. Turkey is also rich in
alabaster (in Turkish, *Hacıbektaş taşı*, from a shrine in central
Anatolia near which it is mined), and this is fashioned into
hideous ashtrays and other bric-à-brac.

Turkey continues to produce good hand-made lace and em-
broidery, which modern Turkish dress designers use to good
effect in their collections. These are beginning to be shown and
to be appreciated in the west. If a visitor has enough time and
money he would be well advised to enquire for Turkish haute
couture dresses (traditional caftans, *entaris* and other styles)
which are made privately or at the state finishing schools
(Olgunlaşma Enstitüleri) and are supposed to last a lifetime.
Much cheaper are the attractive scarves of hand-woven heavy
silk, for which the Mediterranean tourist resort of Alanya is
famous. Turkish factory-made textiles, both wool and cotton,
are also remarkably good and cheap for a young industry. Mohair, the wool of the angora (Ankara) goat, is of course a
Turkish product, but it is better worked in Europe than in
Turkey.

Turkish food and cooking are to be counted among the joys
of travel to Turkey. The country has throughout history been
famous for its agricultural produce and was often an important
exporter of wheat, fish, cereals, fruit and vegetables. In recent
years, the rapid growth of population and the delay in the
introduction of intensive agricultural techniques have made
Turkey a net importer of cereals, but the country is self-suffici-
ent in almost all other foodstuffs and has a surplus in many.

The wheat produced on the Anatolian plateau is of the hard
variety, particularly suitable for the manufacture of *pasta*, as
well as making a delicious bread. Barley, of which Turkey
has exported considerable quantities, is highly suitable for use
in breweries. Vegetables are plentiful. In addition to the more

common varieties, there are aubergines, called by the Turks 'king of vegetables', since they form the basis of a whole galaxy of dishes, okra (or lady's fingers, in Turkish, *bamya*), large disc artichokes, delicious courgettes, as well as the unusual long hanging marrows (*asma kabağı*), grown on trellis. Notable fruits include Bursa peaches, apricots, the hard round pears of Ankara and Beypazar (in central Anatolia), large red apples from Amasya and Niğde (to the north-east and south-east of Ankara), highly-perfumed small bananas from Alanya, Jaffa oranges from Fethiye and the Hatay (on the Mediterranean coast), purple and green figs, a large variety of grapes (the large, thin-skinned *çavuş* being particularly prized), strawberries, (now unfortunately mainly of the large red variety, although the small white, perfumed strawberries named after the Istanbul suburb of Arnavutköy can still be found), round and oblong melons and water-melons, growing to prodigious size in Diyarbakır (in the south-east) where small children are often photographed crouching inside their rinds and camels are apocryphally supposed to be fully loaded when carrying two water-melons, one on each side of the hump. Turkey is the largest exporters of hazel-nuts in the world as well as producing large quantities of walnuts, pistachio nuts (near Gaziantep) and almonds.

Turkey is also the only Mediterranean country left with fish to spare, and since fish migrate from the Black Sea to the Mediterranean through the Turkish Straits, it is a Turkish fisherman who is likely to catch the last fish in this much-abused sea. However, that sad consummation is still some way off. In Turkish estimation the hierarchy of fish is headed by sea bass (*levrek*), followed by grey mullet (*kefal*), red mullet (*barbunya*), bluefish, (*lüfer*, caught in the Bosphorus after dark by fishermen carrying lighted candles or lamps to attract the fish) and swordfish (*kılıç balığı*). These are mainly Istanbul fish, while Izmir is famous for its dory (*çipura*) and plaice (*trança*). Gurnard (*kırlangıç balığı* or 'swallow fish') and the delicate fish known for its poisonous darts as sea scorpion (*iskorpit*) are used in delicious fish soups. Rare, but well worth looking for is sturgeon (*mersin balığı*), served smoked in expensive restaurants. Nor is there a lack of cheap and delicious varieties such as the bonito (*torik*, known in south Turkey as *kuzu balığı* or 'lamb fish' on account of its size) and the baby bonito (*palamut*). Salted bonito steaks (*lâkerda*), as delicate as smoked salmon, are Istanbul's speciality and are served with sweet raw onions. Istanbul boasts of large succulent lobsters, while excellent prawns come from the gulfs of Izmir and Iskenderun. In addition to common red roe, used in an hors d'oeuvre known as *tarama*, Turkey is the largest producer of the luxury botargo, (*balık yumurtası*), hard, salted grey-mullet roe, sealed in beeswax. Turkish black sturgeon caviar is good but extremely expensive.

Outside the large cities meat is often disappointing, although the country produces more and better meat than any of its neighbours and has the only beef worth eating in the Mediterranean area. However, like their neighbours, most Turks prefer mutton and lamb to beef. In the provinces a certain amount of goat meat is also eaten. Game abounds, including wild boar which Muslims do not eat, but which is occasionally available in Istanbul. In the autumn there is partridge (*keklik*), quail (*bıldırcın*), wild duck (*ördek*) and more rarely pheasant (*sülün*). Turks are enthusiastic hunters, and in spite of close seasons and other regulations there are signs that the stock of game is being depleted.

Turkish cooking, or rather Istanbul cooking, is to the Near East – from Yugoslavia to Persia – what French cooking is to the west. It is a metropolitan cuisine developed at and around a royal court and imitated in the provinces. Its excellence lies in the perfect use which it makes of the products of the Mediterranean world, so sadly misused in Spain and elsewhere. A complete traditional Turkish meal starts with *meze*, hors d'oeuvres of infinite variety served with the national drink, rakı. A rakı spread (*rakı sofrası*) is a meal in itself, including such items as fish (*lâkerda, balık yumurtası* and *tarama*, as well as Bombay duck in vinegar, fried mussels, shrimps etc), fried liver, boiled lambs' brains, pasties and cold vegetables in olive oil. Bowls of yoghurt with raw cucumber and garlic are also provided to counteract the toxic effects of alcohol.

The hors d'oeuvres are followed by a hot pastry course, *hamur işi*, meat, spinach or other ingredients wrapped in with rolled pastry. Then comes the meat course, usually a kebab with pilaf rice. The kebab can consist of small pieces of lamb grilled and skewered (*şiş kebap*), larger pieces of meat cut off a central rotating spit (*döner kebap*), stewed squares of meat (*tas kebap*) or a number of other varieties; the rice is stewed in butter or other kinds of fat and may be flavoured with tomato. Then, before the pudding, the stomach is rested with a cold dish of vegetables cooked in olive oil: aubergines, okra, artichoke, beans etc. The pudding is usually fried pastry soaked in syrup – *baklava*, which includes also pistachio nuts and honey, or a variety of sweet shapes known as lady's breasts, lady's thighs, lady's fingers etc. Pudding is followed by fruit and Turkish coffee, i.e. pulverised coffee boiled with or without sugar, the gradations varying from *sade* or bitter, through *az şekerli*, sweetish and *orta* medium to *çok şekerli* or very sweet. The grounds are not filtered but allowed to settle in the cup, and the drinker should therefore know when to stop sipping his coffee.

Few travellers will have the stomach for the full treatment. A popular alternative is *meze* by themselves or followed by a grill (*ızgara*) of meat or fish. Then there are the so-called milk shops (*muhallebici*), serving soup, rice, boiled chicken and a variety of milk puddings. Kebab houses (*kebapçı*) are also popular throughout the country. Hard drinkers resort to tripe shops (*işkembeci*), since tripe soup seasoned with vinegar, garlic etc., is a sovereign remedy for a hangover.

In the provinces food is much simpler. Occasionally the only choice is between 'fried' or 'boiled' meat (*kavurma* or *haşlama*), both being in fact stews containing a variable amount of grease.

But vegetables are always available and so is yoghurt, a Turkish contribution to healthy living and to the international vocabulary. Yoghurt diluted with water and seasoned with salt, known as *ayran*, is the standard drink of Anatolian peasants. Their diet relies heavily on buckwheat (*bulgur*), rice being too expensive and meat to be enjoyed only on special occasions. One Anatolian custom is to start the day with soup. This is a pleasant alternative, particularly after a party, to the usual Turkish breakfast of tea without milk, served with bread, white cheese, black olives and sticky jam. There are many regional variations in cuisine: thus on the Black Sea coast, where the olive tree is not indigenous, the main source of fat was provided by nuts, particularly crushed walnuts. The area has consequently given to Turkish cuisine a dish known as Circassian chicken, chicken covered with walnut purée seasoned with pepper. But the favourite of the inhabitants of the Black Sea coast is the small French anchovy (*hamsi*), which are caught in maximum numbers with the minimum of trouble. The south-east is known for its hot kebabs, spicy raw meatballs (*çiğ köfte*) and mashed chickpeas and other pulses. In food as in other ways it is thus a bridge area leading to the Arab world.

In the cities the traveller has to rely on menus, often written only in Turkish, but in the provinces he is advised, indeed invited, to inspect the food available in the kitchen. He will find there large round shallow saucepans, each containing a different dish: stew, rice, vegetables etc. No eyebrows will be raised if the visitor asks to taste before choosing. An expert can of course order food to be specially cooked for him. Food both cooked and raw is comparatively cheap in Turkey and astonishingly so in the provinces, so that the traveller can experiment with a light heart.

In the cities he will find beer available almost everywhere and wine in most places, as well as rakı, although some sort of a licence is required to serve alcoholic drink. In the provinces, particularly in the conservative central and eastern areas, there are places where drink is refused on principle. More often the infidel traveller is humoured and a boy sent out to buy a bottle of liquor from the grocer. Wine is cheap, less so than in Spain or Italy, but on the whole better than the ordinary varieties in either country. Service in city restaurants is good, since labour is still comparatively cheap and the unemployed numerous; in the countryside it is enthusiastic but rough and ready, waiters being almost invariably young boys, as no self-respecting Muslim would allow his wife or daughter to work in a place of common resort. The Turks also tend to be proud of their brandy and liqueurs, but the former is rough and the latter have their roughness masked by an overdose of sugar. However, both seem to find a market not only in Turkey but in Teutonic countries.

Football is undoubtedly the most popular form of sport in Turkey today, just as the pools (*spor-toto*) are the most prevalent form of gambling. League matches arouse intense emotion which, on occasion, spills over into bloody riots. Of traditional Turkish sports, *cirit*, a form of jousting, has all but died out; wrestling still produces Olympic champions, but is practised less and less. A picturesque form of this sport is 'greasy wrestling' (*yağlı güreş*), in which the contestants, who wear long leather breeches, are covered in olive oil to make holds more difficult. The Kırkpınar greasy wrestling national championships, held annually on an island near Edirne to determine the Chief Wrestler (*Başpehlivan*), attract large crowds of Turks and tourists. One Anatolian spectator sport which some tourists find attractive is camel wrestling.

In popular entertainment the cinema is supreme. It specialises in blood-and-thunder melodramas produced locally in vast numbers on absurdly low budgets. The more civilised arts – the theatre, opera and ballet – have a considerable following and are certainly more developed in Turkey than in most neighbouring countries. While opera and ballet are new imports, the theatre benefits from a local tradition of stylised racy comedies (*orta oyunu*) with stock characters engaged in permutations of stock situations. A popular entertainment in a similar vein is the Turkish shadow play (*karagöz*). Puppets cut out of cardboard or leather are reflected on a white screen. The two main characters are the quick-witted Karagöz and the oafish Hacivat, and their adventures, misadventures and interminable quarrels are reminiscent of a punch and judy show. The dialogue is brisk, often vulgar, and spiced with references to matters of current concern.

Karagöz shows are traditional at circumcision parties (*sünnet düğünü*) and other popular rejoicings. Circumcision, performed when a boy is seven years of age or more, is essentially an initiation ceremony marking the passage from infancy to adolescence. It is, therefore, as much an occasion for rejoicing as is a marriage, the same word (*düğün*) being used to describe the festivities marking the two occasions. And since not everyone can afford to celebrate the event in a fitting manner, it is traditionally an act of piety for a rich man to organise circumcision parties for poor boys or to have a poor boy circumcised at the same time as his own son.

City weddings are today tame occasions redolent of international suburban culture. A brief ceremony at the city hall is followed by a reception at which dulcet tangos are played and vast quantities of sweet soft drinks are offered round. In contrast with romantic urban alliances, village weddings, which are usually preceded by hard bargaining until the bride-price (*başlık*) is agreed, are lively. The bride, veiled illegally for this one occasion, is taken to the bridegroom's house in a procession mounted – if not on horses, then on motor cars or even tractors – preceded by pipers and drummers. There is music, folk-dancing and general merrymaking, the din going on through the night while the marriage is consummated.

Urbanisation has not yet destroyed Turkey's vigorous tradition of folk-dancing, with its many regional variations, its sword-dancers, handkerchief-dancers, dancers in the round, dancers imitating battle and all other possible forms of this art. Folk-dance festivals are often held in the holiday season and are, incidentally, the only occasions on which folk costume can be seen, the sartorial reforms of the Republic – insisting that hat, jacket and trousers are the only form of civilised dress – having otherwise produced a uniform greyness.

The great majority of Turks remain attached to their music, usually described simply as oriental, and stemming, it would seem, from Antioch and elsewhere in Syria, whence it spread west to Byzantium and east to Persia. To western ears it often sounds plaintive and monotonous, and appreciation of it is not promoted by the tinny loudspeakers from which it usually emerges. However, Turkish folk music can be lively and tuneful, while classical Ottoman music has a precision, grace and balance reminiscent of plain-chant, which belongs to the same tradition. It remains nonetheless true that the Turks are addicted to musical tear-jerkers, and many a Turkish outing is enlivened by such pop hits as 'The Consumptive Girl', 'The Prison Warden' or 'Death in Foreign Parts'. Various explanations are offered for this predilection for pleasure in pain, Marxists attributing it to the sufferings of a down-trodden proletariat, and amateur psychologists to sexual frustration in a repressive society. Records both of these pop hits and of more pleasing compositions are readily available, and while the quality of recording is low, so is the price.

Turkish music distinguishes between open-air instruments (*meydan sazları*), largely pipes and drums used in folk music or by the revived janissary band (*mehter takımı*), which can often be seen performing on national holidays, and fine instruments (*ince saz*) whose string sections include the rebeck (*rebap*), the lute (*ut*), the dulcimer (*kanun*), as well as instruments approximating to violins and guitars. The most popular string instrument, which accompanies folk songs, is the *bağlama*, a simple three-stringed guitar, smaller than the *bozuk*, another Turkish instrument recently made famous in Greece where it is known as the *bouzouki*. Classical Turkish music follows a number of traditional modes (*makam*), the full composition (*fasıl*) consisting of a fixed number of ingredients: instrumental, vocal (usualy a poem set to music), fast, slow, cadenzas etc.

Most travellers pick up a few words of Turkish, and reading Turkish text presents no difficulty, since the language is written in Latin characters, the spelling is phonetic and Turkish sounds are fairly easy to master by Europeans. However, grammar and vocabulary are another matter. Turkish is often classed with Finnish, Estonian and Hungarian in the west and Mongolian in the east in a Uralo-Altaic family of languages. With these alleged kinsmen it shares not its vocabulary but its structure, which is based on unchanging roots, usually of one or two syllables. Suffixes are added to these to qualify, extend or define the meaning. Person, case, number, tense, form of the verb (indicative, passive, reflexive, causative and reciprocal), negative, interrogative and other grammatical states are all indicated by suffixes, which are tacked on to each other, often making up words of inordinate length. These can only be spoken without loss of breath if one remembers that in Turkish stress is slight and, in any case, divided and that a Turkish word need not be ejaculated in one gush. The absence of relatives, such as 'who' and 'which', and of the verbs 'to be' and 'to have' and the peculiar syntax which always places qualifications before the word qualified and the verb right at the end, thus producing the effect sometimes called back-think, add to the difficulty and for a linguist, to the fascination of the language. Turkish has been enriched by large numbers of borrowings from Persian, which is an Indo-European, and Arabic which is a Semitic language, Persian and Arabic standing to Turkish roughly in the same relation as that of Greek and Latin to English. Recently efforts have been made to reduce the number of Persian and Arabic loan words, replacing them by newly coined Turkish words and by borrowings from French and other west European languages. West European words which are gaining in international current use are in any case flooding the language independently of any conscious policy of the authorities or of philologists.

Until the last war most members of the small educated élite spoke French. Today many educated Turks speak or understand English. Thousands of Turkish workers who have been to Germany, as well as professional people educated in that country, have naturally learnt German, while French is still taught in the excellent French schools in Istanbul, as well as in Turkish schools and, above all, in the old Imperial Lycée of Galatasaray. Thus in the cities the European traveller will usualy find someone to interpret for him. However, the number of Turks proficient in foreign languages is not all that large and, particularly in the countryside, communication can be a problem. The traveller is therefore well advised to equip himself with a simple phrase book.

22   *Interior of the early Ottoman Great Mosque (Ulu Cami) in Bursa*

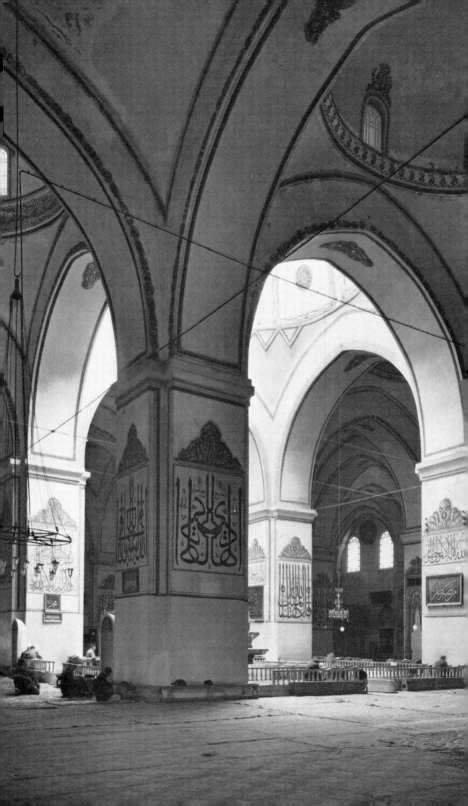

23 *Arch and minaret, Sultan Ahmet Mosque, Istanbul*

4. Thrace

Motorists going to Turkey often choose the crossing at Ipsala on the road from Alexandroupolis (Dedeağaç) in Greek Thrace, to Istanbul, and thus miss the frontier city of Edirne (Adrianople) lying to the north. This is a pity, for Edirne provides a pleasant, although not altogether typical introduction to Turkey. This city, once the second capital of the Ottoman Empire and one of the chief centres of the Balkans, has shrunk to less than half its former size. The absence of population pressure, so obvious elsewhere in Turkey, has allowed the authorities to achieve an unusual degree of neatness, particularly round the central Cumhuriyet Meydanı (Republic Square). This name, as ubiquitous in Turkey as its prototype, Place de la République is in France, usually brings to mind dusty squares embellished by awful little municipal gardens and sickly acacia trees, and overlooked by low square government buildings. Elsewhere in the Turkish provinces Republic Squares exude the tedium of the unemployed and semi-employed who hang around them, of peasants waiting patiently to get a piece of paper signed at government offices, of dilapidated taxis and even more bedraggled horse-carriages waiting for fares, of civil servants who exchange the boredom of their offices for that of some municipal restaurant (Belediye Lokantası), noisy with badly recorded Turkish music relayed through tinny loudspeakers in order to attract customers. Deadly at lunch time, when beer is usually the only drink ordered, these restaurants are not much gayer in the evening, and the rakı that circulates freely after sunset only adds poignancy to speculations about impending transfers and promotions or, when all other subjects are exhausted, to bets placed by customers who seek to predict the exact spot on a wall painting of some improbable Alpine scene on which the largest of the many flies buzzing around is about to land. After a taste of these provincial city centres, the broad sweep of the Turkish countryside, where human endeavour is expressed in the dignity of agriculture rather than the indignity of bureaucracy and of jerrybuilding, comes as a relief and an inspiration.

But in Edirne, Republic Square is overlooked not just by a modern municipality, but by three of the finest mosques to be seen anywhere in Turkey: the fifteenth-century Eski Cami (Old Mosque) and Üç Şerefeli Cami (mosque with three galleries in one of its minarets), and the sixteenth-century Selimiye Camii. The city has another three notable mosques: Yıldırım Camii, the oldest of all, built in 1399, on the foundations of a church; Muradiye Camii, built in 1435-6, and just across the river Tunca, the mosque of Beyazit II (Bayezid II), completed in 1488. Mosques, in which Edirne is so rich, remain to this day the chief architectural ornament of most Turkish cities, their distinction of form and the craftsmanship displayed by their architects, standing in clear and surprising contrast with the cheap and nasty building that is often to be seen around.

The mosques of Edirne have the additional advantage of providing at a glance a summary of the development of Ottoman architecture. The Eski Cami, a smaller version of the earlier Ulu Cami (Great Mosque) in Bursa, still gives the impression of a covered courtyard, its flat roof surmounted by nine small domes. Next, the Üç Şerefeli Cami represents the first step towards the grandiose cathedral mosque, where a large prayer hall is crowned by an equally large central dome, measuring in this instance 78 feet in diameter and 92 feet in height. This central dome is surrounded by four medium-sized and four smaller domes. The mosque of Beyazit II is a large

square building whose height weakens the effect of the flat
dome which surmounts it. Finally the Selimiye is to many
Turks one of the masterpieces not only of Sinan, the most
famous Ottoman architect, but of Ottoman mosque architecture itself, although some critics argue that its four tall minarets
are placed too near the main structure, thus upsetting the
balance between base and elevation. The central dome of this
mosque, more than 100 feet in diameter, resting on eight pillars
and supported by eight buttresses, dominates the composition.
The elimination of half-domes has allowed the placing of a
large number of windows round the central dome, thus giving
an impression of lightness in sharp contrast with the fortress-
like appearance of the mosque of Beyazit ii. All these mosques
are surrounded by outbuildings, which house schools, libraries,
hospitals and almshouses. Most of them, and in particular the
Eski Cami, contain superb examples of Ottoman mural calligraphy – square Cufic, elongated Coranic, flowing Persian etc.
The inscription 'Allah' on the wall of the porch of the Eski Cami
is deservedly famous. Unfortunately most of the original tiles
of Edirne mosques have been destroyed in the many wars and
occupations suffered by the city, but the china panels on the
internal wall of the Selimiye facing Mecca are among the finest
of the kind. Also interesting is the perpetuation by Ottoman
mosque architects of the Byzantine practice of incorporating
into new buildings columns transported from antique ruins.
Thus columns from Syria and also possibly from Athens have
found a final resting place in the cloisters of the Selimiye. Borrowings were not of course limited to materials: the Selimiye
is in some respects a work if not of imitation, then of conscious
emulation of St Sophia in Istanbul, with Sinan clearly priding
himself on the fact that he had exceeded by six cubits the
height of his rival's dome.

Edirne is a city of great mosques. It used also to be a city of
great palaces. Of these little remains but some out-buildings on
the island of Sarayiçi ('Within the Palace') on the river Tunca,

an island more famous today as the venue of the annual 'Greasy Wrestling' championships. The buildings that remain are misnamed Eski Saray (Old Palace), when in fact they belong to the second great palace built by Ottoman sultans. The first had been constructed by Murat 1 in 1365-6, outside the old citadel, but within the modern town (near the Selimiye) and at one time this palace could accommodate 6,000 pages. Today it has completely disappeared. The palace on the island dates back to 1450, and in the seventeenth century it contained 18 pavilions, eight oratories, five audience chambers and 14 baths. It inspired a famous ode by the poet Nef'î (born c. 1572, strangled for an unfortunate satire in 1635), beginning with the lines:

What is this? The city of Edirne or a celestial rose garden?
The Sultan's Castle or Highest Heaven?
And the palace standing in open country,
Is it a mansion of Paradise or a distant Caabah on holy
    ground?
Are these lawns surrounded by streams
Or watered silk bordered with blue?
Are the streams lined with green meadows
Or is the blue-green dome of heaven reflected in the water?
Is the Sultan's person guarded by rivers
Or are these dragons keeping watch over the State treasure?

While Nef'î was composing his oriental hyperboles, Edirne was still visited regularly by the Sultans during the campaigning or the hunting season.

The city, built as it is in a bend of the river Tunca near the point where it meets the wider Meriç (Maritza), owes its importance to two distinct factors. It used to be a considerable inland port serving the Balkan valleys for which it was a natural gateway. Its decline in recent years is thus due not only to the destruction wrought by wars, but to the loss of its hinterland in Greece and Bulgaria. Secondly, Edirne was the first important staging post after Istanbul, from which it is separated by the rolling Thracian steppe, a country which it was as easy to cross on horseback as it is today in a motor car.

The geography and consequently the history of Turkish eastern Thrace is dominated by the fact that along the Black Sea this region is bordered by the Istranca mountains which catch most of the rain brought by the cool northern winds. The northern slopes of the Istranca were as a result covered with thick forests which still survive in places, while to the south the land is bone dry, the spring rains draining away quickly to the Mediterranean through deep wadis cut in the soft limestone. Harsh winters and hot dry summers make inland Thrace a natural prolongation of the Anatolian environment which Turks have found so congenial. Eastern Thrace is, like the Anatolian plateau, a land of dry farming and of fast marches. The Indo-European Thracians who first inhabited it in historical times raided as far east as the borders of Mesopotamia and established themselves permanently in much of Anatolia. The Thracians were later conquered by the kindred Macedonians who gave Edirne its first known name of Orestias. However, the modern city owes its name and its foundation to Emperor Hadrian (A.D. 117-138), traces of whose walls are still to be seen between the Clock Tower and the Gazimihal bridge carrying the main road to Bulgaria across the Tunca. From Hadrian to the city's capture by the Ottomans in 1362, Adrianople was notable mainly for the battles to which it was host and the sieges which it sustained. It was near the city that Constantine defeated his rival Licinius in 323, the year, that is, before he chose Byzantium as the capital of his empire. It was also at Adrianople that in 378 the Roman legions led by the Emperor Valens were broken by Gothic cavalry, a defeat from which neither Rome nor the service of infantry ever recovered, the military supremacy of the horse lasting well into modern times.

Between its martial past and its present role as a tidy museum, Ottoman Edirne had a long stretch of commercial prosperity which not even the Russian occupation of 1829 could destroy. This prosperity attracted and was promoted by a vigorous Jewish community of Spanish origin, although in Edirne as in Istanbul there had already been Greek-speaking Jews in Byzantine times. A small Jewish community survives to this day, one of the few to remain in Turkey outside Istanbul. It is of the peaceable and adaptable Edirne Jews that Turks tell a story typical of Oriental peoples who have learnt the art of survival through the vicissitudes of history. The city was captured by the Russians in 1878, by the Bulgarians in 1913 and recaptured by the Turks in the same year. As Turkish horsemen entered it, a Jew was heard to shout 'Long live, long live!' 'Long live who?' a bystander asked. 'That is not yet clear,' the Jew replied, and he was right, since the Greeks were next to occupy the city in 1918 and the Turks did not re-establish themselves firmly in it until the conclusion of the Treaty of Lausanne in 1923. A small Jewish community, a large Victorian synagogue and a large rebuilt covered market survive from the days of commercial prosperity.

Covered markets – in Turkish, *kapalı çarşı* or *bedesten*, a term more properly applied to the section of the market where valuable goods are sold – are a traditional, picturesque and disappearing feature of Turkish and other Oriental cities. Shops in these markets are grouped by trades: drapers, haberdashers, cobblers, saddlers, carpet merchants, jewellers etc., all have their own sections. Nowadays cheap locally manufactured textiles, clothes made from them and cheap plastics predominate. Since the markets cater largely for peasants, these goods find a ready sale, as does the local eau de Cologne made from Turkish spirit, and strong imported, usually English, artificial scents, of which Turks like other Oriental people make great use. Jewellers specialise in gold bracelets in which craftsmanship takes second place to the value of the gold, since these represent a traditional form of peasant investment and a status symbol for peasant wives.

Tourists looking for typically Turkish goods are offered hand embroideries, leather goods (which are cheap), carpets (usually expensive), silver filigree work (coming mainly from eastern Turkey, particularly Diyarbakır and reasonably priced, provided the articles are well made, which is not always the case), meerschaum pipes, objects carved from alabaster, and in Bursa, knives with buffalo-horn handles and towels, both well worth buying. Most of the goods offered for sale are in fact cheap, nationally distributed consumer goods and as such usually not subject to bargaining. For most other articles the customer is expected to bargain, and it is worth remembering that gold, silver, precious stones and good carpets are cheaper in western Europe, so that the best bargains are medium-priced products of local craftsmanship. Antiques, which are often offered for sale, should be treated with great caution: not only is their export illegal, but the market is so flooded with fakes – from obvious ones sold by children outside archaeological sites to highly sophisticated and highly-priced imitations – that only an expert can distinguish them from the genuine article. Shops usually extend beyond the limit of the covered market, and in particular the noisier trades, such as that of the coppersmiths, are practised outside it. Finally, souvenir hunters have at least one thing to be grateful for: since Turkey severely restricts the import of consumer goods, what there is to buy, however cheap and nasty, is unlikely to have been made in Japan or Hong Kong. In neighbouring Cyprus the reverse obtains.

Outside the neat rebuilt covered market of Edirne, there is a neat street (Sarraçlar Caddesi or Saddlers' Avenue), where the traveller may have his first introduction to Turkish cafés. Turkish coffee, always served with a glass of water which the customer is meant to drink first in order to clear his mouth, local tea served without milk in small glasses, and soft drinks usually manufactured under licence from American firms, which have all but displaced the local *gazöz* or sweetened aerated water, can be bought for a few pence. Very occasionally one can also get beer, brewed locally either by the State Monopoly or, more expensively, by international firms, and very good in both cases. The café may be a quiet one devoted largely to the reading of newspapers (in which case it is called a *kıraathane* or reading room) or the rougher sort frequented by drivers, when it will be noisy with backgammon (*tavla*) and playing cards which the players bend and slap down on the table, producing surprising bangs. Tips are expected in most cafés, restaurants and hotels, but since a service charge is usually added, they need not be very large, and are in any case much lower than the ten or fifteen per cent customary in the west. On the other hand, taxi drivers do not expect tips since they take the precaution of over-charging. But prices are still reasonable, unless the customer looks a simpleton, the driver is a rapacious fiend, or both. Taxis drivers charging by the meter are so rare as to deserve special commendation.

Turkey seems to be the country of origin of the *dolmuş* or shared taxi, serving a fixed route and starting only when it has filled its complement of passengers. *Dolmuşes* ply not only in, but also between towns, some go as far afield as Germany, and there are *dolmuş* motorboats in Istanbul. They are cheap, since they have to compete with even cheaper public transport, and therefore a boon to the traveller, except the motorist who may find the *dolmuş* suddenly pulling up in front of him to allow a passenger to get on or off. Progress has had one unfortunate result in allowing *dolmuş* drivers to instal record-players and to buy cheap plastic pop records, meretricious in lyrics and composition, appalling in execution and hideously recorded. But since the *dolmuş* driver is master of his vehicle, no one can object to his choice nor yet to the volume of the music.

The roads across the Thracian uplands from Edirne and from Ipsala to Istanbul are both dull, except for a feeling of spaciousness which Turkey, like Spain, never fails to inspire, and except in the late spring, when ripening fields of corn and sunflower cover this dry land with splashes of brilliant colour. Sunflower, long cultivated in Bulgaria, is a comparative newcomer to Turkey where it has become a popular crop only recently as a result of the authorities' attempts to limit the cultivation of low-grade tobacco and of the new demand created by margarine producers. As butter is expensive and olive oil in great demand throughout the world and therefore also increasingly expensive, margarine, which is manufactured by the usual international companies, has become a staple of Turkish diet.

The Ipsala road approaches the Sea of Marmara at Tekirdağ (formerly Rodosto), a busy but undistinguished little town which planners are trying to develop in order to relieve congestion in Istanbul. To the traveller it offers little beyond some refreshing seaside restaurants where he may with luck be able to taste local fish. East of Tekirdağ, the Ipsala road joins the Edirne road for the final approach to Istanbul, the last stretch being known as Londra Asfaltı or London Asphalt from its presumed final destination. The suburbs of Istanbul start by the lagoon of Çekmece. However, the village of Küçük Çekmece lies outside the Istanbul municipal boundaries and, for reasons which are not very clear, absence of control has allowed the growth of the best meat restaurants in the city.

The northern shores of the Sea of Marmara are comparatively flat and therefore dull, fit candidates for the extension of ribbon development. However, west of Tekirdağ, the Garros hills have so far proved an effective obstacle to the construction of a coastal road to the Gallipoli peninsula. Much less known and less accessible than Gallipoli is the Black Sea coast of Thrace, north of the Istranca mountains. Yet apart from the difficulty of communications, which is gradually being remedied, this coast with its long sandy beaches, lagoons, forests and mountains, could rival in attraction its northern extension, the Black Sea coast of Bulgaria, home of much-publicised and much-frequented resorts.

A motorist can approach the Black Sea coast of Turkish Thrace either from the west, from Edirne through Kırklareli, or

from Istanbul in the east. The road from Edirne to Kırklareli
crosses the typically bare Thracian hills, cut here and there by
the gullies of the Ergene river and its tributaries. Kırklareli (formerly Kırk Kilise or Forty Churches) is, like so many other
places in Thrace, a garrison town, the whole area being until
recently a vast military camp defending the approaches to
Istanbul. Equally uneventful is the run from Kırklareli to Pınarhisar, notable only for its cement works. However, if the
motorist is brave enough to take the earth road over a spur of
the Balkan mountains from Pınarhisar to Demirköy, he will be
richly rewarded. The southern slopes of the mountain are bare
and deeply eroded, but over the top the scene changes completely. Thick forests of beech, oak and ash stretch into the distance. There are gushing springs by the roadside. The Depart-
ment of State Forests, which controls the whole area, has
opened up a few picnic sites and provided them with rough
wooden tables and benches. The road winds down through
forests and over fast streams down to the neat Alpine-looking
village of Demirköy, inhabited largely by forestry officials.
Then the country flattens out, but it is still green, dotted with
trees and reed beds, between the typically small Black Sea
fields growing maize and flax as well as wheat. Unlike central
Thrace, a typically Turkish land, these edges of sea and mountain had remained until the Great War an enclave of Greeks
and, a little inland, of Bulgarians. Communications were by
sea, and Greeks were predominant as sailors and fishermen.
After the Great War the area was resettled with Turkish
refugees from Greece and Bulgaria, peasants often from mountain homes, who have yet to adapt themselves to their new
environment.

The road from Demirköy ends at the idyllic village of
Iğneada, at the centre of a small bay, sheltered from the north
by a long sandy spit (hence its name meaning Needle Island,
really needle peninsula) and bordered by miles of sandy beach.
Sheltered narrow valleys between the mountains which often

tumble precipitously into the sea, making a coastal road almost impossible, are a characteristic of this charming corner of Turkey. Although the distances are comparatively short, it takes at least two days to explore the whole coast from the Bulgarian frontier to Istanbul, since to move from one coastal village to the next the motorist has to turn inland to rejoin the main Kırklareli-Istanbul road. But the effort is worth while : it affords the visitor the satisfaction of being a pioneer near a great metropolis; it offers an escape from crowds and, in the summer, from heat and dust. There is superb bathing and ample room for camping. What the coast does not offer is anything but the roughest hotels and the plainest Anatolian-type food, usually mutton stew of one kind or another. Fish will remain scarce until the Turkish settlers take to the sea like their Greek predecessors. The beaches are either completely deserted or, as elsewhere in provincial Turkey, frequented by village boys, but taboo to the girls. One can follow the whole Black Sea coast from the Bulgarian to the Russian frontiers without once seeing a girl swimming – except of course from the beaches of Istanbul.

Turkish provincial hotels of the non-tourist variety deserve a separate mention. Since the advent of DDT they are usually free of insects. Otherwise the only amenity which they offer is a bed. The bed is covered with a sheet, often of doubtful cleanliness, and rolled at the bottom of it lies a quilt to which a counterpane is pinned. Traditionally Turks sleep rolled in a quilt, using the bed therefore more or less as a floor, on which formerly bedding used to be spread. Payment is for each single bed, and to ensure privacy one has to hire all the beds in a room, if these happen to be free. This is not usually expensive as the charge per bed can be as low as five or ten lira. Sometimes the hotel is simply divided into two dormitories for the two sexes. Sanitary arrangements are usually primitive, while lighting is provided at night by a weak bare bulb dangling from a fly-blown ceiling. There is no cooking done on the premises, but a boy can usually be sent out to fetch a glass of tea or a cup of coffee. Staying at these hotels one appreciates the insistence of some Turks that they are not so much a nation as an army ready to camp anywhere with the minimum of fuss. 'A bed is a bed,' as an innkeeper at the small Thracian town of Vize said to me when I objected to a suffocating little cubicle without a single window.

Vize, south of Pınarhisar, has some distinguished-looking Ottoman mosques. At night the restaurants are full of lorry drivers and of officers and NCO's from nearby military camps. As usual in the provinces, not a single woman is to be seen abroad after nightfall, and the men can drink rakı to their hearts' content in a spirit of barrack-room camaraderie. Food in inland Thrace is usually better than in other provinces, partly because Istanbul exerts a civilising influence and partly because this is a cattle-breeding area. It is also famous for its yoghurt, preferably the thick and creamy kind made at Silivri not far from Istanbul.

From Saray, the next stop after Vize on the Kırklareli-Istanbul road, a side turning leads to the Black Sea coastal village of Midye, now officially and unimaginatively renamed Kıyıköy, i.e. Coastal Village. In contemporary history it has figured only once, in 1913 when Turkey was pressed by the Balkan allies and their mentors among the Great Powers to accept as its western frontier the line from Midye to Enez, on the Mediterranean at the mouth of the Meriç. As the Ottoman government seemed willing to comply, the Young Turkish leader Enver seized the ministries and then marched to reoccupy Edirne. Midye was at the time a purely Greek village surrounded by Byzantine walls and famous for its monastery cut out of rock. The bare ruins of the monastery are still to be seen, as are the very impressive walls. But inside the walls there is an air of dilapidation: the present inhabitants still behave and feel as squatters. The past of their new home is for them a mystery surrounded by myth. 'There used to be forty bakeries here in the days of the infidels, and still they could not bake enough bread, so populous was Midye,' my local guide said to me as we walked through the shrunken village. Taking me to the ruined monastery, he showed a trough cut in the rock explaining 'And this is where the priests used to wash corpses in wine.' Then a hole in the wall drew the inevitable comment 'From here priests used to watch pretty girls in the congregation.' These stories can be matched by the ignorance of Islam exhibited by Greeks across the border, for after centuries of coexistence the two peoples have become remarkably estranged from each other. In any case, the traveller should realise that descriptions of Christian churches offered by local guides have a strong element of pure myth. In one of the many rock churches in Cappadocia one guide showed me some indentations in a wall and explained, 'This is where the priests used to tie their prisoners before torturing them.' An alien past and its alien monuments thus become the subject of new myths to which repressed urges can be happily consigned.

In spite of its dilapidation, Midye is one of the most attractive spots on the coast. It is built on a headland rising between two beaches, one of which separates the sea from a small lagoon where fishing boats are repaired. At one end, the village hill is joined to the mainland by a causeway, at the other it drops precipitously into the sea, which is overlooked, alas, by a couple of suburban bungalows. Inside the village there is a profusion of mulberry trees, while the hills inland are covered by young trees and scrub, described on maps as degraded forest – all that centuries of charcoaling have left of the magnificent forests which can still be seen farther north. The sale of firewood and charcoal was until recently the main occupation of the local Turkish villagers. Now forests are protected much more effectively and there are savage penalties for unauthorised felling. But in many cases all that the laws preserve are vast areas of unproductive scrub.

The picturesque seaward slopes and cliffs of Midye are all

too often used as a dumping ground for rubbish. This unfortunately is a common practice in Turkey, where urban management is surprisingly backward or simply absent – surprising
because, at its best, Ottoman culture had produced a civilised
style of town life. True, Ottoman private architecture was
mostly developed for and by the rich, who could enjoy their
wooden mansions set in well-tended walled gardens. But the
complexes of public buildings – mosques, schools, bath houses
– and the grouping of shops and bazaars imposed a pattern on
Turkish towns, a pattern which reflected the articulation of an
organised society. Today the destruction of the old social pattern and the absence of satisfactory successors can be seen in
the architectural disorganisation of towns. The departure of the
minorities with their traditional skills, the fall from power of
the old notables with their sense of style, the rise everywhere
of a lower middle-class recruited from the villages, the population explosion – are reflected in messy towns where progress is
signalled by awful suburban bungalows or by badly-built blocks
of flats showing their unfurnished flanks to the surrounding
population and standing like graceless minarets of the new religion of development. The indiscriminate littering of open
spaces is perhaps the result of the carelessness of former peasants used to the vastness of an indestructible countryside, but
it is a carelessness which is encouraged by the absence of any
pattern or style in most towns.

But to return to the Black Sea coast of Thrace – the next seaside village, south-east of Midye, is the newly renamed Yalıköy
with its immense pebble beach. However, here the coast affords
little shelter from the wind or shade from the sun and the
pebbles have their share of tar which tankers continue to dis-
charge regardless of agreements. Since the Turkish Straits are a
major international seaway, the problem of tar pollution is
acute in the Sea of Marmara and round its two exits.

South of Yalıköy comes Terkos where a spit separates the
sea from a fresh-water lake which has for a long time furnished

the European districts of Istanbul with their now inadequate water supply. The Victorian style of the pump house and the surrounding buildings testifies to the European origin of this venerable utility. Then, if the motorist turns off the main Kırklareli road, he can follow uncharted tracks through the forest of Belgrade to the Black Sea resort of Kilyos, just west of the northern entrance of the Bosphorus, and then drive on to Istanbul by a good new road.

The Black Sea coast of Thrace has always been on the edges of history. Not so the south-eastern corner of European Turkey – the peninsula of Gallipoli. To reach it from Istanbul one has to follow the road to Tekirdağ, then turn inland to Malkara and the small garrison town of Keşan, circumnavigating the Garros massif which rises to some 3,000 feet, isolating the wine-growing coastal area of Mürefte. After Keşan the main Gallipoli road climbs the foothills of the Garros through picturesque pine forests. This was the main overland supply route of the Turkish troops defending Gallipoli in the Great War and, ironically, the road was improved by British engineers in the Second World War as a precaution against German attack. From the Garros the road drops down to the Gulf of Saroz on the Aegean side of the peninsula, then rises slightly to the village of Bolayır, situated at the waist of the peninsula and overlooking both the Aegean and the Sea of Marmara. Bolayır had a place in Turkish history well before the Gallipoli campaign of 1915-16. A small and tastelessly-restored mausoleum houses here the tombs of Süleyman Paşa, son of Orhan, the second Ottoman sultan, and of Süleyman's tutor and his horse. It was Süleyman Paşa who had led the first Ottoman troops across the Straits into Europe. The tombs have been restored and furnished with inscriptions in the Latin alphabet which Turkish artists have not yet learnt to handle as artistically as the old calligraphers had handled the Arabic script. Some Muslims are embarrassed by the presence of the horse in the mausoleum. 'Does our religion allow it?' my driver wondered. I did not know the answer, but since

Süleyman is supposed to have died of a fall from his horse, I felt that the animal had been treated generously.

In the mausoleum garden lies the tomb of Namık Kemal (1840-88), the Ottoman 'Poet of Liberty', who provided the main literary inspiration for the Young Turkish coup of 1908. Kemal, who was in turn civil servant, journalist, translator, poet and dramatist, and always a nationalist politician, derived most of his ideas from western Europe where he spent three years editing subversive newspapers, the best-known being *Hürriyet* (Freedom), published in London in 1868-70. He died in exile on the island of Chio, then an Ottoman possession, his body being transferred to Bolayır by the Young Turks who thought it appropriate that the man who had brought European thought to Turkey should lie beside the soldier who had first brought Turkish arms to Europe.

Süleyman Paşa had first crossed the Dardanelles apparently as an ally of John Cantacuzenus, a contestant for the Byzantine throne, established a military settlement in the Gallipoli peninsula, and, when an earthquake had breached the walls of Gallipoli in 1354, occupied the town. Such were the small beginnings of the Ottoman conquest in Europe, but the importance of the undertaking was not lost on Süleyman's contemporaries who saw in it the hand of Providence. A poet close to the court composed a congratulatory ode which read:

Leading your people in holy zeal,
You have made a raft of your prayer-rug,
And taken the coast of Roumelia in your pious hands.

The Byzantine castle of Gallipoli which Süleyman Paşa restored did not stay Ottoman without a struggle. It was captured in 1366 by the Crusaders led by the Duke of Savoy, but the Byzantine Emperor was forced to return it to Sultan Murat I ten years later. From that time until the conquest of Constantinople, Gallipoli was the Turks' main crossing point into Europe,

24   *Late Ottoman Nusretiye mosque, Istanbul, with the Genoese tower of Galata in the background*

and as such the main objective of Christian counter-offensives. 'If the said castle and port are captured,' the Frenchman de Lannoy wrote in 1422, 'the Turks will have no secure passage left from one side to the other, and the land which they have in Greece will be lost.' However, attempts by the Venetians to capture Gallipoli failed, and the local fortress known as 'The Abode of Warriors' remained as the main Ottoman naval base until a new arsenal was constructed in Istanbul in 1515. In the seventeenth century the Ottomans pushed their defences forward to Seddülbahir (meaning the Sea Rampart) near the tip of the peninsula and, opposite it on the Asiatic side, to the new fortress of Kumkale (Sandcastle), and Gallipoli became a rear base, a function which it performed for the last time during the Great War. Nevertheless the town remained prosperous as a centre of both overland and sea trade; it was for some time the administrative centre of Turkish possession in the Aegean, and it levied dues on ships passing through the Straits. Today its population of some 13,000 lives largely by fishing and sardine canning, the chimneys of the cannery rivalling in height the ruins of the historic castle. There are some pleasant seaside fish restaurants frequented by discriminating weekenders from Istanbul, who are attracted by the view, the quality of the fish and its comparatively low price. As a first port of call and clearance station for ships going through the Straits Gallipoli has been supplanted by its Asiatic rival Çanakkale, the administrative centre of the province spanning the Dardanelles. Çanakkale Boğazı (the Straits of Çanakkale) is in fact the Turkish name for the Dardanelles, and the Gallipoli campaign is known to the Turks as the Battle of Çanakkale.

Gallipoli lies at the eastern end of the Dardanelles, a channel some forty miles long and with a width ranging from five miles to less than one mile. Known in classical times as Hellespont, it owes its present western name to Dardanus, the mythical ancestor of the Trojans and their genealogical link with mainland Greece, as he was said to have been a king in the Peloponnese

25 *Quayside scene in Istanbul*

before emigrating first to Thrace and then to Asia. The nar-
rowest point of the Straits is between Çanakkale and the castle
of Kilitbahir (literally Key of the Sea), corresponding to the
ancient Abydos and Cestos. Abydos was the home of Hero,
priestess of Aphrodite, and Cestos the nightly starting point
of her clandestine lover Leander, who swam across the Straits
guided by a light from Hero's tower, until the inevitable end
when the lamp was left unlit, and he lost his way and was
drowned. Today incidentally the name of Leander's Tower has
been transferred in western usage to a structure at the southern
entrance to the Bosphorus. It was also at the narrow neck of
the Dardanelles that Xerxes, the Persian Great King, is said to
have crossed into Europe, marching his troops over two pon-
toon bridges, at the start of his unsuccessful attempt to conquer Greece. Here again Alexander made an eastward crossing
when he set out to fight and destroy the Persian Empire. Lord
Byron, who swam across the 1,250-yard channel in 1810, followed the romantic tradition of Leander rather than the martial one of the two emperors. Today, a Turkish car ferry plies
between the village of Eceabat (formerly Maydos), west of
Kilitbahir, and Çanakkale, sailing past a huge inscription stating
'The Dardanelles cannot be crossed'.

This of course refers to the failure of the Allied attempt in
the Great War to force the Dardanelles, break through to
Istanbul and link up with the Russians. The first attack was
made in February 1915 by warships which had to turn back
after suffering heavy losses from Turkish mines and land
artillery. Then on 25 April 1915, landings began at Arıburnu
(literally Bee Point, but better known as Anzac Cove). Mustafa
Kemal, who played an important part in holding the Allies, had
his divisional headquarters at Eceabat.

The road from Gallipoli goes on to Seddülbahir, running
close to the battlefield, and to the many military cemeteries
which mark it today. The main fighting was for the hills dominating the Aegean coast of the peninsula from Cape Helles, at

its tip, to Suvla Bay – hills such as Kireçtepe (Limestone Hill), Tekketepesi (Monastery Hill), the Anafarta ridge, scene of Mustafa Kemal's victory and therefore commemorated today in the names of countless streets and shops in Turkey, Sarıbayır (Yellow Slope) and others. The Turks could not be dislodged from these hills or, in the few instances where they were, they succeeded in fighting their way back. And since the Allied Fleet could not be expected to give indefinite cover to the troops on the lower slopes, the operation had to be called off.

The Gallipoli campaign is remembered as a clean and chivalrous battle, the blood and the blunders having been whitewashed by the passage of time, and its fiftieth anniversary was marked by mock landings of Anzac veterans who were met in friendly welcome by their former Turkish enemies. In English-speaking countries the Gallipoli battles gave rise to admiration for the soldierly qualities of Johnny Turk, and these feelings were not dissipated by the bitterness of the Mesopotamian campaign and of the siege of Kut. The failure of the Allied landings prolonged the war, prevented adequate contact with the Russians and may thus have been a factor in the outbreak of the Russian revolution two years later. But to the Turks it was a famous victory which prepared them and their leader for the final successful effort to establish their independence on secure foundations.

From Cape Helles to the Bulgarian frontier, from Edirne to Istanbul, Turkish Thrace has long been a battlefield. The battles here were for control of a land bridge, a transit area, which is what Thrace remains for the modern traveller. As he speeds on from Greece or Bulgaria to Istanbul, and from Istanbul to Troy, Pergamum and Izmir, memories of these great battles may add interest to the scenery of bare hill and coast, just as a knowledge of the difficulties overcome by the Turks in conquering, keeping, settling and resettling this land may relieve the human sameness that now seems to pervade it.

5. Istanbul

Geographical advantage alone does not make great cities. In spite of the incomparable excellence of its site, Byzantium had to wait for centuries until the emergence of the right historical conditions and the personal choice of one man turned it almost overnight into a world metropolis.

The site of Byzantium-Constantinople-Istanbul lies at the crossing of the east-west land route from Asia to Europe and the north-south sea route from the Black Sea to the Mediterranean. Here Europe and Asia are separated by the narrow winding channel of the Bosphorus, a flooded fault in the hill barrier which lines the southern shores of the Black Sea. On the European side, the edge of the Thracian plateau is cut by yet another flooded fault, the sea inlet of the Golden Horn, which joins the Bosphorus at its southern end, thus forming a large natural harbour and surrounding on three sides a hilly promontory which dominates it. This promontory, selected by geography for an easily defended human settlement, was the site first of a Thracian village and then of the small city of Byzantium, founded, according to tradition, in the middle of the seventh century B.C. by Greeks from Megaris, a stretch of hilly coast between Athens and Corinth. Byzantium was from the first a trading settlement set at a strategic point on an important sea route, and it could also rely on ample local resources – on the fish which abounds in the Bosphorus, on the corn grown on the Thracian plateau, on the fruit and vegetables produced in the small sheltered valleys leading down from the plateau to the sea and in the flatter country along the north-eastern shore of the Sea of Marmara. However, the Bosphorus does not provide the only possible crossing from Asia Minor to the Balkans. A more southerly route crosses the Dardanelles, and since this lay nearer the older centres of civilisation, with Troy situated in its immediate neighbourhood, it was at first used more frequently. The Bosphorus on the other hand suffered at first the disadvantage of lying in the middle of wooded country inhabited by the warlike Thracians, after whom it was called Thracian Bosphorus, to distinguish it from the Cimmerian Bosphorus (the Straits of Kerch, between the Crimea and the northern Caucasus). But when Macedonia emerged from barbarism, conquered and absorbed the European Thracians, and when the Thracians in Asia Minor – in Bithynia – were in turn civilised, the Bosphorus came to divide two prosperous agricultural areas which were later drawn into the imperial economy of Rome. A new route developed through the Balkans to central and thence to western Europe, a route much used by the legions as they were switched from one threatened point to another along the exposed northern periphery of the Roman Empire. Moreover, the newly civilised countries which were crossed by this route, and above all Illyria (Yugoslavia/ Albania), provided new leaders for the empire. The centre of gravity, which moved north for strategic reasons, also shifted east for reasons both of defence and of economic convenience, since Asia Minor, including the newly prosperous Roman provinces of Bithynia and Pontus, became the main granary of the civilised world.

Byzantium was slow to profit from this change. Its importance was at first subordinate to that of Adrianople in the west and in the east to that of Nicomedia, the seat of the empire under Diocletian. Byzantium backed the wrong contestant in a Roman civil war, with the result that the winner, Septimius Severus, besieged it for three years (A.D. 191–3), razed its walls to the ground and subordinated it to the small city of Heracleia in Thrace (Marmaraereğlisi, between Istanbul and Tekirdağ). However, this misfortune only served to stimulate the growth of the city. Septimius Severus himself had the walls rebuilt round an enlarged area, and Byzantium, renamed Antonina Augusta, was soon more prosperous than ever. Then once again it favoured the wrong Roman general, Licinius against Constantine, who was, like Diocletian, a native of what is now Yugoslavia. This second mistake made the city's fortune. Having captured it, Constantine chose it for his capital.

Byzantium-Constantinople had the best and most strategic-ally-placed harbour in the area, but this advantage too was not felt immediately. The harbour was at first too large. It was the diminutive bay of Chalcedon (Kadıköy), on the Asiatic side of the Strait, which had attracted the first Greek settlers, later, in the light of hind-sight, described as blind in the famous prophecy advising the Megarians to settle opposite 'the country of the blind', i.e., on the better site of Byzantium. And as later Constantinople grew and prospered, it could still content itself with small harbours in the indentations of the peninsula which it occupied – Neorion (today Eminönü) at the entrance to the Golden Horn, Contoscalion (Kadırga Limanı) and the port of Eleutherius (Langabostan) on the Marmara, and little bays such as that of Sycae (Galata) on the Golden Horn.

Constantine laid out the new walls of Byzantium in A.D. 324, two miles west of those of Septimius Severus. In 330 he proclaimed the city as the new capital of the empire. It was called the New Rome or Constantinople, it was built like its predecessor on seven hills or thereabouts, and in the spirit of the age it was bigger and flashier than its prototype. More important, it was to be better fortified, for in spite of its central position it was a march city, always subject to attack by the northern barbarians and later by eastern and southern foes. The fortifications were improved and extended in 413, in the reign of Theodosius II, when powerful new land walls were built a mile or so to the west of those of Constantine.

The Theodosian walls enclosed an area of some five square miles, as much as the city needed in ages of prosperity and much more than it could fill in periods of decline. They were, however, farther extended in the twelfth century to take in the imperial residence of Blachernae. This lay in the extreme north-western corner by the Golden Horn where it is commemorated in the names of the districts of Ayvansaray (Porticoed Palace) and Balat (which derives from the demotic Greek *palati* i.e., palace). All attempts to storm the land walls failed until 1453, when they fell to the Turks, who subsequently repaired them, and they still stand today except where recent neglect and still more recent economic development have breached them.

Constantine built his first palace between the Hippodrome (At Meydanı) and the Sea of Marmara on a site most of which is now covered by the mosque of Sultan Ahmet and its outbuildings. Byzantine emperors lived in this palace for some 800 years. 'It was rebuilt, altered, enlarged and embellished countless times to suit different needs and tastes. The result was a vast irregular agglomeration of reception and banqueting halls, pavilions, churches and chapels, residential quarters, baths, colonnades, sporting grounds and gardens, all enclosed within a strong wall; in fact something not unlike the Turkish seraglio of Istanbul' (Cyril Mango, *The Brazen House*, Copenhagen 1959, p. 13). This palace, like the prosperity of Byzantine Constantinople, was ruined by the Latin crusaders in 1204, and when the Greek Emperors regained the city they transferred their residence to Blachernae. Today almost nothing remains of the Great Palace, except for some mosaic paving (preserved at the Museum of Mosaics near Sultan Ahmet). Of the Blachernae complex, on the other hand, one large building has survived, the Tekfur Sarayı. (*Tekfur*, a word of Armenian origin, was used by the Turks to designate local Christian rulers or princelings, among whom the Byzantine emperor came to be counted.) Here a ground floor, probably dating back to the twelfth century, is surmounted by two storeys built under the last Byzantine dynasty of the Palaeologi. The palace was constructed in the usual Byzantine manner of alternating layers of stone and brick. The Ottomans used it for a time to house the potteries which they had transferred from Iznik (Nicaea).

While little is left of royal palaces and nothing of Byzantine private mansions, many churches, above all the Great Church – as the basilica of St Sophia was known – have survived. This is natural, since the Byzantines, like the Turks after them, built more solidly for God than for themselves. But the layout and the aspect of the Byzantine city can be reconstructed with fair accuracy. The tops of the many hills were covered with public buildings, rich mansions and city squares, while the poor had the slopes and the valleys. Access to the hills was provided by innumerable stairs. The city's two main arteries formed a Y, one arm leading to Adrianople (through what is now Edirnekapı i.e. the Adrianople Gate) and the other to the large military encampment of the Campus Martius on the northern shore of the Sea of Marmara, and then on to Hebdomon (Bakırköy). The population, estimated at over 100,000 excluding slaves and servants, in the fifth century, must have grown more or less constantly until the Latin conquest of 1204, when the city was denuded of people as well as of treasure. The Byzantine reconquest did not arrest the decline of Constantinople and by 1453 the number of its inhabitants had dropped to perhaps as little as 50,000

As an imperial capital, Constantinople must have always had a mixed population, with the two main ethnic groups, Slavs from the Balkans and Armenians from Anatolia, contributing many recruits who were, however, sooner or later Hellenised, for Constantinople was a Greek city and a centre of Greek learning. But since religion was the basic criterion of identity, Hellenisation applied mainly to Eastern Orthodox citizens. Latin traders retained their separate identity. Latins began to establish themselves in the city, and across the Golden Horn, certainly from the tenth century. Merchants from Venice, Amalfi, Pisa and Genoa had their own districts on the southern shore of the Golden Horn, which thus came into its own as the city's natural harbour. Together with Lombards and Jews they occupied what has remained to this day a commercial area – the area lying roughly between the present Galata and Atatürk bridges. Eminönü, at the southern end of Galata bridge, was a Jewish district until the seventeenth century when the Yeni Valide Camii mosque was built and the Jews were moved to Hasköy, on the northern shore of the Golden Horn, opposite the old Jewish ghetto of Balat.

It was under the Byzantines that Istanbul acquired a bad name as a centre of intrigue, deviousness and hairsplitting. Intrigue was the natural result of the centralisation of the administrative system which concentrated all power in the hands of the emperor. The all-powerful emperor was all-vulnerable in case of failure and had always to guard his position with complete ruthlessness. Rival contestants were a constant danger to the holder of central power – hence the murder, blinding and maiming of pretenders. Ottoman sultans, who found themselves in a similar position, introduced the even more drastic custom of killing all the brothers of the reigning sovereign lest division enter the realm. One of the weaknesses of the Byzantine Empire was that it relied largely on mercenary foreign troops – warlike tribes from the great north European plain, Varangian Normans, Slavs, Turks, Caucasians. It was a short step from the recruitment of these barbarians for the empire to their enlistment in the service of a pretender, who naturally hoped that he would be able to dispense with them once his ambition was satisfied. In the event, both the Latin conquest and spoliation of Constantinople in 1204 and the Turkish crossing into Europe in the middle of the fourteenth century were the direct result of Byzantine dissension. But perhaps even if Byzantine factions had not invited these invaders, the changed balance of power – the rise of western

Europe from the tenth century onward, the Turkish flood let loose by the Mongols in the thirteenth century – would sooner or later have made themselves felt. The manipulation of power, calling in new worlds to redress the balance of the old, was the means by which Constantinople was kept inviolate for almost 900 years, but that policy could not succeed for ever. What appeared as deviousness to the barbarians who were being manipulated was to the Byzantines a perfectly licit means of pursuing their messianic hopes. Constantinople started as the New Rome, but it soon saw itself as the New Zion, which only had to defend religious truth in order to survive to the end of the world. In the Byzantine Empire the heritage of Greece and Rome was consecrated to biblical ideals. Certainly from the ninth century onwards the Byzantines, like the Jews, saw their salvation depending on loyalty to a fully developed static truth. This conservative view of life has not been without its uses to the cause of civilisation. To the conservationist efforts of Byzantine Constantinople we owe a great deal : the broad stream of Christian orthodoxy, which, however, would have been fossilised without the adaptability of Rome; the texts of the classics; a hieratic art whose every work, whether church, icon or decorative object, was meant as an expression of an unchanging universal order. In the continuum of Byzantine Constantinople, extremes met : the fixer was also the uncompromising religious fanatic.

Three classes of building have come down from this mediaeval world : fortifications, public monuments and utilities, and churches. The provision of water was, of course, a major concern to the rulers and defenders of the great walled city. The main supply of water came from the hills beyond Kağıthane at the head of the Golden Horn, and was conveyed by an aqueduct built by the Emperor Valens (364-78) and repeatedly reconstructed by his Byzantine and Ottoman successors. Large sections of this aqueduct (known in Turkish as Bozdoğan Kemeri or Grey Hawk Arch, after the name of the village in the

Thracian hills to which it can be traced) have survived between the third and fourth hills of Istanbul, where they form an arch over the new Atatürk Boulevard with its busy airport traffic. For emergencies the city had to rely on cisterns. The largest one to have survived is the underground Cisterna Basilica (in Turkish Yerebatan Saray or Buried Palace), where the visitor can have a boat ride among its 336 columns. The now dry Binbirdirek cistern, north-west of St Sophia, had only 224 columns and not one thousand and one as its Turkish name implies. However, the columns were much higher than those of the Basilica. Then there are the large open cisterns in the western districts, near the land walls. These cisterns were later used as market gardens, hence the name Çukurbostan (Sunken Garden) by which they are known to the Turks. The southernmost of the Çukurbostans, situated on top of the seventh hill, was originally the largest cistern of Constantinople, that of Mocius. Going south, the next is the cistern of Aetius near Edirnekapı, which is now used as a football ground. Finally, next to the mosque of Sultan Selim lay the cistern named after the Gothic general Aspar who is said to have built it in 459.

The Goths have given their name to another Istanbul monument, the 50-foot granite column in Gülhane Park near Seraglio Point. A Latin inscription on this column commemorates a victory over the Goths, although no one quite knows which one. There are several other famous columns; such as the monolithic Egyptian obelisk of Tuthmosis III (fifteenth century B.C.), brought from Heliopolis by Theodosius I in A.D. 390 and placed on the raised spine (*spina*) of the Hippodrome. The Emperor, his wife and two sons, and the games which they watched are pictured on the pedestal of this obelisk. Also in the middle of the Hippodrome stands the Greek bronze Serpentine Column representing three interlaced snakes. This was originally erected outside the temple of Delphi, where it commemorated a victory over the Persians. The Turks, like the Byzantines before them, considered it a *tılsım* or talisman, an object possessing magical properties and granting miraculous cures. The third monument standing in the Hippodrome is the imitation obelisk, of which we can say with certainty that it was restored in the tenth century. Originally covered with gilt bronze plates, which the Latin crusaders plundered, it presents today a somewhat moth-eaten appearance. There are two other famous columns in Istanbul: Çemberlitaş (Column with Hoops, the latter having been placed on it in the eighteenth century to keep the monument in one piece after a fire from which it derives its western name of Burnt Column), erected by Constantine I, not far from the present Nuruosmaniye Mosque; and Kıztaşı (the Maiden's Stone, since it was supposed to provide an infallible test of virginity, a property which this column shared with other similar phallic objects). Kıztaşı was put up by the Emperor Marcian (450-57) near the aqueduct of Valens.

The Turks, who thus derived many magical benefits from the preservation of secular classical monuments, were even better guardians of Byzantine churches. Of these churches only one, the thirteenth century St Mary of the Mongols (in Greek, Moukhliotissa) standing a little way inland from the modern Greek Patriarchate at Fener on the Golden Horn, is still used for Christian worship. The others were converted into mosques, thus continuing to serve for worship until modern times when, in some instances, they were turned into museums.

The main Byzantine churches of Istanbul are St Sophia (Aya Sofya), dedicated in 537, since when it has been repeatedly repaired; St Irene, rebuilt completely in the eighth century and later incorporated in the grounds of Topkapı Palace, where it was used as an arsenal; Sts Sergius and Bacchus (Küçük Aya-sofya), built, like St Sophia, in the reign of Justinian I on a site between the Imperial Palace and the Sea of Marmara; the ruined monastery of St John of Studion (Imrahor Camii or Mosque of the Chief Constable), founded in 463 between Sam-atya and the south-western corner of the land walls at Yedi-kule (the Castle of Seven Towers, where in Ottoman times ambassadors of unfriendly foreign powers were kept in prison to induce a change in their masters' behaviour); and a group of churches, built or rebuilt after the Byzantine reconquest of the city in 1261. To this group belong Kaariye Camii (St Saviour in Khora, i.e. in the Fields, built in the twelfth and extended in the fourteenth century); Christ Pantocrator (Mollazeyrek Camii), going back to the twelfth century; St Constantine Lips (tenth century) and St John Panachrantos (fourteenth century), forming the one mosque of Feneriisa Camii; St Theodosia (Gül Camii), a ninth-century church much altered by rebuilding; Vefa Kılıç Camii, probably consecrated to St Theodore and certainly rebuilt in the fourteenth century; St Andrew in Crisei (Kocamustafapaşa Camii), built in the thirteenth century; the thirteenth-century church of the Virgin Pammacaristos (Fethiye Camii), and others.

Students of architecture or of the history of art may wish to visit all or most of these buildings. The ordinary traveller will probably content himself with two; St Sophia and Kaariye Camii, both now administered as museums. They lie at opposite ends of the town – St Sophia just outside the limits of ancient Byzantium, south of Seraglio Point, and Kaariye Camii by Edirnekapı in the north-western corner of the Theodosian walls. Between them they cover the whole Byzantine achievement from the sixth to the fourteenth centuries, for although the main structure of St Sophia was completed in 537, the dome was repeatedly brought low by earthquakes and had to be rebuilt. The present dome dates back to the fourteenth century, when external buttresses were also added. More buttresses were built in the sixteenth century by the Ottomans, who also of course added the minarets, the first in the southeast corner, immediately after the conquest, and the other three in the century that followed it. The mosaics in the church span the centuries of its Christian existence from the sixth to the fourteenth.

Like the other Byzantine churches in Istanbul, St Sophia

owes its survival to the care taken by the Turks to preserve it as a place of worship, and to the fact that Muslim ritual requires the minimum of alteration beyond the removal of images and the addition of a prayer niche and a pulpit. Moreover, since the simplest way of removing images was to paint them over with whitewash, many mosaic panels, which might otherwise have suffered from exposure, have been preserved intact. Heavy when seen from the outside, St Sophia looks vast and mysterious within. The vastness was intended by the architect Anthemius and by his imperial patron who wanted to recreate the Temple of Solomon and to exceed it in grandeur. The mystery is at least partly the product of history. Windows have been blocked, gleaming silver and gold removed, mosaics and other decorations lost, so that the interior has become darker, the shafts of light that fitfully illuminate part of it do not flatten detail, but rather bring out the effects and ravages of time – the unevenness of the floors, worn out by countless generations of worshippers, of doorways shaken by earthquakes, the marks left on the walls or columns by the removal of Christian decorations, the variety of colour and shape of the columns assembled by the builders from widely scattered classical sites. The great Muslim shields inscribed with the names of Allah, the Prophet and the Caliphs, which Atatürk removed but which were later replaced, and the other memorials to Muslim religious use, emphasises the continuity of worship until modern agnostic times. In this atmosphere it is easy to believe that the last Greek Patriarch and his clergy were swallowed up by the walls as the Turks approached the building, that the conqueror's horse left a hoof-mark half way up one of the columns as it trod on layers of bodies, that sterility can be cured by touching another column. Above all, St Sophia has been spared that architecturally accurate but artistically inept restoration which is turning monument after monument in Turkey into Hollywood sets of unweathered stone and cement joints. Art and time have made St Sophia: the enthusiasm of its architects and designers, gradually overlaid by the patina of age and restrained by the reticence of Muslim sensibility, has after a millennium and a half produced a unique effect, which no catalogue of the dimensions of the structure, impressive as they are, or description of its decorative features can define. The mosaics – of Christ, the Virgin, saints and emperors – can probably be seen more clearly in expert photographs than in the semi-darkness of the narthex, but no description can reproduce the total impression of awe left by the building on a sensitive visitor.

Kaariye Camii is different both through accident and design. It is of course a product of late Byzantine art. It is smaller. It is accidentally better lit. Here the recently uncovered frescoes and mosaics, contrasting with the remaining whitewash, show up brilliantly, recreating the art and sensibility of fourteenth-century Constantinople. Here we have the faith in pictures which have to some extent unfrozen from the hieratic pose of the icons. They are grouped in three cycles, the life of Christ, the life of the Virgin Mary and, in the funerary chapel, a symbolic cycle showing saints, the Church and the Day of Judgement. These cycles were not unique to Kaariye Camii, but nowhere else have they been preserved so well. They have been described as a work, sometimes as the masterpiece, of Byzantine Renaissance, and the description is apt. Colour – brilliant blues, and reds contrasting with whites – as well as form are fresher and freer than in other surviving Byzantine pictures. Whether there is here a first effect of nascent western art, itself deeply affected by Byzantine iconography, is for art historians to decide. What is not in doubt is that fourteenth-century Constantinople was in constant communication with the Latin west; that it was at times almost a client state of the Latins and that it had the Genoese on its doorstep.

This doorstep was the district of Galata at the northern entrance to the Golden Horn, opposite the commercial district within the walls, where Italian merchants had established themselves as early as the tenth century. Galata, originally part of the district of Sycae (Fig Trees), had for centuries functioned as a small auxiliary port. It had also long contained fortifications, from which a chain could be stretched to a tower in the modern district of Sirkeci, thus barring the great natural harbour. The name of Galata is variously derived from a Galatian, i.e. inhabitant of the country round Ankara, who is supposed to have had a house there; or from a demotic Greek word meaning 'milkman'. But whatever the antecedents of the settlement and of its name, the real history of Galata and of the hill at the back of it starts at the end of the thirteenth century, when the Genoese were allowed to settle there after the Byzantine reconquest of Constantinople. Originally confined to the tip of the peninsula, they gradually extended their town to the hill top of Pera, a Greek word meaning 'beyond (the Golden Horn)', which came to designate the Latin and later Levantine settlement opposite the old city of Istanbul.

Galata was and looked Italian. It had tall mansions built in stone and brick, strong walls which have now almost completely disappeared, and a thick round Genoese tower which survives to this day as one of the landmarks of the Istanbul skyline. With the Genoese came the friars. The Dominicans took over and rebuilt a small Byzantine church, keeping it for over two centuries until 1453 when Mehmet the Conqueror assigned it to Muslim refugees from Andalucia, after whom it was named the Arab Mosque (Arap Camii). Later, Franciscans, Jesuits, Lazarists and a host of other orders carried the banner of west European spirituality opposite the venerable walls of Constantinople-Istanbul.

As a port, Galata had from the first a cosmopolitan population. In addition to the dominant Italians, there were Greeks, Armenians and Jews. After the conquest they were joined by Turks and other Muslims who occupied the waterside districts to the west and east of Galata – Kasımpaşa and Tophane, famous for their shipyards and naval arsenals. But Galata and

26   *Bithynian landscape: looking towards the sea of Marmara from the Bursa road*

27 *Girl drawing water from a village well near Muğla, south-west Turkey*

28 *Anatolian shepherd*

the hill of Pera, rising steeply from the harbour, remained until after the Great War largely non-Muslim, although there were some Turkish notables who were attracted by its clean country air and built their mansions there. From one of them Pera derived its Turkish name of Beyoğlu (Bey's Son). After the conquest, ambassadors of Christian powers were allowed to build their residences in Pera, where they could be kept at a safe distance from the Sultan's subjects. Venice, the Holy Roman Empire, France and England gradually acquired their own 'palaces', mansions set in walled gardens enclosing also chapels and sometimes schools. As for Galata, the Italians there were largely assimilated into the Levantine mass and swamped by Jews and Greeks. The district at the foot of the Tower of Galata (Kuledibi) was taken over by the Jews who, as else-where, provided most of the money-changers and money-lenders of the capital, while Greek sailors, chandlers and, above all, tavern-keepers were concentrated in the waterside district of Galata.

'The people of Galata are grouped in trades,' the seventeenth-century Turkish traveller Evliya Çelebi wrote. 'The first group are sailors, the second merchants, the third artisans, the fourth carpenters and caulkers. Most of them are dressed like Algerians (in short embroidered jackets, baggy trousers and tasselled hats). Quite a few are Arabs. They have marvellous captains. The tavern-keepers are Greek, the pedlars Armenian, the pro-vision merchants Jews. The tavern-keepers and the merchants are rogues. "Galata" means "tavern" (Allah forgive us) ... and men of standing go there to forget their cares and engage in intimate conversation. But they waste their fortunes to no purpose ... It is a devilish mill producing vast wealth.'

The women of Galata were as desirable to Muslims as its wine. Mehmet the Conqueror himself wrote a poem in praise of a woman of Galata, 'a sun-faced angel, the moon of the world, whose black tresses are the sighs of her lovers; a graceful cypress, a resplendent moon dressed in black; the sovereign in beauty of the Kingdom of the Franks'. And the Conqueror ended sadly 'Do not delude yourself that the beloved, pretty as a picture, will submit to you, for if you are the Sultan of Istanbul, she is the Queen of Galata.' However, not all the women of Galata were inaccessible, and for lovers whose sentiments were less elevated, the district has always provided a large number of brothels.

The Genoese in Galata remained neutral during the siege of Constantinople, and it was just outside their ramparts, and certainly under their eyes, that the most daring Turkish manoeuvre was executed – the transfer of the Sultan's ships over land from the entrance to the Bosphorus (Fındıklı is a likely starting place) to Kasımpaşa on the Golden Horn. The chain barring the entrance to the Golden Horn was thus circumvented and the net round Constantinople tightened until the final assault on 29 May 1453 brought the two-month-old siege to a victorious conclusion. The walls were breached in the northern sector between Topkapı (Cannon Gate, after Mehmet the Conqueror's great cannon cast by a Hungarian renegade) and the Golden Horn. The valley of the stream called Lycus (Bayrampaşa) between Topkapı and Edirnekapı was the weakest point of the defences, which the Ottomans stormed, possibly breaking through at Hücum Kapısı (Assault Gate, earlier known as the fifth Military Gate). However, according to one tradition, the janissaries first broke through at the no longer existing postern of Kerkoporta (near Kaariye Camii), which the Greek defenders forgot to close after a sortie. The last Byzantine Emperor, Constantine XI, is said to have died fighting somewhere near Topkapı.

The population of Constantinople had reached it lowest level on the eve of the conquest. The deportations which followed reduced it further. To make good the losses, Mehmet and his successors settled Turks from Anatolia in the newly-captured capital. The districts of Aksaray and Çarşamba are thus said to derive their names from towns in central and northern Anatolia, whose inhabitants were moved to Istanbul. Muslims from Anatolia, from newly conquered Roumelia and even from as far afield as Spain, gave Istanbul a Muslim majority almost immediately after the conquest. But Greeks and Armenians also moved in, so that the few Christians left in Istanbul today are descended from post-conquest immigrants and are no more indigenous to the city than their Muslim neighbours. Istanbul was too large to allow the usual practice of settling Christians outside the walls of newly conquered cities. Instead, Greeks and Armenians congregated in separate and, usually, relatively distant districts within the walls – Fener on the Golden Horn, and the shore of the Sea of Marmara from Kumkapı to Samatya. With the passage of time Fener became the seat of the Greek Patriarch and Samatya that of his Armenian peer and rival. The buildings and churches occupied today by these two dignitaries are comparatively modern.

As imperial Istanbul prospered, the number of non-Muslims grew if anything faster than that of the Muslims. The latter represented some two-thirds of an estimated population of 75,000 in 1477, but just under 60 per cent of the 120,000 households established in the city in the middle of the sixteenth century. Thereafter, while the population grew, the proportion remained roughly the same, the last census before the Great War showing 580,000 Muslims (60 per cent) to 243,000 Greeks (25 per cent) in the province of Istanbul. But by that time the city had spread well beyond its old confines, with the mass of Christians concentrated in the new city of Pera/Beyoğlu.

The opening up of Istanbul was one of the consequences of the conquest. Another was a complete change in its aspect. Wood replaced brick and stone as the principal material of private dwellings, which were squeezed tightly together in typical Turkish neighbourhoods of winding streets and overhanging eaves. But in spite of the expansion of population there was, until recently, room for orchards and market gardens within the walls, the best known being at Langa, the filled-in Byzantine harbour of Eleutherius.

Public buildings were, however, the glory of Ottoman Istanbul – the imperial mosques (*selâtin camileri*) first of all, with their schools, hospitals and almshouses, and then the palaces, covered markets, baths and fountains. Mehmet II built his first palace (Eski Saray) at Beyazit, the Byzantine Forum Tauri, a district settled under Theodosius I in the fourth century and marked with a marble column which no longer exists. The old palace later became derelict and its site was used for the Ottoman Ministry of War (Serasker Kapısı), which now houses Istanbul University. Beyazit occupies the top of the third hill, and the seventeenth-century marble tower standing in the present University gardens is a pendant to the Genoese tower of Galata across the Golden Horn, both affording superb views of the Bosphorus and the Sea of Marmara. The Beyazit mosque, built between 1501 and 1505 by the architect Yakup Şah, is in fact the oldest large mosque in Istanbul, if one excludes converted churches. Like the earlier and smaller mosque built by the same Sultan (Beyazit or Bayezid II, 1481-1512) in Edirne, it has a rectangular plan, the squareness of the building being emphasised by the bareness of its eastern and western walls. A central dome, 56 feet in diameter, supported by two half-domes, surmounts a large square prayer hall, measuring 118 feet along each side.

The mosque named after Mehmet the Conqueror, Fatih Camii, which stands on the summit of the fourth hill, northwest of Beyazit, is in fact a more modern building dating back only to 1771, the original mosque having been destroyed in the earthquake of 1766. The Conqueror's tomb and the nearby library belong to the same period. Fatih Camii stands on the site of the large Byzantine church of the Holy Apostles, a famous shrine built by Constantine I and rebuilt by Justinian. It was the burial place of most early emperors, including Justinian, and it performed its last service to the Greek Church between 1453 and 1461 when it housed the Greek Patriarchate after the loss of St Sophia.

The Turks significantly thus made their first impact in Istanbul on the hills lying away from the shore. However, the advantages of the commanding site at the tip of the peninsula, originally occupied by the acropolis of classical Byzantium, soon impressed themselves on the Conqueror and he built himself a palace there in 1462, surrounding it with walls which fitted into the curve of the Byzantine sea walls. It was a truly imperial site, overlooking the junction of the Bosphorus, the Sea of Marmara and the Golden Horn, whereas the Byzantine Emperors, with their palace a little to the south, had contented themselves with a view over the Sea of Marmara alone. Inside the Conqueror's walls there gradually grew up an elegant compound of pavilions, summer-houses, audience rooms, residences, libraries, bath houses, kitchens, stables, fountains and, of course, barracks. The apartments were as usual divided into the *harem*, reserved for the Sultan's wives, concubines, serving women and the black and white eunuchs who attended on them, and the *selâmlık* where male officials were allowed to transact the Sultan's business. The whole compound gradually became divided into four courtyards, separated by interior walls or screens of buildings. The Imperial Gate (Bab-ı Hümayun), built in 1478, led to the first of these courtyards, where the palace guards (known as *bostancı* or gardeners) had their quarters, and which served as a general concourse for visitors. The Middle Gate (Ortakapı, otherwise known as Babüsselâm or Gate of Peace) gave access to the second courtyard used primarily for the business of government, as conducted by the Grand Vizier. The buildings of the Divan (Privy Council) were situated in one corner of the courtyard, which was flanked on the north side by the stables, and on the south by the labyrinthine kitchens of the palace. Then the Gate of Felicity (Bab-ı Saadet) opened on to the third courtyard, containing a throne room, the royal treasury, a treasury of relics and libraries, and giving access to

the *selâmlık* and thence to the *harem*. The last and fourth courtyard, in the south-eastern corner of the palace grounds, overlooked the Sea of Marmara, and was dotted with small pavilions and summer-houses. Beyond lay the sea walls and then a
landing stage and boat-houses. These shore installations disappeared when the European railway system extended its fur-
thest tentacle to Sirkeci, at the entrance to the Golden Horn.
One of the casualties was Cannon Gate (Topkapı, not to be con-
fused with the gate of the same name in the Byzantine land
walls), after which the Turks called first the summer pavilions
and then the whole seraglio Topkapı Sarayı, this term replacing the older name of New Palace (Yeni Saray) which used to
distinguish it from the Conqueror's old palace. But to the Europeans this seat of the sultans was always known simply as the
Seraglio (from the Turkish word *saray*, meaning palace) or
sometimes the Grand Seraglio. It was for centuries a place of
romance and mystery, since official business with foreign ambassadors was transacted at the house of the Grand Vizier (Bab-ı
Âli or Sublime Gate, which gave to the Ottoman government
the western name of The Sublime Porte) outside the palace, and
occasionally in the Vizier's audience room in the second courtyard. Consequently few foreigners managed to penetrate the
inner courtyards. Among the lucky ones was the Italian
Domenico Hierosolimetano, employed as a palace physician
under Murat III (1574-95), the Englishman Thomas Dallam who
in 1599 presented an organ to the Sultan and assembled it in
the Seraglio, and others. The accounts which they have left
stress the beauty of the 'perfumed gardens', the magnificent
decorations of the pavilions and the labyrinthine layout, with
the absence of a monumental central building. The foreigners'
interest was however centred mainly on the secluded beauties
of the *harem*, the eunuchs and on tales of cruelty relating to
the drowning of unfaithful wives off Seraglio Point or the
beheading of Grand Viziers in the infamous prison of Balıkhane
(Fish Store) in the south-eastern corner of the palace grounds.

Accounts of the palace became more numerous in the eighteenth and early nineteenth centuries, when European chief gardeners were employed. The eighteenth century witnessed the penetration into Turkey first of European tastes and then of European ideas, and Ottoman architecture was deeply influenced, developing hybrid styles known as Turkish baroque and Turkish rococo, which are represented in the Seraglio in the dining room of Ahmed III, the room of Abdülhamit I and the kiosk of Abdülmecit (1840). The sultans finally transferred their residence to the palace of Dolmabahçe on the Bosphorus in 1853. The change symbolised the decay of Constantinople/ Istanbul, which had become the Old City, and the growth of the new city of Pera/Beyoğlu. Although Dolmabahçe was situated on the Muslim shore, it was overlooked by the Franks of Pera, among whom the Sultan had now taken up his residence. Thereafter the Seraglio suffered a fire in 1862, was truncated by the railway in 1871, was thrown open to visitors after the Young Turkish revolution of 1908 and was gradually transformed into a museum under the Republic, an archaeological museum having already been built in the palace grounds at the end of the last century.

Today curious visitors can see a coach museum in the old stables, Turkish china in the Clerks' room of the Divan, weapons in the old Inner Treasury (as well as the inevitable cannon in the first courtyard leading to the Middle Gate), chinese porcelain and Turkish glassware in the old imperial kitchens, miniatures, embroideries and costumes in the library of Ahmet III, treasures of all kinds – from diamonds the size of an egg and a golden cradle to the hand of St John the Baptist and to a hideous nineteenth-century gold candlestick on which a bankrupt sultan wasted his borrowed money – in the Privy Treasury. (English-speaking visitors should not be misled by the caption 'braces' applied to long pendants which must have dangled from the ceiling and could not possibly hold up anyone's trousers.) More impressive than these secular collections of expensive bric-à-brac are the Muslim relics in the Apartment of the Honourable Cloak (Hırka-i Şerif Dairesi). The Prophet's cloak to which the name refers is encased in a gold reliquary made in the sixteenth century and incorporating the crescent in its design. The crescent, which is said to be related to the moon symbol of Artemis and Astarte and which certainly appeared as a royal symbol on pre-Islamic Persian coins, has for centuries been singled out by Christians as the emblem of Islam. But Muslims themselves used it fitfully and often in association with other symbols, such as the sun. The uniform use of the crescent by the Muslims today is thus a by-product of European choice. European influence has also played a part in the evolution of the Turkish flag which shows a star and crescent against a red background. This flag was first designed for the European-style New Army of Sultan Selim III at the beginning of the nineteenth century.

Other exhibits in the Seraglio include the Prophet's staff, sword, bow, a hair from his beard, and a letter allegedly written on his instructions to the ruler of the Copts in Egypt urging him to become a Muslim. The swords of the first four Caliphs are in the same building. As a notice warns the visitor, this collection of relics has been considered for centuries as a holy place, the repository of a supernatural power which strengthened the arm of Ottoman warriors.

Byzantine Constantinople had also been rich in relics and miraculous icons which preserved the city, and in holy wells (Greek *haghiasma*, Turkish *ayazma*) which safeguarded the health of the citizens, and the Turks maintained this reliance on the magical power residing in objects. Even within the walls of the Seraglio there was a holy spring which had originally lain within the Byzantine church of St Saviour, and its water was conducted outside the sea wall to the continuing benefit of the Sultan's Greek subjects.

The *harem* quarters are usually out of bounds to visitors, but there is more than enough architectural interest in the other buildings. The main chamber of the Privy Council (known as Kubbealtı or 'Underneath the Dome') with its Italianate pointed tower, forming the highest pinnacle of the Seraglio buildings, and above all the elegant seventeenth-century pavilions named after Ottoman victories at Baghdad and Erevan (now the capital of Soviet Armenia), with the nearby small building used for the circumcision of princes, are beautifully proportioned, perfectly suited to function, richly but not overwhelmingly decorated. A conquering, martial state thus developed at its centre a garden architecture, clothing in refinement the realities and the cruelty of power. The gardens of the Seraglio have been truncated by the separation of the Gülhane Park (Park of the Rose Pavilion) on the slopes leading to the Golden Horn and extending as far as the tip of Seraglio Point, where Atatürk is today commemorated by a large statue, the prototype of hundreds of similar memorials throughout the country. The park of Gülhane also houses the municipal zoo, which is descended from the Sultan's menagerie, much praised and minutely described by European travellers. In the palace compound itself the gardens are far from impressive. The effect intended by the architects is thus largely lost, the ensemble tending to disintegrate into its constituent parts.

Within the outer walls of the Seraglio are situated the Museum of Antiquities and of the Ancient Orient and Çinili Köşk (the China Kiosk, originally called Crystal Palace), built in 1472 as a residence for the Conqueror. One of the oldest Turkish buildings in Istanbul, it continued the architectural style of Bursa with its reliance on china tiles for internal and external decoration. It is now used as a museum of the Conquest. The Museum of Oriental Antiquities shows works of Sumerian, Assyrian and other Near-Eastern civilisations and it is said to have the second largest collection in the world, of cuneiform inscriptions, Near-Eastern archaeology having luckily started before Turkey lost its Arab provinces. The main Museum of Antiquities has an impressive collection of Greek and Hellenistic art, including the immense sarcophagi found in Sidon (now in the Lebanon) and dating back to the fifth century B.C. The attribution of one of them to Alexander the Great is doubtful, but the great conqueror is represented by a more than life-size statue found near Manisa. The museum has retained its Ottoman-Victorian character, partly because so many objects in it come from outside the borders of the Republic, partly because the core of the collection has remained largely unchanged. This is no drawback: the Istanbul Museum of Antiquities is rich enough as it is, and the decision to concentrate in Ankara on pre-classical antiquity, as well as leaving important collections in local museums has made for balance and has reserved unexpected pleasures for the visitors to Turkish provinces.

The traveller on a conducted tour, as well as the independent traveller trying to economise on time and fares, will probably take in the mosque of Sultan Ahmet, known to foreigners but not to Turks as the Blue Mosque, in a day's trip round the museums. Standing on the site of the Byzantine Great Palace, south of St Sophia, this mosque affords a superb view over the Marmara, a view which the architect Mehmet Ağa brought into the building. Light flooding in through 260 semicircular windows is reflected by vast expanses of blue and green china tiles. The colour of the tiles with their stylised flowers – hyacinth, tulip and carnation – is set off by the ornate marble of the prayer niche and pulpit. The mosque is large. It was obviously meant to be the most imposing building in the capital, but the vast rectangle of its central prayer hall, measuring 174 feet by 167 feet and surmounted by a dome 90 feet in diameter, is reduced in size by thick ornate columns. Were it not for the large southern windows with their sea view, the heaviness would perhaps have been excessive. Seen from the outside, the majestic bulk of the mosque is balanced both by the height of the six minarets and the distance separating them from the central dome. The base of the composition is extended by an immense marble-paved courtyard and by the usual outbuildings. The rise is gradual from the covered portico with its 36 granite columns and 30 small domes to tiers of half-domes, leading to the main dome, surmounted by the gilt spur which culminates in a crescent. The Sultan Ahmet Mosque was built between 1609 and 1616, its royal patron dying the following year and being buried in the nearby mausoleum. His reign had been spent in constant wars – in the west, where he secured his predecessors' conquest of Hungary; in the east, where he was less successful against Persia, and at sea, with variable fortunes. These exertions were beginning to tell and Anatolia was racked by revolt. New customs were setting in: the use of tobacco became common. The Sultan is also remembered for having broken with custom by refusing to have his brothers killed on his accession. Thoughts were probably turning to peace. But peace of satiety was denied the Empire which was called upon, and ultimately failed to defend its conquests.

The mosque of Sultan Ahmet thus symbolises immense achievement, but achievement already past its peak. In architecture the peak was reached by the architect Sinan in the reign of Süleyman the Magnificent. His two best-known mosques in Istanbul are Şehzade Camii, begun in 1544 and finished in 1548, and above all Süleymaniye, begun in 1550 and completed in 1557 – both built therefore before the Selimiye in Edirne. Şehzade Mosque (the Mosque of Mehmet the son of Süleyman the Magnificent) is situated between Beyazit and Fatih, near the new municipal offices. It is a geometrically perfect construction: the courtyard exactly balances the mosque, the dome (62 feet in diameter) is balanced by four half-domes, the prayer hall is square, each side measuring 125 feet. The rectangular character of the building, with the high projection formed by the courtyard wall is reminiscent of the severe mosques of Beyazit II in Edirne and Istanbul.

The Süleymaniye mosque, with its lofty central structure rising high above the courtyard and the outbuildings, represents a breakthrough, a triumphal upward thrust of Ottoman architecture. The wall round the courtyard is low, so as not to detract from the mosque. At its four corners there are four lofty minarets, the two taller ones adjoining the mosque. An enormous central dome, 87 feet in diameter and 174 feet high, rests on four pillars and is buttressed by two half-domes. Underneath, the rectangular prayer hall is divided by columns into a nave and two aisles. This makes it look both larger and higher than in the other mosques in Istanbul. It is also extremely light, and the decoration, more restrained than in Sultan Ahmet, achieves a quality of pious majesty which to most Turks symbolises the spirit of their classical culture. With St Sophia originally an alien masterpiece and now a museum, and Sultan Ahmet a work of slightly self-conscious grandeur with largely ceremonial associations, Süleymaniye is the architectural monument nearest and dearest to Turkish hearts. The mosque is situated on top of the third hill, overlooking the Golden Horn, and its terrace offers a panorama of urban Istanbul including the infidel Pera/ Beyoğlu, from which it appears as the most notable monument of the old city. The mausolea of Süleyman, of his wife Roxelana (Hurrem Sultan) and of the architect Sinan himself are in the vicinity of the mosque, while one of its former colleges now houses the Museum of Turkish and Muslim Arts which contains rich collections of manuscript Corans, miniatures, carpets and china.

Another imperial mosque sometimes attributed to Sinan is the Selimiye, built in 1522 at the orders of Süleyman the Magnificent to commemorate his father Selim 1, known as the Grim (Yavuz), the conqueror of the Arab Near East. Nearby are the mausolea of Selim 1 and of a very different Sultan, the weak, pleasure-loving and civilised Abdülmecit, the first Sultan to speak a west-European language, which was, of course, French. The Selimiye Mosque overlooks the Golden Horn from a hill inland from Fener. Square and fairly simple, it is noteworthy for having nine small domes around the main one, thus representing a step in the transition from the flat roof covered by a multiplicity of domes of early Ottoman mosques to the later pyramids of dome piled on dome of classical mosque architecture.

Istanbul has many mosques and many of them have some special feature or claim to fame. No visitor can avoid the large Yeni Cami (New Mosque, 1598-1603) in Eminönü Square dominating Galata Bridge. Less conspicuous is the mosque of Rüstem Pasha between Galata and Atatürk bridges, famous for the quality of the Iznik china tiles which line its prayer hall. Then there is the brave attempt to fuse Turkish and baroque in Nuruosmaniye Camii (The Light of the Ottomans Mosque, 1748-1756), which is situated at the entrance to the covered market. It has pseudo-Ionic columns, a profusion of plaster decoration and an oval courtyard in front of a rectangular building. Western influence, still discreet here, runs riot in the rococo Lâleli Camii (Tulip Mosque, 1763) between Beyazit and Aksaray. Outside the walls of Istanbul there is the famous shrine of Eyüp, near the head of the Golden Horn, sacred to the memory of a companion of the Prophet, who is said to have fallen there in the unsuccessful siege of Constantinople by the Arabs in 670. The present mosque dates back only to 1800. Of more interest are the tomb of Eyüp, which draws large numbers of pilgrims, the large Muslim cemetery and the hill behind the mosque which was made famous by the romantic French novelist Pierre Loti. He is commemorated today in the name of a street and of a café from which the visitor can admire the Golden Horn. On its banks factory chimneys compete today with minarets, and slums with mosques, while its water is foul and poisonous. The northern shores of the Golden Horn and then, after rounding the point of Galata, the shores of the Bosphorus, are punctuated by noble mosques: the mosque of Piyale Paşa (1537) in the dockyard district of Kasımpaşa, noted for its dirt and its toughs; the mosque of Azapkapı (Gate of the Azabs, the latter being a military corps which provided marines and pioneer troops), built by the great Sinan in 1577, and then another Sinan mosque, that of Kılıç Ali Paşa (1580) in the Tophane (Arsenal) district on the Bosphorus. Across the Bosphorus in Üsküdar (Scutari), Sinan built the elegant Mihrimah Camii (commissioned by a daughter of Süleyman the Magnificent, whose name means 'Sun and Moon'). Nearby is one of the oldest mosques in Istanbul, the Rumi Mehmet Paşa Camii (1471), and another work of Sinan, the mosque of Şemsi Paşa. Also in Üsküdar are the mosques of the two Queen Mothers, the Old (Atik Valide Camii, 1583) and the New (Yeni Valide Camii, 1710); and a small mosque known for its tiles, Çinili Cami (China Mosque, 1640).

The markets are part of the heritage of Ottoman Istanbul. Since they were particularly prone to fires, they have been repeatedly restored, but although most of the building is new, the layout is old and the atmosphere traditional. The most famous market is the covered Grand Bazaar with its eighteen gates leading to some 3,000 shops. Its core is the Eski Bedesten, a large rectangular building, where shops dealing in precious goods were concentrated. Near Eminönü Square is the completely rebuilt Spice Market (Mısır Çarşısı, Egyptian Market), now visited largely for its expensive, expense-account restaurant. The Grand Bazaar contains one of the best known inns, the Zincirli Han (Chain Inn). The older Kurşunlu Han (Lead Inn), near the Mosque of Rüstem Paşa in the commercial district south of the Golden Horn, dates back to the reign of Süleyman the Magnificent.

One of the effects of the Turkish conquest was the integration of Istanbul with its countryside, now safe from enemy incursion and available to serve the needs of the city in food, rest and recreation. In Üsküdar a whole new city arose which replaced Kadıköy/Chalcedon as the starting point of caravans and expeditions to Asia. The Turks were also particularly attracted by the Bosphorus where they sought and developed places of shade and refreshment, trying to recreate in their new home the Near-Eastern vision of Paradise. The shores of the Bosphorus were gradually filled with large wooden summer mansions (*yalı*), set in walled gardens and often easier to reach by sea than by road. Most of the *yalıs* are gone today, but the nineteenth-century stone palaces survive. There is first of all Dolmabahçe Palace, remembered not so much as the centre of the court in the era of reforms (Tanzimat) or the place from which the last Ottoman Sultan slipped away in 1922 to board a British battleship, as for the fact that the first President of the Republic, Kemal Atatürk, died there on 10 November 1938. The room where he died is kept as a shrine, with all clocks stopped to show the hour of his death.

Further up the Bosphorus in the suburb of Beşiktaş is situated the mausoleum of Hayrettin Barbarossa, the Grand Admiral (or to Europeans Grand Corsair) who conquered Algeria for the Sultan in 1516. On a hill a little to the north stands the palace of Yıldız (the Star), built by Sultan Abdülhamit II (1878-1909) and overlooking the seaside palace of Çirağan, where Abdülhamit kept confined for twenty-seven years his deposed, and by all accounts, demented brother Murat V. Like Topkapı, Yıldız is a collection of pavilions and barracks set in a walled garden. It bred isolation and rumour, but also detachment. The Oriental despot whom it housed was fed on a diet of police denunciations, but was wise enough to extract from them enough information to keep his enemies divided and his realm intact. When he was finally deposed by his own army, the park of Yıldız was thrown open to the public, while the palace buildings served a number of purposes – the soldiers keeping their barracks, a short-lived gambling casino being installed in one of the pavilions, etc. Abdülhamit himself spent his last days on the Asiatic side of the Bosphorus in the palace of Beylerbeyi, another product of Ottoman wedding-cake rococo, where the Empress Eugénie had once been entertained by the Sultan Abdülaziz. It was Abdülaziz who visited the Great Exhibition in London, and whose features are preserved in some pub signs bearing the name of 'The Turk's Head'. On the same shore, north of Beylerbey, stands the eighteenth-century summer palace of Küçüksu. This was built at a noted recreation spot, the meadows of the Sweet Waters of Asia, famous in the nineteenth century as a place for clandestine assignations with secluded Ottoman ladies. Today the palace overlooks one of Istanbul's bathing beaches, beaches that are patently insufficient to meet the demands of the city in summer time.

Küçüksu has been luckier than Kâğıthane (the Sweet Waters of Europe) at the head of the Golden Horn, where two small streams complete their journey from the Thracian hills to the sea. This was the site of the summer palace of Saadabat (Abode of Felicity), associated with the Tulip Era (reign of Ahmet III, 1703-27). During this era European tastes penetrated the court, the first Muslim printing press was established, the prohibition of drink was widely disregarded, and the tulip, reimported from Holland and valued above all flowers, became the symbol of pleasure and elegance. Tortoises with lighted candles fixed on their shells were set loose among the tulip beds during night festivities. Circumcision celebrations reached proportions never seen before. Alas, the cost in extortionate taxation and undefended frontiers was high, and Ahmet III was deposed by a popular rebellion. Saadabat palace no longer exists and Kâğıthane is today the polluted site of an industrial estate.

But to return to the Bosphorus – above Küçüksu is the castle of Anadolu Hisarı, built in the closing years of the fourteenth century by Beyazit I, its function of controlling shipping through the Straits being complemented in 1452 by the much larger fortress of Rumeli Hisarı (originally known as Boğazkesen or Strait-cutter), which Mehmet the Conqueror constructed on the European shore before embarking on the siege of Istanbul. Rumeli Hisarı is today restored to serve such purposes as theatrical performances or pageants, while across the Straits, Anadolu Hisarı sprouts houses like fungi, as is the case with most ancient walls and fortresses in a country where an

29 'Fairy Chimney' in Göreme valley, Cappadocia

30 (overleaf) Traditional Turkish wooden houses in Malatya, south-eastern Turkey

increasing population is chronically short of a place to lay its head.

The shores of the Bosphorus were architecturally most pleasing at the turn of the century. The settlements at each twist of the Strait were still distinct villages, most easily reached by sea. The *yalıs* of the rich still retained their caiques, long rowing boats with uniformed oarsmen, although regular communications were ensured by the Clyde-built steam ferries of the Şirket-i Hayriye (the Beneficent Company), reputedly the first Muslim joint stock venture, owned by the high and mighty of the Empire, including the Sultan's family. The national character of the various villages was still preserved: inland the population was almost uniformly Muslim, except for the still existing Polish refugee settlement at Polonezköy, east of Beykoz on the Asiatic shore of the upper Bosphorus. On the coast there were rich European families on Kandilli hill, a notable vantage point of the middle Bosphorus, and on the European shore, ambassadors' summer residences at Tarabya (Therapia), and American missionaries already established in their colleges above the castle of Rumeli Hisarı, as well as in Arnavutköy and at Üsküdar. The villages on the shore of the Sea of Marmara and the islands were still predominantly Greek. It was in the nineteenth century that Princes Islands acquired their large wooden villas, their carriages and their romantic reputation, superimposed on memories of a distant Byzantine past when they had served as a place of exile for unlucky and usually maimed princes and other dignitaries.

In the city itself Pera/Beyoğlu, although never a place of beauty, had substantial and well-kept houses for its rich merchants. Its prosperity and the foreign airs which it gave itself were resented by nationalist Turks. One of them, the writer Yakup Kadri Karaosmanoğlu, lambasted it as 'a nest of ugly creatures, a place whose plan was drawn by pork butchers, whose foundations were laid by wine merchants, whose decoration was provided by grocers and which stands as an irritating monument to bad taste and degeneracy opposite the silent and modest form of true Istanbul.' Nevertheless Turkish nationalists resorted to Beyoğlu for their pleasure and finally settled in it after the Republic was proclaimed.

Before the Great War Istanbul was truly cosmopolitan. The influence of the European Great Powers was strong, and their extra-territorial powers (the so-called capitulations) extensive. However, it would be an over-simplification to say that the Turks were not masters of their capital, which only reflected the multi-national character of their empire, and at best the co-operative division of skills and functions which lay at the roots of Ottoman civilisation. For the various religious communities and national groups did not stay aloof in their neighbourhoods, but came together in work, not least in the creation of artistic monuments. Thus the achievement of Muslim mosque architects, whose immense edifices marked a clear technical advance on the work of their Byzantine predecessors, would not have been possible without the skill of Armenian stonemasons, nor the works of Turkish ceramic art without that of Armenian potters. It is nevertheless right to describe the results of this cooperative endeavour as an Ottoman civilisation, for it was the Ottoman dynasty, with its civil and military arms, which provided the framework and gave its distinctive character to this mixed human society. It was a society that the West destroyed with its nationalist creed, but it also helped Istanbul to live through its last, and by no means contemptible, age of imperial existence. Victorian Istanbul was never a great cultural centre, but it was visited by European theatrical companies and orchestras; and European influences, mediated largely by Armenians, mingled with Turkish art to lay the foundations of contemporary theatre, music and painting.

Ottoman Istanbul absorbed a mass of Muslim refugees after the defeat which the Ottoman Empire suffered at the hands of the Russians in 1878. A second and larger wave reached it in the Balkan wars of 1912-13, and before these could be settled, the Great War broke out, bringing hunger and privations. Defeat in the war brought Allied armies of occupation to Istanbul and a vaster than ever flood of refugees – Muslims from the war zones, but also thousands of Armenians from Anatolia, and finally the remnants of White Russian armies with their camp-followers. Between 1918 and 1923, Istanbul lived its most cosmopolitan age, but a cosmopolitanism without balance or grace. The city became another Shanghai, over-crowded, under-policed, with totally inadequate services, a disorderly mixture of profiteering and destitution.

Order returned in 1923 with the imposition of the authority of the government in Ankara. The Allied armies of occupation departed, the White Russians drifted away, indigenous Greeks were allowed to stay within the city limits, but many, their hopes of a revived Byzantium finally destroyed, preferred to join their brothers in Greece. Before long economics was added to politics as a reason for emigration. After the Bolshevik revolution, entrepôt trade with Russia decreased. Then after the crisis of 1929 the foreign trade of Turkey collapsed. No longer the capital, Istanbul suddenly became a backwater.

Revival and change came after the Second War. As population and prosperity increased, blocks of flats sprouted everywhere, filling the waste land within the walls of the old city, stretching in a ribbon along the European and Asiatic shores of the Sea of Marmara, marching along the crests of the hills overlooking the European side of the Bosphorus. Between 1935 and 1965 the population of Istanbul increased from three-quarters of a million to a million and three-quarters within the municipal boundaries which, however, have become meaningless as the city spread beyond them. Today the population of the Istanbul conurbation is estimated at two and a half millions and growth is still continuing. Private blocks of flats have been supplemented by low-cost cooperative housing and even lower-cost shanty towns, where hundreds of thousands of peasant immigrants are learning the ways of a city. In the 1950's Prime

Minister Menderes assumed the role of a Turkish Haussmann and opened up new arteries and squares, but he was overthrown before completing the task.

The Menderes reconstruction briefly relieved the traffic, while changing the character of the city, not always for the better. The European shore of the Bosphorus, now accessible through a fast motor road, lost its distinctive village atmosphere. A coastal road by the sea walls of the old city remains a dusty scar. Squares opened up in front of the main monuments are still desolations of tarmac. In the meantime, the city centre of Beyoğlu has become a sleazy slum; the ancient malodorous tanneries still separate the castle of Seven Towers from the garden suburbs along the Marmara coast, and now the Bosphorus bridge is threatening the Asiatic shore of the Bosphorus, which, because of poor communications, has so far preserved its old houses and walled gardens. In the absence of effective town-planning, builders can approach landowners with attractive propositions to exchange their land or small houses set in gardens for a flat or two in new blocks. Gardens are thus disappearing one by one, and streets become deep canyons cut through high buildings, with narrow pavements used as parking lots. With city beaches inadequate and the sea polluted, middle-class citizens have started taking holidays in distant Anatolian resorts. But for the well-to-do Istanbul remains a pearl among cities. They can admire the view from their town flats overlooking the Bosphorus and from their summer houses in the islands or outer suburbs. They can take to their yachts and motor-boats to escape the polluted beaches or drive to the Black Sea resorts of Kilyos and Şile.

The pleasures which Istanbul affords the rich and the room which it offers for their enjoyment can create social and personal problems. With its distinct northern and southern climates, its hills and its sea, its modernity and its history Istanbul is, *mutatis mutandis*, like Paris and the Riviera rolled into one. When so much is at hand, why go anywhere else? The prizes that it offers are so desirable that ruthlessness can become natural in their pursuit. For the rich it poses only one problem – that of maintaining their riches. For the intellectuals it becomes a beguiling talking shop. Discussion of the problems of Anatolian peasants is often an hors d'oeuvre at rakı parties held on the shores of the Bosphorus.

This, however, is only one side of Istanbul life. For the majority of the citizens life is frustrating and uncomfortable. Housing, transport, sanitation, schools and recreation facilities are all inadequate. Istanbul is a megalopolis, but one lacking the social organisation which megalopolitan living requires. However, its immense and immensely beautiful site offers room for orderly expansion. Istanbul has more natural advantages than almost any other great city. And if the recent boom has destroyed the fine balance between man and environment which Ottoman civilisation had achieved, the loss need not be permanent, nor is it complete. There are still a few corners of the old city where the old ease can be felt. Parts of the Bosphorus and the islands are as attractive as ever. If parks and public gardens are inadequate, there are scores of waterside restaurants, where the view, the air, the food and the drink meet in a unique and euphoric combination. The city walls, churches and above all the mosques stand in all their glory. Although no longer cosmopolitan, Istanbul is vigorous and thrusting. Like the rest of Turkey which it represents as it never did before, and whose problems and possibilities, experiences and inadequacies, pride and impatience it concentrates, it will probably have to sustain many shocks before it settles down in a technological world. Like all great cities, Istanbul demands discrimination, knowledge, patience and sympathy. A visitor who can muster these qualities will not be disappointed by it.

6. The Coasts

In Istanbul tranquillity can be enjoyed only if one keeps to one's hotel or to a house in the suburbs. But since most visitors will want to see the city, the noisy and crowded discomfort which is inseparable from metropolitan living will sooner or later tire even the most energetic. It is then time to move on to Anatolia.

The motorist's journey to Anatolia, like that of the sultans' messengers of old, starts at Üsküdar. From the ferry the traveller will see the white Tower of Leander, set on a tiny island some 200 yards from the coast of Asia. The building is new, the legend, from which it derives its Turkish name of Maiden's Tower (Kızkulesi) old. Leander belongs more properly to the Dardanelles, while the heroine of the Bosphorus, Io, who swam across it in the shape of a cow (and gave it its Greek name, meaning ox-ford), has singularly failed to fire the romantic imagination. As for the Turkish maiden, she belongs to Anatolia and her story illustrates the simple moral that fate cannot be evaded. A prophecy having foretold that she would die of a snake-bite, her father had a tower built for her in the middle of the sea. However, the snake penetrated the enclosure – hidden in the building materials, or according to a variant, in a basket of grapes – and the maiden was stung to death according to plan. Like the story of the king who fled to China and into the arms of the Angel of Death whom he was trying to evade in his own country, this cautionary tale never fails to impress and console the Oriental mind.

Üsküdar is of course the Scutari of the Florence Nightingale story which preaches the opposite moral. She proved the value of struggle and exertion in the barracks of Selimiye, named after the unfortunate Selim III, whose reforming zeal cost him his throne. Inside the barracks, a witness to the failure of the Ottoman reformer and of the success of the more determined Englishwoman, Florence Nightingale's room is preserved as a museum complete with a replica of her lamp, while a more apt memorial has been built in Istanbul in the shape of a modern college of nursing. The road from Üsküdar skirts the cemetery of Karacaahmet, the largest in Istanbul – an attractive forest of cypresses and head-stones, the latter until modern times surmounted by hats to show the rank of the deceased: clerics' turbans, civil servants' fezzes, janissaries' tall hats. The town of Üsküdar itself is inhabited by people of modest means, junior and retired civil servants in the main. The road to Anatolia goes on through the back of the more prosperous suburbs of Kadıköy and Moda, then over the malodorous Kurbağalı Dere (Frog Stream) to the neat districts of Erenköy and Suadiye, once exclusively summer resorts, but now increasingly sheltering middle-class refugees from the dirt of the city centre. Across the sea lie the Princes Islands, which still fill up every June and empty every September, but which are particularly attractive in May when the flowers in the gardens of the locked villas are in bloom, and the drivers of the horse-carriages (cars are luckily banned) greet every prospective fare as a benefactor.

On the Asiatic side, suburb follows suburb along the Ankara road. The road swerves inland to avoid the hill of Dragos (the Dragon), covered with villas like the rest of the coast, and then descends to the attractive village of Kartal. From there the car can be put on the ferry to Yalova, across the mouth of the Gulf of Izmit. The gulf itself is a busy and dirty waterway full of tankers serving a large petrol refinery and of warships, since the main base of the Turkish fleet is at Gölcük, opposite Izmit. Factories are gradually filling every available plot on the road to

Izmit. Pendik, the last village in Istanbul province, is still attractive and famous for its fish restaurants, romantically known as the Moonlight, the New Moonlight etc. However, a shipyard will soon put an end to all that.

Gebze, the first town in the province of Kocaeli (Izmit) and the last stop on the electrified suburban railway from Istanbul, is remembered as the place where Hannibal committed suicide when he learned that his host, the Thracian king of Bithynia, was about to hand him over to the Romans. It is now a growing industrial suburb. A little farther, Hereke, picturesquely situated below the road which follows here a fairly steep escarpment, is a textile centre like Karamürsel facing it across the gulf. These were the outposts of the Bithynian weaving industry, based on Bursa. Hand looms, which were to be found in almost every cottage throughout the region, gradually disappeared when the Ottoman Empire opened it gates to cheap European imports, and production now is concentrated in factories built since the 1930's.

Izmit, lying at the head of the gulf, is an undistinguished town of some 100,000 inhabitants, already drawn into the economic orbit of Istanbul. Situated on the Istanbul-Ankara road and railway and enjoying good sea communications, it seems assured of a prosperous future. In the past it was one of the three great cities of Bithynia, the other two being Iznik (Nicaea) and Bursa (Broussa, Prusa). The layout of the region to the south of the Marmara, with small basins separated by ranges of hills and usually centred on lakes, favoured the emergence of self-contained cities. Izmit (Nicomedia), like the other Bithynian cities, grew in Hellenistic times and prospered under the Romans and the Byzantines. It was founded in 266 B.C. by King Nicomedes I, replacing Nicaea as the capital of Bithynia, passed to the Romans with the rest of the kingdom in 76 B.C., was chosen as the administrative centre of the Roman province of Bithynia and Pontus (Pliny the Younger was its most famous governor), became briefly the capital of the Empire under Diocletian, served as a royal residence for Constantine I, and from being one of the main cities of the Empire gradually declined, being overshadowed by Nicaea in Byzantine times. The Seljuks held it for a short time at the end of the eleventh century and it was finally captured by the Ottoman Sultan Orhan in 1399. Always an important staging post, Izmit triumphed over its rival Iznik when the Anatolian railway was built, replacing the old caravan route through the Lefke (Osmaniye) Pass to the plateau.

East of Izmit one can turn right from the Ankara highway and follow the recently surfaced road along the southern shore of the gulf to Yalova, which is fast becoming a suburb of Istanbul. Yalova Spa lies a little farther west. This is the first of the many spas that lie along the southern shore of the Marmara and are fed by hot mineral springs in the Uludağ massif and its outer ridges. Yalova, known earlier as Thermae Pythiae, was frequented by Justinian I who built baths there. Its present fame dates back to Atatürk who took a fancy to the place towards the end of his life, had a hotel built, and used it along with Florya, a beach on the northern shore of the Marmara just west of Istanbul, as a summer residence and a venue for his interminable rakı parties. The gaiety which he introduced evaporated under his dour and careful successor Ismet Inönü, but Yalova Spa has remained the most accessible watering place for the Istanbul bourgeoisie. Much afflicted by the consequences of over-eating and over-drinking and by the modern fear of heart disease, rich Istanbul businessmen have been making increasing use of the natural hot springs lying on their doorstep. And whatever the rival merits of sulphur, phosphorus, iron salts and radio-activity, present in different proportions in various establishments, there is no denying that a few days of swimming in modern Turkish mineral baths provide excellent relaxation. Hotels are comparatively cheap, food, drink and service excellent; there are lovely views and pleasant walks; and with the spectacular improvements in communications – fast ferries from Istanbul to Yalova, an even faster air-shuttle service to Bursa, and good roads leading to the main towns, this region should become an important holiday centre. It is less hot than the Aegean and Mediterranean coasts, while being sheltered from cold north winds. There are olive groves and vineyards in the plains, Mediterranean maquis on the dividing hills, and impressive forests in the Uludağ mountains which border the region in the south. And as Istanbul grows and becomes more and more a city to visit but not to stay long in, the advantages of the countryside round it should become obvious.

From Yalova the Bursa road crosses a range of hills before descending to Orhangazi (named after the second Ottoman sultan), at the western end of the lake of Iznik. The road round the lake is good, the countryside pretty. In autumn there is wild duck to shoot and an abundance of fresh fruit to eat. The grapes growing along the southern and prettier shore of the lake are particularly good. Iznik itself is today a small market town of 8,000 inhabitants. As in the rest of Bithynia, its population, depleted by the departure of the Greeks, has been made up by Turkish refugees from the Balkans. At present it is so small that the shape of historic Nicaea, a neatly planned round (or octagonal) city intersected by two main arteries, can be seen perfectly. It was built on the site of an obscure Thracian settlement (the legend ascribing the foundation to the Thracian wine god Dionysus is appropriate) and was named after Nicaea (Greek for Victoria), the wife of one of Alexander's generals, Antigones the One-Eyed. After being incorporated in the kingdom of Bithynia and passing with it to Rome, Nicaea took second place to Nicomedia before emerging as a great city under Constantine and his successors. In spite of recurring earthquakes, it maintained its importance as a fortress and then a political and intellectual centre throughout the Byzantine period. It hosted two oecumenical councils, the first under Constantine in 325, which drew up the Catholic creed, and the seventh which re-established the use of images in churches. Its walls were made progressively stronger and, having withstood the Arabs, kept the city inviolate until 1081, when the Seljuks were introduced into it by a Byzantine pretender. The Latins of the first crusade restored it to the Byzantines in 1097, with the unforeseen consequence that when Constantinople was taken in 1204 by the plundering hordes of the Fourth Crusade, Nicaea became the Byzantine capital in exile, the centre of a Greek revival and the base from which the Palaeologi recaptured the old imperial capital in 1261. The importance of the city inevitably declined thereafter, although it remained a formidable fortress guarding the approaches to Istanbul. The Ottoman conquest in 1331 gave Nicaea many notable monuments, but did not reestablish its importance, the primacy of Bithynia passing irrevocably to Bursa with its richer plain and more commanding position.

The Roman-Byzantine walls still stand more or less intact and immensely impressive, with many inscriptions and reliefs, particularly over the beautiful Lefke Gate. The Byzantine cathedral of St Sophia, which dates back to the fifth or sixth centuries and was the venue of the seventh council (the first met in a palace), has been repeatedly restored and rebuilt both before and after becoming a mosque. It was last rebuilt by the great Sinan himself, who repaired the ravages which it had suffered under Tamerlane in the previous century. Sinan's work more or less coincided with the foundation of the famous Iznik potteries by craftsmen brought from Persia by the Ottoman government. Iznik produced the finest china made in Turkey, and its wares decorated with simple floral designs in blue, green, red and the rarer yellow, can be seen in the mosques of Istanbul and the collections of western museums. In the eighteenth century the potteries were transferred to the Byzantine palace of Tekfur Saray in Istanbul and thereafter declined. However, Iznik had an earlier tradition of pottery as witness the green china tiles and enamelled brick decorating the fourteenth-century Green Mosque (Yeşil Cami). This is a beautiful building with a marble prayer hall and a central dome, one of the first Turkish mosques to have one. Opposite the Green Mosque is the local archaeological museum which has a good collection of Graeco-Roman inscriptions and sarcophagi.

The roads from Orhangazi to Bursa passes through Gemlik, and a small detour will take one to the sea front of this delightful village which still preserves something of its Greek character. There is a new hotel and seaside restaurants serving fish and hors d'oeuvres to go with their rakı in the best Istanbul manner. Gemlik lies at the head of the bay of Mudanya, with another resort, Armutlu, situated at its northern entrance. Mudanya itself is the main port of Bursa, but it is less busy now that land and air communications have improved. The narrow-gauge railway which used to link it with Bursa, panting over olive-clad hills, has been dismantled and replaced by regular bus and *dolmuş* services. It was at Mudanya that on 11 October 1922 the Turkish nationalists signed the armistice which ended the fighting with the Greeks. The latter had already left Anatolia, but there were British troops at Çanakkale, and a clash between them and the advancing Turks seemed imminent. The crisis was averted by a hair's breadth at Mudanya, where arrangements were also made for the return of Turkish troops to eastern Thrace and the departure of Greek soldiers and civilians. The Greeks never signed the Mudanya convention, but were obliged to accept it. The following year the treaty of Lausanne formally put an end to the war, the remaining Allied troops were withdrawn and Turkish troops entered Istanbul on 2 October 1923.

The road from Gemlik to Bursa goes past another hotel with its own natural springs, crosses another hill barrier and then descends to the plain of Bursa. On the outskirts there is a new industrial estate, where cars are now manufactured. Bursa has always been famous for its knives and the local skill in metalwork has for many years been applied to the manufacture of car bodies. In the noisy workshops on the outskirts of the town, imported lorries are converted into buses and then sent out to ply their dangerous trade on half-made Anatolian roads. Along with other cities in western Anatolia, Bursa suffered considerably in the fighting with the Greeks after the Great War, and also from the departure of its skilled Greek and Armenian citizens. To remedy the economic decline which followed, the Republican Government reintroduced the textile industry, for which the city had once been famous, and other enterprises were later set up. Industry has not spoiled the look of Bursa, mainly because the factories are in the plain, and the town rises above them in a sea of greenery on the lower slopes of the Uludağ. Bursa is now of course a purely Turkish town, and it has always been the most Ottoman town in Turkey, the first capital of the dynasty, the burial place of its first kings, and a town which owed its prosperity to the Ottoman conquest. Its conservative tranquillity has for many years drawn to it retired civil servants, so that it is a Turkish Cheltenham rising above its new industrial base. It is also attracting increasing numbers of holidaymakers from Istanbul and from abroad. It is particularly popular with Arab dignitaries who find its Muslim atmosphere as congenial as its mineral springs are beneficial. It was while recuperating in Bursa that the aged King Idris of Libya lost his throne – he could not have heard the sad news at a nicer place. Industry, tourism, catering for the retired, coupled with progress in agriculture and communications, have caused the population of Bursa to triple in one generation. It now has over 200,000 inhabitants, and is the fifth largest city in the country.

Bursa owes its name to one of the many early kings of Bithynia, called Prusias, and to distinguish it from other cities bearing the same royal name it was usually referred to as Prusa ad Olympum, Olympus being the classical name of the Uludağ mountain. The city was the natural centre of the rich agricultural plain which it overlooks, and has always had an important asset in its hot springs, which the Romans and their

Byzantine successors prized highly. Nevertheless, it took third place to Nicomedia and Nicaea, gaining in importance only immediately before the Ottoman conquest, during the revival of Greek life in north-western Asia Minor under the Palaeologi. It had a strong castle on a foothill of the Uludağ, which withstood Ottoman raids for some twenty years until it finally succumbed in 1326. The Greeks were thereafter removed from the walled city, but together with the Armenians and the Jews who were attracted by the prosperity born of the Ottoman conquest, they stayed on in the districts outside the walls until after the Great War.

The political importance which Bursa acquired as the first Ottoman capital was soon lost, but its commercial importance grew. A starting point of Ottoman expeditions to the Near East, it became also the most important centre along the so-called diagonal caravan route stretching through the Cilician Gates to Syria, as well as on the horizontal routes to Persia. From Persia it obtained the raw silk used in its looms, and from the Far East through the Arab Near East, spices, sugar and dyes which it re-exported to Europe. It was visited by merchants from India and Persia as well as from Europe, the Italians being particularly active. A large number of caravanserais bearing such names as Silk Inn, Cocoon Inn and Rice Inn, catered for the needs of these visitors. European merchants usually exchanged their woollen cloth against the silken stuffs produced in Bursa, the number of looms in the city exceeding one thousand in the sixteenth century, when a French traveller noted 'Bource is still at present as rich and populous as Constantinople and, dare we say it, richer than Constantinople.' When wars with Persia interrupted the supply of Persian raw silk, the silkworm was successfully introduced and bred in the Bursa region, so that gradually from exporting woven silk Bursa became a provider of raw silk for Europe, whose finished products it then imported. Hand looms disappeared in the nineteenth century in the face of European competition, to be replaced by power looms, grouped today in a few major factories which use artificial silk and other man-made fibres as well as natural silk, wool and cotton. Some 1,700 tons of raw silk were still produced in the region in 1968.

Bursa is by local standards prosperous, neat and well organised. To the tourist it provides more natural hot baths than any other Turkish spa, walks, mountaineering and, in the winter, ski-ing on Uludağ, as well as all the treasures of Ottoman architecture. The baths are in the suburb of Çekirge, originally inhabited mainly by Greeks, and now more or less joined to the city. In addition to the natural hot water swimming pool at the excellent Çelik Palas hotel, built, like the Yalova spa, at the orders of Atatürk, and since extended, there are many old Turkish baths – the large Eski Kaplıca (Old Baths) put up by the Turks in the fourteenth century on the site of a Byzantine establishment, the sixteenth-century Yeni Kaplıca (New Baths), the Kükürtlü Hamam (Sulphur Baths), Kaynarca Hamamı (Boiling Baths) and others. The waters differ in mineral content and in presumed medical effect, while some are more pleasant to drink than others. However, all are equally restful.

On a hill between Çekirge and the centre of Bursa lies Muradiye, a compound containing the mosque, seminary and tomb of Murat II, set in the most famous garden in Bursa. Murad II was the author of the Turkish victory over the Christian allies in the great battle of Varna in 1444, and according to his last wish, his tomb in Bursa is covered with earth and open to the rain, through an opening in the dome. Nearby lies the tomb of the unfortunate Cem, an Ottoman prince who had failed to wrest the throne from his brother Beyazit II, and who then fled to Europe, where he was used as a bargaining counter against the Ottomans.

The centre of Bursa is dominated by the Great Mosque (Ulu Cami), built between 1396 and 1399. A large, simple and impressive building, it consists basically of a rectangular prayer hall (223 feet by 184 feet) divided into five naves by fifteen square pillars, and surmounted by twenty small domes. The domes, which give the building a slightly Byzantine appearance, are more or less of the same size. Inside the mosque, the size of the prayer hall, the forest of columns, the way in which the eye is drawn horizontally to the depth of the building, rather than upwards, bring to mind the masterpieces of early Arab religious architecture. The ornate ablutions fountain is, unusually, inside the mosque which is also famous for its carved walnut pulpit, cunningly joined without the use of a single nail, and for the calligraphy of the Arabic inscriptions on the walls. The central mosque of an essentially conservative city, it has preserved an atmosphere of fervour and even of intolerance, although this is directed not at foreigners but secularist Turks.

Next to the Ulu Cami stands the smaller and older (although much restored) mosque of Orhan, the conqueror of Bursa. Built of alternate layers of stone and brick in the Byzantine style, it also shows Byzantine influence in its T-shaped prayer hall. The mosque of Orhan is the oldest monument in Bursa: the Greek church inside the castle has disappeared, and the tombs of Osman, the founder of the dynasty, and of his son Orhan are modern. However, the buildings in Bursa that attract most visitors are the Green Mosque (Yeşil Cami) and the Green Mausoleum (Yeşil Türbe). The mosque was built in 1419-20 for the Sultan Mehmet I who reunited the Empire after its defeat by Tamerlane, and who lies buried in the Green Mausoleum. Green refers of course to the colour of the tiles which line both mosque and mausoleum, and which were designed by Persian artists from Tabriz. Unfortunately, where the beautiful original tiles were missing, bright and flashy modern imitations have been substituted, and far too much modern cement meets and offends the eye. The Green Mosque is situated on a small hill to the east of that of the citadel, and from its terrace there is a panoramic view over the city and the plain. Still farther east is the mosque of Beyazit I, known as the Thunderbolt (Yıldırım), who triumphed over the crusaders in Nicopolis, but was defeated by Tamerlane at the battle of Ankara. His mosque was built between 1391 and 1395 and is said to have influenced the architecture of the Green Mosque.

Uludağ (the Great Mountain), whose 8,000 foot peak rises above Bursa, has become the winter sports centre for Istanbul. In the high summer when the sheltered plain of Bursa is baking in the heat, every turn of the winding road leading to a cluster of hotels just below the summit brings relief and refreshment. The road goes through a series of *yaylas*, a Turkish word originally meaning summer camping grounds, but used today in the sense of mountain plateau. The *yaylas* are frequented by *yörüks*, Turcoman nomadic tribesmen with their herds of sheep and goats. There are still *yörüks* in Turkey, although the attempts to settle them, made by every single government from the first Seljuk conquerors of Anatolia to our day, are about to reach a successful conclusion. These dwindling bands of nomads are a reminder of the vast masses of roaming Turcomans, with even vaster flocks, who became an integral part in the life, culture, economy and politics of Anatolia after 1071. The *yörüks* have preserved archaic Turkish words, customs that are said to derive in some cases from the distant pre-Islamic past, and, more obviously, traditional skills in carpet-weaving and cheese-making. Less admirably, they and their goats are mainly to blame for the destruction of forests, and if much of the plateau of Uludağ is today open pasture land, the *yörüks* are largely responsible. On the lower and middle slopes of the mountain there are, however, trees in plenty – first oaks and chestnuts, then conifers. Finally, after the grassy plateau, the easily accessible peak rises above a rocky waste.

Uludağ made its main impact on history in Byzantine times, when it was a favourite haunt of hermits. In addition to self-mortification and contemplation, these were much addicted to ecclesiastical politics, upholding, for example, the use of images against iconoclasts, or championing Patriarch Ignatius against his rival, the brilliant and worldly-wise Photius, in the feud which led to a first split between the Western and Eastern Churches. The hermits must have survived into Turkish times, as the mountain had until recently the alternative Turkish name of Keşiş Dağı, meaning Monks' Mount. Today there are hardly any traces left of their occupation of the steep northern slopes.

East of the Uludağ, the road to Ankara crosses Ahı Dağı, or Mountain of the Akhis. The latter word designated the members of craft guilds of religious inspiration which were paramount in many Anatolian cities in the period between the Mongol invasion and the establishment of Ottoman power. After leaving the plain of Bursa, the Ankara road enters a fertile valley full of fruit trees. The whole region of Bursa is famous for its fruit, particularly its large peaches which have recently begun to be exported. Inevitably the exported article lacks the lusciousness of the fruit which can be bought locally, and equally inevitably it costs more than the few pence a kilo which it usually fetches in Bursa. However, Inegöl, the small market town on the northern side of the Ahı Dağı, is known not so much for its fruit as for its meat. Throughout Turkey makers of meatballs, known as *köftecis*, proclaim on their shop-fronts that they hail from Inegöl. With high mountain pastures lying in the neighbourhood this is, of course, an area suited for cattle-breeding. Furthermore, this feeling for meat may have something to do with the fact that the local inhabitants are largely Circassians, Muslim refugees from the Caucusus settled in Anatolia in the second half of the last century. Circassians are particularly numerous further north in the wooded country between Adapazarı and Gerede on the Istanbul-Ankara road, and their attachment to the sultans posed a difficult problem for Atatürk at the beginning of his military struggle, for while all Circassians detested the infidel Greek invaders, some of them suspected the nationalist authorities in Ankara of even more dangerous infidelity. Following the promptings of the Sultan's

government in Istanbul, they rose against nationalist commanders who had to mount punitive expeditions to put them down.
In any case these tribesmen of the mountains saw their independence threatened by the modernising and centralising policies
of the nationalists, and when Atatürk attempted to form a
regular army out of the bands of resistance fighters, even those
Circassians who had originally taken the field against the
Greeks began to waver. In the end Ankara triumphed over
Circassians of both persuasions, over Anzavur who sided with
the Sultan, as well as over Çerkes Ethem, the formidable guer-
rilla leader, who was one of the first to raise the standard of
resistance to the Greeks, but finally went over to them rather
than submit to control from Ankara.

Inegöl and the villages on the Ahı Dağı still preserve their
picturesque wooden or half-timbered houses, with projecting
upper storeys, often whitewashed in bright colours – ochre,
blue, pink and purple. Here nature and art provide the last
splash of colour before the great monochrome expanses of the
Anatolian plateau. But before one reaches the plateau there is
the broken country of the middle Sakarya river. This is the
Bithynian march, where Ottoman power was born at the
beginning of the fourteenth century and where the Greeks
suffered their first reverses in 1921, in the last war to be fought
on Anatolian soil. There are now very few trees left in this
country, and only the courses of the streams are marked by the
inevitable poplars and willows (*söğüt*) which gave their name
to the large village, not far from the Bursa – Eskişehir road,
where the founder of the Ottoman dynasty held his first fief.

But to explore the Mediterranean coastlands of Turkey, one
must take the road from Bursa to the west, through the central
Bithynian plains, past the large lake of Uluabat (or Apolyont/
Solidus Apollonias) and then either cut across the base of the
mountainous Troad peninsula or follow the Marmara coast to
the busy port and military airbase of Bandırma. This has given
its name to a borax ore called pandermite, which is found in

the country south of lakes Uluabat and Manyas. Production of this mineral has been developed by a British-owned company, much to the displeasure of Turkish nationalists and socialists, always in search of a good xenophobic issue to endear themselves to their compatriots. Lake Manyas is associated with another – now forgotten – controversy. A group of Russian cossacks who disagreed with the Czarist government on religious and possibly other grounds, since they belonged to the sect of Molokans or Milk-drinkers, were allowed by the sultans to settle near the shores of this lake and lived there in concord with their Muslim neighbours until a few years ago when they returned to Soviet Russia, saying that there were not enough Russian girls left for them to marry, but, more likely, because a modern secular republic is less tolerant of eccentric exceptions than the traditional society which it has replaced.

A branch road from Bandırma leads to the growing seaside resort of Erdek, frequented by middle-class families from Istanbul. Erdek is near the ruins of ancient Cyzicus, a city founded by Milesians, which stood in perpetual opposition to the masters of the interior, whether Persian, Arab or Turk. Like other Anatolian Greek cities it was particularly prosperous under the Romans, when Strabo described it as one of the first cities of Asia for extent and splendour. Cyzicus stood near the narrow isthmus of a peninsula, which was originally an island until Alexander the Great advised the citizens to build a causeway to the mainland, now made safe by his conquests. The peninsula of Cyzicus (known today as Kapıdağı or Gate Mountain) is separated by a strait from the large and mountainous island of Marmara (Marmara Adası, 46 square miles in area and with a population of only 6,000, now that the Greeks have left). Both peninsula and island were famous for their marble quarries, which have given the Sea of Marmara its present name. The ancient Greeks called it Propontis or Fore-Sea.

From Bandırma, the road turns inland to Gönen, on the river of the same name, a small town known for its hot springs, probably the hottest in the region, and therefore recommended for sufferers from rheumatism and arthritis. Parallel ranges of hills separate Gönen from Biga (whose name, derived from the Greek Pegae or Springs, testifies to the existence of yet another spa), on the Çan Çayı (Bell Stream), the ancient Granicus river, where Alexander scored his first decisive victory over the Persians.

From Biga one can drive to Çanakkale either through Çan and the Mysian mountains or by the coast through Lâpseki (Lampsacus), opposite Gallipoli, at the eastern entrance to the Dardanelles. The coastal plain from Mudanya to Çanakkale is noted for its olives, which are used largely for salting and are served as an indispensable ingredient of the Turkish breakfast, the production of olive oil being concentrated farther south at Ayvalık on the Aegean coast. Çanakkale, or briefly, Chanak, as it was known in English at the time of the Great War, is a busy town, the administrative centre of a province which extends to both sides of the Dardanelles as well as to the two offshore islands of Imroz (Imbros) and Bozcaada (Tenedos), and a frequent port of call for ships going through the Straits. The town is of Turkish origin, Mehmet the Conqueror having built a fortress there which was known originally as Kale-i Sultaniyye or Sultan's Castle, and only later as Çanakkale, Pottery Castle, after the best-known local manufacture. To the Turks it is associated with the Gallipoli campaign, while to modern historians it recalls the Çanakkale Affair of 1922, when Britain came face to face and made terms with Turkish nationalism. To the visitor it is the doorway to Troy, reached more frequently by car from Istanbul and then by ferry from Eceabat. In either case it is worth stopping at Çanakkale, but only for a visit to the museum and for a meal at one of its fish restaurants. To the traveller arriving by sea, Çanakkale gives a foretaste of Istanbul and the Bosphorus, with the added advantage that it leaves most pleasures in store, for Çanakkale is, except for its food, an undistinguished town, while the Bosphorus is immensely more beautiful than the Dardanelles with their bare and monotonous hillsides.

Delightful pine forests appear farther south on the hilly road to Troy, and there is at least one pleasant motel set among trees on the precipitous hillside overlooking the mouth of the Dardanelles. The ruins of Troy are situated on a hill dominating a well-farmed coastal plain. The presence of modern villages, visible from the ruins, and, inevitably and increasingly, of tourists with their cars and coaches and of establishments catering for them, the absence finally of the wealth uncovered in the excavations and whisked away to Berlin, make Troy visually less exciting than the other archaeological sites of Turkey, where the ruins, being generally of later date, are more impressive, where the countryside is grander and usually more deserted and the continuity of past and present more direct. For Troy is a rediscovery of a past which has lived on abroad in European civilisation, and is being gradually reimported with that civilisation into Turkey. The Turkish name of Truva is simply a phonetic rendering of the French Troie and still sounds alien to the Turks. Increasingly, Turks from Istanbul, Ankara and Izmir visit the site, but its appeal to them is intellectual rather than emotional.

Although it was for a time cast unhistorically as a champion of Asia, Troy belongs to Europe. The nine cities which occupied the site contributed their achievements to or drew their sustenance from the main stream of European civilisation. The neolithic Troy I, built not of stone, like the successor cities, but of unfired brick set on stone foundations, developed some time in the third millennium B.C. the prototype of the Homeric palace, the *megaron*, a house having a portico which gave access to a courtyard. Troy II has left us imposing stone fortifications and the ruins of a royal *megaron*, near which Schliemann, the self-taught and cantankerous German discoverer of the site, found the famous treasure of Priam. This proved that at about 2250-2000 B.C. the Trojans were consummate craftsmen in copper, bronze, tin and gold, and that they had developed and used to good purpose the potter's wheel. This culture was overwhelmed by European invaders, at about 1900 B.C., and incorporated into the civilisation which produced the prosperous city of Troy VI with its Mycenean-style walls and its well-built houses standing separately on concentric terraces. Destroyed by an earthquake and immediately rebuilt, this city engaged with Greeks of the Mycenean age in a struggle for supremacy. The victory won by the Greeks at about 1250 B.C. provided them with a national epic and the beginnings of a sense of common identity, which survived the destruction of Mycenean civilisation by the Dorian newcomers. From then on the history of Troy continued outside the city. Having given Greece a shared historical experience, it furnished Rome with a mythical noble origin in rivalry with that of Greece, the legend of Aeneas, noble Trojan emigrant to Rome, symbolising both the incorporation of Rome into Greek culture and its attempt to define itself within it. Troy lived on abroad – from the Iliad through the Aeneid to the Lusiads, from the tragic and memorable Aeneas to the comic and forgotten Brut (founder of Britannia and presumably ancestor of Lud, who is at least remembered in pub names), from Hellenistic novelettes to the twelfth-century *Roman de Troie* and then through Boccaccio, Chaucer and Lydgate to Shakespeare's *Troilus and Cressida*.

Meanwhile, back in real Troy, the victory of the Greeks was quickly followed by the Thracian invasion and the eclipse of civilisation throughout northern and central Anatolia. Troy could then be justly placed in the Thracian-ruled country of Phrygia, as in Shakespeare's prologue where the Greek 'princes orgulous, their high blood chaf'd ... from the Athenian bay put forth towards Phrygia: and their vow is made to ransack Troy'. As the Thracian darkness lifted, the Greek city of Ilium (Troy VIII) appeared on the scene, its importance enhanced by a popular sanctuary of Athena, the divine patron of the Greek destroyers of the original prehistoric Troy. Ilium was visited by Alexander, shared in the urban development which took place in Hellenistic and Roman times (particularly as Caesar and his successors paid with gifts to the real Ilium for their claim to descent from the mythical Aeneas), and, it is said, nearly became the capital of the Empire under Constantine, who, however, soon saw the superior geographical advantages of Byzantium. Ilium continued to give its name to a Greek bishopric, although the Turks probably found little to preserve when they penetrated this corner of Anatolia in the beginning of the fourteenth century. The Troad peninsula at first formed part of the Turcoman principality of Karasi, centred on the inland town of Balıkesir (the Byzantine Palaeocastron or Old Castle), which had the advantage of lying in a rich agricultural area. The principality was short-lived, being quickly annexed by the Ottoman Orhan, but the name of Karasi was kept to designate an Ottoman province (*sancak*) until the beginning of the last century.

Troy disappeared in the mound of Hisarlık (near the village of Tevfikiye, whose name, meaning Divine Assistance, betrays its recent foundation by the Ottoman government for the settlement of refugees), until Schliemann started his excavations in 1870. Troy then re-emerged from the *musée imaginaire* of European cultural tradition and assumed material form in the uncovered ruins and the objects discovered in them. At the same time it performed its last service by vindicating the validity of that cultural tradition against nineteenth-century 'higher criticism'. The Iliad was proved to be a better guide than the theory that the Trojan war was but a version of a common European myth symbolising the struggle between night and day and 'the victory of the solar hero around the walls and battlements of the sky'. Although in recent years the discovery of the Dead Sea Scrolls has similarly vindicated the Massoretic text of the Old Testament, the lesson has yet to be learned by the de-mythologisers.

So the European visitor can see today the plain where the battles of the Trojan war were actually fought, satisfy himself that the Greeks' island base of Tenedos (Bozcaada) is actually visible from the Trojan shore, examine, if he is so inclined, the building methods of his cultural ancestors, feel the continuity of culture from a remote neolithic past to the last and, naturally, best-preserved Roman theatre. Scientifically-minded doubting Thomases should certainly visit Troy, particularly as one needs a scientific mind to disentangle the levels of occupation or even to follow the guiding arrows in the maze of paths and ditches. The museum has some interesting fragments of Greek pottery, and hideous modern wall decorations.

The road south from Troy goes through some pine forests as it curves its way round the 5,200 feet high Mount Ida, known in Turkish unromantically as Kazdağ or Goose Mountain. Not far from Ayvacık, where the road begins to turn east, following the outlines of the gulf of Edremit, lay the ancient port of Assos. Aristotle taught there, and St Paul sailed from it after he had seen in a dream a Macedonian who prayed to him and said 'Come over into Macedonia to help us' (Acts 16, 9). Assos was an Aeolian settlement, like the rest of the Greek cities from the mouth of the Dardanelles to Izmir, the Aeolians having arrived in this area from their home in Thessaly not long after the Trojan war.

The road then descends to Edremit which is at sea-level, but some way from the sea, and which derives its name, although not its exact site, from the ancient Adramyttion. A short run leads one to the somewhat rough and ready bathing establishments and ancillary eating-houses on the shore. The coast from here to Ayvalık and beyond has recently become a popular holiday resort for civil servants from Ankara, while young Germans are, as usual, spear-heading a more substantial foreign invasion.

Edremit is a prosperous market town at the northern end of the largest olive-growing region in Turkey. Having in the manner of so many Turkish towns turned its back on the sea, it looks inland to Balıkesir to which it is administratively subject and thence to Istanbul for its trade and its culture. I found the shops well-stocked with tinned goods, and the citizens prosperous, since olive oil is in great demand throughout the world and prices are soaring. But the Belgian-trained young Turkish civil servant who took me round told me the usual tale of provincial boredom and frustration: meetings with girls were impossible, even with fiancées – and he had no intention of marrying a local girl – local notables considered any young bachelor as a ravening wolf to be tamed or driven away; at parties, such as they were, the sexes were rigorously segregated; talk was confined to local gossip and reading to the mass-circulation daily *Hürriyet*. He had found an escape in long shooting expeditions on the wooded slopes of Goose Mountain, but my driver, who gossiped with the locals while we were talking, informed me as soon as we had left, that the young man had a most deplorable reputation since girls had been seen visiting his office. 'But what can he do?' he added generously, 'it is not for nothing that young men are called *delikanlı* (mad bloods).' Not only young bachelors, but married Turkish intellectuals, even if they are of local origin, find it hard to live in the provinces for any length of time. They complain that the locals are all fanatics, and mutual hostility flares up the moment that tongues are loosened by alcohol. Since traditional Turkish culture is largely repressive, alcohol does provide a release, and often an explosion, and the foreign visitor should take great care to exercise tact on such occasions. His companions, although bound by the rules of hospitality, are always ready, as the Turkish expression goes, to consider themselves insulted if he so much as mentions a cloud, since clouds lead to rain, rain collects in puddles, geese wade in puddles, and therefore a passing reference to clouds is tantamount to describing the company as a gaggle of stupid geese.

The feeling of boring provincial isolation, which towns like

Edremit inspire in the educated residents, is partly the result of the division of the natural unity of the Aegean basin after the expulsion of the Greeks in 1922. A neighbouring different culture can provide an escape from the frustrations of one's own way of life. 'Our leadership is, of course, right to insist that we should deal only with our own people,' a Turkish-Cypriot friend complained to me some time ago, 'But how can we find girls in our own community, where everyone knows us?' And frustrations increase when part of a society is alienated from the mass, as is the case with Turkish intellectuals, and finds itself in a minority, for only in the three large cities are there enough like-minded emancipated Turks to form a satisfying sub-culture.

The delightful seaside town of Ayvalık, with its pretty off-shore island of Alibey, was almost purely Greek and surrounded by Greek villages before 1922. The bitterness which Turks felt against the local Greeks is easily understood if one remembers that one Greek village alone produced an armed detachment of 400 men to join the invaders, while a whole Greek division was formed by Aegean Greeks to fight their Turkish neighbours. Incidentally this concentration of Greeks on the Aegean coast had not been continuous since classical times. Until the middle of the eighteenth century, the coastal towns, including Izmir, were largely Muslim, and Turkish was the language spoken in the Smyrna market. It was only later that the local population was swollen by Christian immigrants from the interior and from the Greek islands and mainland; immigrants who found in the Empire of the reforming sultans a fruitful field for the exercise of their commercial skills. It was at Ayvalık on 28 May 1919 that a regular detachment of the Turkish army disregarded the *diktat* of the victorious Allies and made its first stand against the Greek landings, before withdrawing into the interior to organise bands of popular resistance fighters – the so-called *kuva-yi milliye* or national forces.

Some way south of Ayvalık, a side turning from the main

Izmir highway leads to Bergama (Pergamum), the northern-most of the great classical sites of Turkey. The site has been occupied continuously at least from early Thracian times, its foundation being ascribed to a king of Mysia. Greeks from the mainland took it over during the Trojan war, and the small town preserved its Greek character under Persian rule from which it was wrested by Alexander in 334 B.C. It was under Alexander's successors that the 1,100-foot high hill of Perga-mum rose to world fame. Lysimachus, who had made himself master of Thrace and western Anatolia, deposited there a hoard of 9,000 gold talents which he unwisely left in the charge of the eunuch Philetaerus. The latter promptly allied himself with another of Alexander's generals, Seleucus King of Syria, appro-priated the treasure and laid the foundations of Pergamene independence and prosperity. Both derived from the fact that Pergamum lay between the zones of influence of the two main successor states – Syria in the east and Macedonia in the west. In their balancing act between the two, the kings of Perga-mum later successfully enlisted the power of Rome, to which the last king of Pergamum, Attalus III, finally bequeathed his kingdom in 143 B.C., a precedent which was to be followed in 76 B.C. by King Nicomedes IV of Bithynia. Pergamum continued to prosper and develop, first as the capital and then the second city of the Roman province of Asia. The local Christian com-munity was numbered among the seven churches of Asia, and the city survived the decline of Anatolian urban civilisation in the third century A.D., the destruction wrought by the Arabs in the eighth century and other vicissitudes. It remained an im-portant Byzantine fortress until it was captured by the Turco-man Emir of Karasi at the beginning of the fourteenth century. In Ottoman times Bergama was a busy market town, renowned for its carpets. As usual, the local Greeks were replaced by Turkish refugees from the Balkans at the end of the Great War, the population then gradually rising to its present level of 25,000.

In world history Pergamum figures as one of the main centres of Hellenistic civilisation and, as such, a link between classical Greece and Rome. It produced a distinctive and dramatic school of sculpture whose masterpieces, commemorating the defeat of the Gauls in 231 B.C. by the second king of Pergamum Eumenes I, are now to be found in the Pergamum Museum in Berlin. Some less well-known but nonetheless beautiful statues are exhibited in the small local museum. The Gauls had come from the plateau round Ankara, to which they had given the name of Galatia, and their defeat was followed by the golden age of Pergamene independence under Eumenes II (197-159 B.C.). This king set up the famous library which is said to have contained 200,000 volumes when Anthony gave it to Cleopatra. The Pergamene contribution to the written word is commemorated by the term 'parchment', a material which is said to have been first developed locally from animal hides, to overcome the effects of the Egyptian ban on the export of papyrus. Pergamum was also one of the main medical centres of antiquity. It was the birthplace of Galen (A.D. 130-200), who developed the principles first laid down in the fifth century B.C. by Hippocrates of Cos (Turkish Istanköy, a Greek island off Halicarnassus/Bodrum). Through his Arab and Italian translators and commentators, Galen of Pergamum dominated medical practice until the birth of scientific medicine.

Pergamene medicine was practised in the large compound of the Aesculapium (or temple of Aesculapius, the divine 'blameless physician'). In accordance with a sensible and hygienic tradition, this was built outside the city, on a small plateau lying about a mile away from the lower town of Pergamum. The ruins which one can see there today formed part of a building erected by the Romans in A.D. 142. The indispensable sacred spring was set in the middle of a large porticoed courtyard and connected by a tunnel with the temple proper. Next to the Aesculapium there were two theatres, one of which has been restored. The third theatre, near the top of Pergamum hill, was built by Eumenes II and enlarged by the Romans. Precariously perched on a precipitous slope, it commands a breath-taking panorama of the valley of Selinus (Bergama) Çayı. The theatres of Bergama are today used for a folk festival held in May and for occasional theatrical performances. The theatre on the hill was surrounded by a group of public buildings – the temples of Athena and Trajan, the library and, next to the Agora, the altar of Zeus, decorated with the famous reliefs which are now displayed in Berlin. Lower down the hill was the temple of the earth goddess Demeter, patron of the Eleusinian mysteries. Nearby stands one of the best-preserved Greek gymnasia in the world.

The impression left by Bergama depends partly on size – the gymnasium lecture hall alone could hold 1,000 listeners, while the Roman theatre outside the Aesculapium could seat 30,000 – partly on the beauty of the ruins, as in the elegant columns enclosing the Aesculapium courtyard, but largely on the beauty of the site: the majestic hill, surmounted by its Acropolis, balanced by the perfect ensemble of the Aesculapium, with the modern town in between, and at the foot of the hill, on the banks of Bergama Çayı, the great red bulk of the Christian basilica which had earlier been the temple of the synthetic Graeco-Egyptian god Serapis. Pergamum was a first product of the civilisation of large cities – a civilisation which had of course its brutal side, as witness the remnants of the amphitheatre (between the Aesculapium and the Acropolis) used for gladiatorial fights, but which gives an impression of balance deserving the vogue epithet 'psychosomatic'. It made ample provision for training the body, instructing the mind and entertaining the whole person, for curing the patient and also resting and amusing him. And, as elsewhere in Turkey, the clean break between town – in this case both the ruins of ancient Pergamum and the buildings of modern Bergama, and country – the fertile valley of the Caicus (Bakır Çayı or Copper Stream) with its surrounding hills, defines the product of human endeavour in its natural and largely unchanged setting.

The country between Bergama and Izmir – a country rich in olives, fruit trees and tobacco, and on the hill-sides dotted with the gnarled form of the valonia oak, whose acorns are rich in tannin and are consequently valued in the manufacture of leather – was known in classical times as Aeolis. Very little remains of Cyme, the main city of the region. Cyme was a seaport, standing on a site known now as Namurt Limanı, a bay lying south of that of Aliağa, where Turkish planners have placed a Soviet-built oil refinery. South-east of Cyme, near the point where the Izmir road crosses the Gediz (Hermus) river, there are some ancient ramparts which may or may not have guarded a city known as Aeolian Larissa. More exciting visually – as a site, for very little has survived of classical antiquity – is Eski Foça (Old Phocea), a small port lying just off the main Izmir road. Phocea was an important Ionian settlement in Aeolian country. It declined in post-classical times, but was redeveloped in the thirteenth and fourteenth centuries as a trading settlement by the Genoese, who also founded Yeni Foça (New Phocea) some six miles to the north. The importance of the district derived from the local deposits of alum, which the Genoese Zaccharia family started developing around 1275. Alum, used extensively in dyeing, tanning and medicine was essential to the European textile industry, and Anatolia was one of the main centres of supply of this mineral.

The only modern Turkish town between Ayvalık and Izmir is Menemen, just south of the Gediz. This town of 17,000 in-habitants is remembered in Turkey for a religious riot in 1930, in which a young officer named Kubilây (who is commemorated by a statue) was set upon and killed by a mob led by dervishes. The riot led to a tightening of Atatürk's secularist repression and fed the conviction of educated Turks that democratic freedom would always be exploited by religious fanatics, as well, of course, as threatening their own privileged position.

The dervishes had come from Manisa, a town of some 70,000 inhabitants, which lies some way inland on the Gediz. In classical times it was known as Magnesia ad Sipylum, Sipylus (Manisa Dağı) being a 5,000-foot high mountain dominating the town. In history it is famous for the battle fought near it in 190 B.C., in which the Romans defeated the Seleucids of Syria and became masters of Asia Minor. But the prosperity of the town dates from the fourteenth century when it became the seat of the Turcoman Saruhan dynasty. To this period belongs the Ulu Cami (Great Mosque), built in 1366-7, which occupies an important place in the development of Turkish architecture. The plan is roughly square, half the square being occupied by the mosque proper and the other half by a porticoed courtyard. The columns used in the building were obtained from Byzantine churches. The minaret is built of glazed bricks of different colours and has the appearance of a Turkish rug.

Izmir (Smyrna) is the natural centre for visits to sites of archaeological and historical interest in western Turkey. Pergamum in the north, Manisa and Sardis in the east, Ephesus, Priene, Miletus and Didyma in the south, are all within a day's drive from Izmir. The city has many hotels, and those placed in the first class are cheaper and more restful than equivalent ones in Istanbul. Izmir fully deserves the adjective 'beautiful' (*güzel*), which Turks apply to it, and which replaces its former popular nickname 'Infidel Smyrna' (Gâvur Izmir). The city is situated at the head of a deep gulf, which penetrates 46 miles inland from the Aegean sea. As a result of its post-war expansion Izmir extends almost without a break from the modern garden suburb of Karşıyaka (the Opposite Shore), on the northern shore of the gulf, to Inciraltı (Underneath the Fig Trees) on the south shore. The central part is dominated by the castle of Kadifekale (Velvet Castle, the classical Mount Pagus), while Manisa Dağı in the north-east and Iki Kardeş (Two Brothers) in the south provide a distant backdrop. In spite of its long and distinguished past Izmir is a largely modern city, and the fire which destroyed its commercial cosmopolitan centre, after its recapture by the Turks in September 1922, has allowed an ampler lay-out with wide tree-lined avenues. It has a population of over 400,000, making it the third largest city in Turkey, and it is growing fast. In addition to its traditional function as a port through which the produce of western Turkey is exported and many of the imports are handled, it has become a considerable industrial centre. The international trade fair held every year from 20 August to 20 September attracts many foreign exhibitors and many more local visitors, and the tourist in search of peace and quiet is best advised to give Izmir a wide berth at that time, particularly as the weather is scorchingly hot, in spite of the sea wind known as Imbat. Izmir is also the headquarters of the south-eastern command of NATO land armies, a headquarters which has the difficult task of securing some co-operation between Turkish and Greek forces under the aegis of the Americans. With all these modern activities, Izmir, however beautiful, is not itself a holiday centre. The gulf is a busy and polluted harbour and bathers have to go to beaches lying some distance away on the road west to Çeşme, or across the base of the Urla peninsula, to Gümüldür in the south. The latter is situated near the sites of Colophon, Notium and Clarus. The last two contain interesting ruins, those of the temple and oracle of Apollo at Clarus being particularly impressive.

Before the Great War, 'Infidel Izmir' had a non-Muslim majority, one estimate made at the beginning of the century putting the number of Greeks alone at 130,000 out of a population of a quarter of a million. One reminder of the cosmopolitan past is the suburb of Bornova, originally a preserve of European and Levantine merchants, many of whose villas and a few of whose descendants have survived to this day. However, it would be wrong to assume that Izmir has always been a great international commercial centre. Its modern importance really dates back to the eighteenth century when it replaced Bursa as a centre of eastern trade with Europe. It seems that it was also in the eighteenth century that the local Greek population began to grow until it overshadowed the Muslim character which the city had undoubtedly had from the beginning of the fifteenth century.

Izmir – at least on its present site – is a Hellenistic creation which first attained to prosperity and importance under the Roman Empire. Earlier there had been an Aeolian and then an Ionian settlement in the area at present occupied by the northern suburb of Bayraklı, but apart from the possibility that it may have been Homer's birthplace it made little impact on history and was finally destroyed by the Lydians in the sixth century B.C. The new Smyrna, founded by Alexander's general Lysimachus, proved more lasting. Under the Romans it became one of the three most important cities of western Asia, the other two being Pergamum and Ephesus. When Ephesus finally lost its harbour in Byzantine times, as the result of the silting up of the estuary of the Cayster (Küçük Menderes), Smyrna remained the only large port in the area. Turcomans first appeared on the scene immediately after the Seljuks' victory at Malazgirt, and Smyrna became for a time the lair of the redoubtable Turkish pirate Çaka. However, the Byzantines returned, only to cede the city to the Latins, represented mainly by the Genoese. In the late thirteenth century Smyrna was reconquered by the Turcomans of the Aydın dynasty, and in the beginning of the fourteenth century Çaka's exploits were repeated by the 'Sea Ghazi' Umur Bey, who wrought such havoc that a crusade had to be mounted against him. As a result, the Knights of Rhodes established themselves in the city until Tamerlane retook it for Islam in 1402. Ottoman rule dates from 1415. The cosmopolitan interval which culminated in the Greek occupation between May 1919 and September 1922 was bound to be an ephemeral phenomenon, like the fourteenth-century Latin interval. The prosperity of Izmir, as of the other cities of the littoral, depends on that of the hinterland, whose political fate it is bound to share in the long run.

Little remains of classical Smyrna apart from the Roman Agora and, of course, the exhibits in the two archaeological museums, whose best pieces come, however, from farther afield – Ephesus, Sardis and Hierapolis. It is to these sites that the historically-minded tourist will turn. Three important Ionian cities used to stand on the Urla peninsula west of Izmir: Clazomenae on the site known today as Urla Iskelesi, Teos (Sığacık, which retains its Genoese fortress) and Erythrae (Ildır). Almost nothing is left of them today. Çeşme at the tip of the peninsula, opposite Chio, is of modern foundation. It is dominated by a fortress built by the Genoese and enlarged by Sultan Beyazit II in 1508. The small town is mainly remembered for the great naval battle fought near it on 5 July 1770, in which the Ottoman fleet was defeated and set on fire by the fleet sent to the Mediterranean by the Russian Empress Catherine the Great. The visitor may be more interested in the excellent sandy beach, the hot springs at nearby Ilıca and the views, which are pleasing on all sides.

The Lydian capital of Sardis lies near the small market town of Salihli (30,000 inhabitants), just off the Izmir-Ankara road, which follows the natural highway from the Aegean to the Anatolian plateau, formed by the Gediz valley. This is the road which the Lydians followed to the west when they sacked Smyrna and conquered some of the other Greek settlements on the coast, and to the east when they advanced to conquer Phrygia and suffer defeat at the hands of the Persians beyond the Kızılırmak (Halys) river. It was also the road taken by the Greeks after the Great War during their advance into Anatolia which ended in their crushing defeat at Dumlupınar on the plateau, between Uşak and Afyon, on 30 August 1922.

Sardis, like so many Anatolian cities, lies at the foot of a high mountain (Tmolus/Bozdağ, some 6,500 feet high). Built on a strategically important site on the main highway, and commanding a fertile valley, Sardis had the added advantage of lying on a stream (Pactolus, a tributary of the Gediz) from which gold could be extracted. This was used in what were apparently the first coins ever minted by civilised man, coins made first of an alloy of gold and silver, and then, under the last Lydian king Croesus, of these two metals separately. Apart from being inventors of coins, the Indo-European, probably Thracian, Lydians are also said to have invented gambling games. After their conquest by the Persians, they struck out in a new direction and produced skilful musicians, hence the Lydian mode of musical composition. Although Sardis is one of the few cities in the region to have decreased in size in Græco-Roman times, the most impressive ruin to be seen locally is the temple of Artemis, a Hellenistic building, altered by the Romans, and famous for its superb Corinthian columns. Parts of the fortifications of the city have also been uncovered. But by far the most common monument left by the Lydians are their tombs – the tumuli of Bin Tepe (Thousand Hills), some six miles north of Sardis on a ridge overlooking the Gediz valley; a tomb in the shape of a stepped pyramid near the Acropolis; and tombs cut out of rocks. The Lydians shared this concentration on elaborate burial places with the Egyptians, but also with other Anatolian peoples, such as the Phrygians (the fortress-like building known as Taşkule/Stone Tower, near Eski Foça, north of Izmir, is probably a Phrygian tomb) and the Carians and Lycians, whose tombs are to be found all over western and south-western Anatolia.

The decline of Sardis may perhaps have been hastened by the rise of Alaşehir (Philadelphia), a Hellenistic foundation on the other side of the Tmolus, which became an important Byzantine fortress and had the distinction of being the last city in western Anatolia to be conquered by the Muslims, in the person of Tamerlane himself in 1402. However, the local Greeks had long become familiar with the language and the ways of their Turkish neighbours, and provided interpreters and go-betweens used by Muslim Emirs in their dealings with the Christians.

North of Sardis, on another tributary of the Gediz, lies the market town of Akhisar, the ancient Thyatira, famous as the site of one of the seven churches of Asia. We are here on the edges of the plateau, the old border between Phrygia and Lydia. This area and the mountains south of Izmir, particularly round Aydın, saw the birth of Turkish popular resistance against the Greek occupation in 1919. First in the fray were the outlaws, known as *zeybek* or *efe*, who at times frightened their friends as much as their enemies. They are remembered today for their exploits; their lively dances are played at all folk festivals. But their excesses, which obliged the first Turkish resistance congress at Alaşehir to proclaim piously 'We denounce banditry as odious', and which led to a suppression of the *efes* by the nationalist leaders themselves, are mercifully forgotten. Western Anatolia has in fact a long tradition of Muslim urban culture, developed in such centres as Manisa, Aydın, Birgi, Denizli and Muğla – towns that passed into Muslim hands at the end of the thirteenth or the beginning of the fourteenth century – and their citizens had no sympathy with outlaws of peasant origin. Today the visitor will probably pass through them quickly on his way to archaeological sites or to seaside resorts and, particularly after the destruction wrought in the Greek-Turkish war, there are few Muslim monuments of note. However, the Ulu Cami (Great Mosque) in Birgi, near Ödemiş, and some attractive old houses in Muğla deserve attention.

Of the sites south of Izmir, Ephesus has pride of place, followed by Miletus, Didyma and Priene. We are back here in Ionia, the coastal country between the Hermus and the Maeander. The road from Izmir to Ephesus (Efes, near the small town of Selçuk, where the ruined but interesting early mosque of Isa Bey deserves a visit), runs through a fertile plain and crosses a hill barrier before dropping down to the valley of the Küçük Menderes (Cayster). Ephesus had a fertile hinterland, and the Cayster valley provided a convenient route to the interior. But the river also deposited large quantities of earth near the city, which had consequently to move its harbour at regular intervals. In Ionian times, Ephesus was famous for its sanctuary of the goddess Artemis, continuing the local tradition of the worship of the Anatolian mother goddess. Dating back to the eighth century B.C., the sanctuary was repeatedly rebuilt, the most famous occasion being after 365 B.C. when Herostatus set fire to it as the only way he could devise of immortalising his memory. It was after this gratuitously-caused reconstruction that it came to be numbered among the seven wonders of the world, of which only one other, the mausoleum of Halicarnassus, lay in the territory of Turkey. Throughout all these vicissitudes, the temple of Artemis retained its site, while the city was repeatedly moved, first by the Lydian Croesus from the coast to the vicinity of the sanctuary, and then by Alexander's general Lysimachus, who chose for it a new harbour, now also embedded in the alluvial plain.

The impressive ruins which one can see today, possibly the most impressive in Turkey, belong to the Hellenistic city, which was developed by the Romans as the capital of their province of Asia and grew into a thriving metropolis with a quarter of a million inhabitants. Within the Hellenistic walls are scattered the bones of a great city, standing clean and clear like a marble-strewn cemetery of the immediate predecessors of our own civilisation. On either side of the celebrated Marble Street, there are the ruins of a theatre, gymnasium, stadium, agora, library, baths, museum, odeon and the characteristically elegant temple of Hadrian. Objects found in the excavations are shown in the beautifully arranged small museum. Turn left as you enter, and you see a large collection of heads of Roman notables, pompous in a particularly Victorian way; turn right and you face a statue of the great Artemis of Ephesus, the Asiatic, barbaric-looking goddess whom these civilised notables worshipped or professed to. Covered with a multiplicity of either breasts or eggs – the experts are not sure which – with wild animals carved on her two legs joined together to form a pedestal, Artemis represents primitive Anatolia incorporated into the Greek world. Gradually her cult, headed by a eunuch chief priest, served by vestal virgins, acrobats and mountebanks, became an anachronism in her own city, so that St Paul's words 'There be no gods which are made with hands' quickly found an echo and 'so mightily grew the word of God and prevailed', in spite of the uproar raised by one Demetrius who 'made silver shrines for Diana' (Artemis) and 'brought no small gain unto the craftsmen' (Acts 19; 26, 20, 24). The triumph of Christianity in Ephesus is represented by the church of the Virgin Mary, the product of a fourth-century conversion of the pagan Museum (it is in this church that the third Oecumenical Council was held in 431), by the magnificent church of St John built under Justinian on high ground (near the modern township of Selçuk) and by the House of the Virgin on Aladağ mountain, five miles south-west of Selçuk. The House of the Virgin, now restored as a chapel, and with a Catholic priest usually in residence, provides a refreshing postscript to a tour of Ephesus. It is situated on a delightfully wooded spur of the mountain, in a spot ideally suited for the holy picnics which the Turks, like the Byzantines before them, enjoyed so much. The house was first described in a vision by Catherine Emmerich and identified in 1891 by a Lazarist priest. Today it is recognised as a place of pilgrimage, although belief that this was the Virgin's last abode on earth or even that she was ever taken to Ephesus by St John is not incumbent on Catholics.

There is, of course, no doubt that St John himself was a very early visitor to Ephesus, and the basilica built over his tomb became such an important place of pilgrimage in the Middle Ages that the name of Ephesus itself disappeared from current use, to be replaced by Hagios Theologos (Saint (John the) Theologian), a place-name that the Italians changed to Alto Luogo, and the Turcoman conquerors of the city more accurately to Ayasoluk. Turcomans and Latins, represented mainly by Catalan mercenaries, fought for posses

sion of mediaeval Ephesus, and it is perhaps this struggle which
finds an echo in Shakespeare's 'Comedy of Errors' when the
Duke of Ephesus declares:

> *It hath in solemn synod been decreed,*
> *Both by the Syracusians and ourselves,*
> *To admit no traffic to our adverse towns:*
> *Nay, more,*
> *If any born in Ephesus be seen*
> *At any Syracusan marts or fairs,*
> *Again, if any Syracusan-born*
> *Come to the bay of Ephesus, he dies...*

In fact, however, traffic between Ayasoluk/Alto Luogo and
the Latins continued in spite of intermittent hostilities, and
was transferred to Kuşadası/Scala Nuova, after the harbour of
Ephesus had been completely silted up. Kuşadası, meaning
Birds' Island, after the small island, now joined to the mainland, which is surmounted by a castle, is a pretty and growing
holiday resort. It is ideally situated for visits to Ephesus and
other archaeological sites, and offers in addition good bathing,
excellent views, reasonable hotels and restaurants and at least
a sniff of Turkish atmosphere in its market.

A short drive over the hills, south-east of Kuşadası, takes one
to Söke, a prosperous market town in the valley of the Maeander (Büyük Menderes), once marshy but now drained to form
one of the richest cotton-growing areas in Turkey.* Another
short drive separates Söke from the ruins of Priene, the birthplace of Bias, one of the seven sages of antiquity. The city,
originally founded by Ionians, was transferred to the present
site at the time of Alexander. The ruins which one can see
today are largely Hellenistic, since the city did not grow much
under the Romans. The main buildings of the city can be easily

---

* Agriculture is incidentally gradually decreasing the supply of the wild
licorice root for which Söke and its environs were famous.

visualised: the sanctuary of Athena, the theatre, the stadium, the gymnasium and especially the well-preserved Council House. It is a pretty and compact site standing in deserted open country.

To reach Miletus one has to turn back to the main road from Söke to Milâs and then turn right again towards the sea. Miletus, which lay originally at the mouth of the Maeander, now finds itself some five miles inland. It was founded by Ionians on a site first occupied by local Carians, became the maritime capital of Greece in the sixth century B.C., was the birthplace of the sage Thales (the author of the advice 'know thyself') and of the geographer Anaximander. The first golden age of Miletus ended when it was destroyed by the Persians in 494 B.C. It was then rebuilt on its present site, was captured by Alexander and prospered under the Romans to whom we owe the theatre and the baths of Faustina, the two most impressive buildings on the site, each probably the best surviving specimen of its kind. Miletus was visited by St Paul, became the seat of a Byzantine archbishop and survived into Turcoman times when it was visited by Venetian merchants. As with other cities on the coast its doom was sealed when its harbour silted up.

A coastal road, first built by the Romans, joins the ruins of Graeco-Roman Miletus with the great temple of Apollo at Didyma. In the sixth century B.C. this was already a famous sanctuary, and the 'sacred road' from the landing stage to the temple was lined with statues, some of which can be seen today in the British Museum. The temple was destroyed by the Persians, after Darius had defeated the Ionian revolt in 494 B.C. Work on the new and much larger temple started under Alexander's successor Seleucus in 300 B.C. and went on for a couple of centuries, in spite of attacks by Gauls and pirates. The temple was patronised by the Romans, enjoying great fame and riches until the third century A.D., when it was converted into a fortress to resist the marauding Goths. It subsequently became a battlefield between pagans and Christians, the victory of Christianity being signalled by the construction of a church in the temple sanctuary. The prophetess of Didyma, like the priest sitting by the *omphalos*, the navel-stone of Claros, then fell silent. But the temple building was too massive to perish, and its ruins stand today as an impressive monument to Hellenistic engineering and, as some would have it, to Hellenistic taste.

Didyma is the last important Ionian site. Farther south the resorts of Güllük and Bodrum are in the neighbouring province of Caria. The main road south skirts the large fresh-water lake of Bafa, which was once a sea gulf, and which is today famous for its delicious *botargo* and for its place in the daemonology of Turkish radicals, since the fishing rights are privately owned and the local peasants often clash with armed guards employed by the owners. On the opposite shore of the lake, which can be reached by motor boat, stand the ruins of the Carian city of Heracleia at the foot of the 4,000-foot high Mount Latmus (Beşparmak Dağı or Five Finger Mountain). The strong sea ramparts put up by the Carian king Mausolus still survive. Heracleia also boasted of the sanctuary of the deathless Endymion, the lover of the moon goddess Selene. Near the ruins of this building there is a profusion of Carian tombs, carved out of the rocky mountainside.

Milâs, once the capital of Caria and then of the Turcoman Menteşe principality, has three fourteenth-century mosques, one of which was built with the marble débris of earlier monuments. From Milâs a road leads first to Güllük on the bay of the same name, on whose shores lie the ruins of the Greek cities of Iasus and Bargylia, and then to Bodrum (Halicarnassus). There is hardly anything left of classical Halicarnassus, a city colonised by the Dorians but chosen as the capital by the Carian king Mausolus, whose tomb, the original Mausoleum, was counted among the seven wonders of the world. The last remaining stones of this monument are said to have been used by the Knights of Rhodes in 1415 when they built their im-

pressive Castle of St Peter (Bodrum Kalesi). This was captured
by the Ottomans in 1522 and later served as a prison. In the
past the people of Bodrum, like their neighbours on the Greek
island of Calymnos, derived a precarious income from sponge
fishing. Today tourism provides a better livelihood.

The climb into the Carian mountains begins immediately
after Milâs. After Muğla, a typical Turkish town of the plateau
(*yaylâ*), the road to the seaside resort of Marmaris is said to
contain as many bends as there are days of the year. It has now
been surfaced and can be negotiated with reasonable safety. It
offers splendid views of mountains, a distant sea, and pine
forests with clearings usually dotted with beehives.

The south-western corner of Turkey, where the high mountains meet the sea, is indented with deep gulfs, separated by
peninsulas, whose shores are broken by masses of little bays.
Even the millions of tourists whom the Turkish authorities are
trying to attract will never swamp this shore. Marmaris, situated on a small peninsula projecting into an almost completely
land-locked bay, is undoubtedly the most attractive resort on
this coast. It has a small castle built by Süleyman the Magnificent as a preparation for his assault on Rhodes, and surrounded
by tumbledown old Turkish houses which are gradually being
replaced by tourist pensions. There are pine forests around and
also eucalyptus trees, planted a century ago when the coastal
marshes were drained.

An adventurous drive takes one from Marmaris along the
long narrow neck of the Reşadiye peninsula to the seaside village of Datça. Thence a hair-raising road follows the spine of
the peninsula to the ruins of Cnidus, a site first settled by
Dorians. Cnidus had a strategically-placed small natural harbour, and the added advantage of being almost inaccessible by
land. It prospered in the classical period, and particularly under
the Romans, and was famous for its medical school and the
artists and scholars which it bred. Today the natural site at the
wind-swept tip of the peninsula is more impressive than the

ruins. The most famous work of art found locally, a large recumbent lion and a seated goddess, are in the British Museum. The northern slopes of the peninsula are barren and wild, the southern contain narrow isolated valleys, producing olive and citrus. In the centre wild boar still roam the hills and can occasionally be seen darting across the road.

A coastal road is being built from Datça to Marmaris, and thence to Köyceğiz, Fethiye and Antalya. However, even before it is completed, intrepid drivers can reach Köyceğiz by the track used by lorries carrying chrome ore from the many mines which export their produce through Fethiye, farther east. Köyceğiz, situated romantically on a large lagoon, famous for its fish-traps (*dalyan*) is little more than a village, lying on the frontier between Caria and Lycia. Fethiye, on the other hand, is a beautiful little town at the head of a bay dotted with pine-covered islands. The new municipal building displays a few antique inscriptions, among them a nineteenth-century Jewish gravestone, which, my guide assured me, provided a perfect example of the lost Lycian alphabet.

From Fethiye the road continues over the hills, still abounding in jackal as well as wild boar, to the ruins of Xanthus, the ancient capital of Lycia on the Kocaçay river. The valley of the Kocaçay is already part of tropical Turkey – the valleys and plains south of the Taurus mountains, settled in prehistoric times, prosperous in Graeco-Roman days, and then ruined by Arabs, malaria and neglect until the current development of the Turkish countryside. Farther east, DDT, drainage, the cultivation of cash crops and tourism have made the Pamphylian plain one of the fastest-growing regions of Turkey. The isolated valley of the Kocaçay is, however, still virgin land and the hill of Xanthus with its impressive remains – Graeco-Roman walls, acropolis, theatre, inscribed pillars, sarcophagi and Byzantine basilica – stands in a hot, scrub-covered empty valley, visited by a few tourists in the summer and by nomads from the mountains in the winter. The most famous local finds – the Lycian throne supported by lions (the lion was the symbol of Lycia), the frieze from the monument of the Sirens, carvings from the monument of the Nereids – are all in the British Museum.

Little, apart from the Roman gate, remains of the port of Patara, at the mouth of the valley. The modern road curves east to the little port of Kalkan, built on the slopes leading steeply down to a sheltered cove, perfect haunt of pirates and smugglers, who gave the coast a bad name in antiquity and also in recent times. The population of these seaside villages and small towns was largely Greek until the Great War, and is now made up of Turks from the plateau and refugees from the Balkans. Cut picturesquely and dangerously in the scrub-covered seaward slopes of the Taurus, the road goes on to the lovely port of Kaş, on the site of Antiphellus, whose Hellenistic theatre is well-preserved and which, like all other settlements in the region, is surrounded by Lycian rock tombs. A little out to sea lies the Greek island of Castellorizo (Megiste/Meis), administered as part of the Dodecanese and therefore an Italian possession from 1912 to 1944.

Demre, which lies west of Kaş on the way to Finike, is the ancient Myra, the Christian metropolis of Lycia. The relics of St Nicholas, the famous local bishop, were whisked away to Italy in the eleventh century, the modern church built over the saint's tomb has fallen into ruin after the departure of the local Greeks, but the Turkish authorities have been making strenuous efforts to attract to Demre west Europeans and Americans, in whose mixed-up mythology Santa Claus occupies a soft spot. Eschewing the traditional Turkish form of Aya Nikola, with its Greek associations, the tourist authorities have called the local tourist saint Noel Baba (from the French Père Noël), a name which the Turkish inhabitants instantly Islamicised into Nâil Baba. The captain of the caique which took me to Demre explained that Nâil had been a Bektashi dervish (hence the title Baba or Father, characteristic of that order), famous for the sanctity of his life and for the miraculous cures effected at his tomb. I felt privileged to be present at the birth of a new myth expressing old values.

Finike stands at the centre of a small fertile plain famous for its oranges and providing a foretaste of Pamphylia from which it is separated by the 9,000-foot high Bey mountains, part of the Western or Lycian Taurus. The wild and wooded slopes between Cape Gelidonya (Swallow Point) and the western approach to Antalya are dissected by narrow valleys, rich in classical and Byzantine ruins, in camping sites set among wild rhododendrons on sandy beaches, and, increasingly, in market gardens producing out-of-season fruit and vegetables. Of these valleys that of Kemer (the name meaning 'arch' testifies to the presence of ruins) is nearest Antalya and has, therefore, been the first to share in the development of modern Pamphylia.

Antalya is of course reached more easily by air or sea, or again by roads crossing the interior of Anatolia. The main road from Izmir through Denizli and Burdur affords an opportunity of visiting one of Turkey's show places, Pamukkale/Hierapolis. Hierapolis lies on the plateau overlooking the Maeander, some thirteen miles north of Denizli. It was founded in Hellenistic times and, of course, prospered under the Romans. Its main assets were the natural hot springs, bubbly with gas, and so rich in minerals that they are said to deposit more than seven tons of limestone annually, producing cataracts of chalk-white cliffs from which the name of Pamukkale (Cotton Castle) is thought to derive, although it may also have something to do with the cotton plantations in the valley below. Round these springs the Romans laid out a large spa, while paying tribute to this miracle of nature by a religious cult, complete with an oracle. Today it is possible to swim in the pool formed by the central hot spring among débris of Roman columns. However, progress in irrigation has led to a fall in the water table and the output of the spring has decreased visibly.

The road from Denizli to Pamukkale passes by the huge site once occupied by Laodicea, one of the most important cities of

Asia under the Romans. Christianity spread here quickly, probably through the presence of a large Jewish community, but prosperity tempered the fervour of the local church, one of the seven of Asia, drawing from St John the Divine the rebuke 'So then because thou art lukewarm, and neither cold nor hot, I will spew thee out of my mouth' (Rev. 3, 16). Is there here a reference to the lukewarm streams flowing from the springs of nearby Hierapolis?

Below Burdur, on the way from Afyon or Izmir to Antalya, a side road leads to Korkuteli and then on to Elmalı on the high plateau dominating the south-western corner of Turkey. These Lycian highlands, much frequented by nomad Yörüks and by the kindred Shiah *tahtacıs* (woodcutters), were the centre of the Turcoman Tekke principality in the fourteenth century. With the rest of the Anatolian plateau they are thus part of the Turkish core of Turkey. The same is true of the lake country to the north-west, the ancient Pisidia, centred on the towns of Burdur, Eğridir and Isparta. This land became Muslim even earlier, at the time of the Seljuk conquests in the early thirteenth century, while in the fourteenth century it was ruled by the Hamit Turcomans, who had their military capital at Eğridir, picturesquely situated on a promontory in the lake of the same name. Like other traditionally Turkish areas, Pisidia was famous for its carpets, particularly those made at Isparta. In the nineteenth century Muslim refugees from Bulgaria introduced the cultivation of roses, and today the French scent industry draws many of its raw materials from the *vilayets* of Burdur and Isparta.

The extreme south-eastern outpost of Pisidia was at Termessus, a stronghold occupied by proverbially warlike people. Perched on a 3,500-foot high mountain which overlooks the road from Antalya to Korkuteli, Termessus resisted Alexander, preserved its independence under his successors and enjoyed considerable autonomy under the Romans, to whom it was officially allied rather than subjected. The impressive remains of

a theatre, temples and, of course, walls belong to the Hellenistic and Roman periods, mainly the latter. Both periods are
well represented in Turkey and the interest of the site lies
mainly in its wild mountain setting.

The mountain provinces were Hellenised late in history, and
probably imperfectly. Not so the plain of Pamphylia, where,
according to tradition, Greeks of diverse tribes settled after the
Trojan wars. The main classical cities of Pamphylia, where
Greeks met local Anatolian – probably Hittite – influences are
Perge, Aspendus and Side. Antalya (Attaleia/Adalia) is a product of the development of the area begun under Alexander's
successors and continued under the Roman Empire. The city
was founded by Attalus II, King of Pergamum, who ruled over
Pamphylia by grace of the Romans, after the defeat of their
common enemy, the Seleucids of Syria. Roman rule, which succeeded the brief Pergamene period, gave Pamphylia prosperity
unequalled until our own days. After declining in Byzantine
times, when it suffered from Arab raids, Pamphylia had the luck
of being annexed fairly early – at the beginning of the thirteenth century – by the Seljuks of Konya, for whom it offered
a natural gateway to the Mediterranean and who left their mark
in a mass of architectural monuments: castles, mosques, medreses and caravanserais. The Seljuks were succeeded by the
Turcomans of the Hamit dynasty and then, before Ottoman rule
was imposed, by a troubled interregnum: the Latins, in the
person of Pierre de Lusignan, King of Cyprus, held Antalya
between 1361 and 1373, while, farther east, Alanya came under
the Karaman Turcomans and then briefly under the Egyptian
Mamluks. The present prosperity dates from the eradication of
malaria after the Second War, the introduction of the cultivation of cotton and the opening up of good communications with
the interior. The population of Antalya increased from 23,000
to 72,000 in thirty years, while that of the province as a whole
has reached half a million inhabitants.

The plain of Antalya rises step by step, forming two main

terraces, and the thirty or so streams which flow through it from the Taurus mountains proceed by a series of waterfalls, the most famous being that on the Manavgat (Melas) river, or occasionally disappear in potholes (*düden*) to re-emerge a few miles later. The sound of running water flowing through the city or tumbling into the sea over the cliffs to the east of it, is one of the most pleasing features of Antalya, particularly to Turks from the arid plateau. The visitor has a choice of beaches, among them the long pebble beach at Konyaaltı to the west of Antalya, and the fine sand beach at Lara, east of the town and of the Düden waterfall. Lara is the site of the ancient Magydus and bathers can easily pick out the ruins of the artificial harbour and of some of the city buildings.

Antalya has a well-arranged local museum, rich in Lycian and Pamphylian sarcophagi and proud of its modern reliquary of St Nicholas brought from Myra. Near the museum rises the town's famous landmark, known as the Fluted Minaret (Yivli Minare). Other Seljuk monuments include a mosque incorporating the remains of a Byzantine basilica and usually referred to as the Cut-off Minaret (Kesik Minare), and the thirteenth-century mosque of Karatay. The city's Roman past is represented by the lovely Gate of Hadrian (Üçlü Kapı/Three-fold Gate). The citizens of Antalya are particularly proud of their modern park overlooking the town and harbour from the eastern cliffs. This does indeed afford impressive views of the bay and of the Bey mountains in the distance, but with its concrete paths, neat palm trees and hideous modern statues, it is a prime example of provincial municipal taste. Much more attractive is the walled old city on the slopes leading down to the small harbour protected by two breakwaters. Here, traditional large Turkish houses with overhanging upper storeys, often directly reached by outside staircases from enclosed gardens, their large rooms usually arranged in the shape of a cross to make maximum use of every breath of air, remind us of the days when Antalya was a small Ottoman harbour, less prosperous than today but with a way of life suited to the environment. Motor-boats can be hired for trips to the waterfalls, caves and beaches. Visitors used to be warned against sharks, which were apparently attracted by the effluent of a slaughterhouse curiously perched on the sea cliffs, but this menace has receded.

Rich visitors can travel by caique as far as Side. This is, however, much more easily reached by the fast modern road, and a day's trip can easily take in also visits to Perge, Sillyum and Aspendus. The ruins of Perge lie near the banks of the Aksu (Cestrus) river, which was wide enough to allow small ships to reach this inland port in classical times. It is traditionally one of the cities founded by the early Greek settlers, who preserved the local cult of a black stone, probably a meteorite, later surmounted by a bust of Artemis. The symbols of the goddess, the star and the moon, appear on local coins and provide a coincidental link with modern Turkey. The moon (Selene) and the sun (as Phoebus) are repeatedly shown in the ruins of this beautiful compact Graeco-Roman city, whose walls, monumental gates, main streets and public buildings are neatly outlined on the sun-drenched plain. Inscriptions, mostly bilingual in Latin and Greek sing the praises of local dignitaries, above all of a rich benefactress called Plancia Magna. In spite of the passage of almost two thousand years, the marks left by stonemasons' chisels are clean and clear.

East of Perge a side turning leads to Sillyum, built on a 700-foot high flat-topped hill. It is famous for its inscription in the Pamphylian Greek dialect, but the visitor who is not a philologist will probably be more interested in the impressive fortifications and the ramp leading to them. Because of its natural position, Sillyum was a Christian stronghold in troubled Byzantine times, and most of the remains, including that of the basilica, belong to that age.

Aspendus (called in Turkish, Belkıs Harabeleri, i.e. the Ruins of the Queen of Sheba, for only a great personage could have been presumed to have built it) is easily reached by a hard-surface road. The site is famous for its huge and extraordinarily well-preserved theatre, shored up by the Seljuks and restored recently to serve as the venue of folk and pop music festivals. It is colossal rather than beautiful, rising monumentally on a flat and well cultivated plain. Nearby flows the Köprü Su (Eurymedon). This stream provided a passage to the Mediterranean, but does not seem to have been an adequate source of fresh water, which was consequently brought to the city from the foothills of the Taurus by an aqueduct, whose ruins are still standing. A track leads inland to the Pisidian stronghold of Selge (Zerk), the constant rival of Termessus until the Romans spread their mantle over both cities and allowed them to achieve the prosperity to which the extensive ruins bear witness. As at Termessus, the site of Selge excites by its distant mountain setting, nearly 2,000 feet up in the Taurus.

Side is pleasing in a different way. Here sandy beaches lie within a stone's throw of the beautifully-preserved ruins of the ancient town – a large seaside theatre, walls, colonnaded streets, temples, a basilica and Roman baths restored to house a rich local museum. There are hotels, pensions, reasonable seaside restaurants – facilities that presage the tourist city which is soon to cover the whole site. At present, before the marina, golf course, large hotels and service industries have made their appearance, Side has achieved a pleasant balance. It has adequate comforts, while the local people – Muslim refugees from Crete for whom the Ottoman government had built the village of Selimiye – have not yet completed the transition from hospitality to catering. The ancient city, named after the pomegranate and preserving a pre-Greek language much longer than its neighbours, flourished under the Roman Empire, enjoyed a revival in the fifth and sixth centuries under the Byzantines, and was finally brought low by the Arabs, its abandoned ruins being known locally as Eski Antalya (Old Antalya).

Side lies a little away from Manavgat, a flourishing if undistinguished market town on the river of the same name. Above the falls, famous for their width rather than their height, a hydro-electric station has been built to supply power to the aluminium smelter at Seydişehir, south-east of Konya. What effect this will have on the trout for which the river is also famous remains to be seen.

Manavgat river formed the frontier between Pamphylia and Rough Cilicia (Tracheotis), the former overlooked by Pisidia, the latter by Isauria. The barbarous Isaurians often raided the coast, establishing nests of redoubtable pirates, whom even the Romans had difficulty in subduing. However, the western foot-hills of the maritime central Taurus are fairly low, and the long and narrow plain of Alanya is easily reached. Long sandy beaches on either side of this Gibraltar-like fortress have at-tracted more motel builders than any other stretch of the Turkish coast. Alanya is extremely impressive – a rock 820 feet high, made impregnable by the Seljuks who obtained it in 1220 by way of exchange from its Byzantine-appointed Armen-ian governor. The present name derives from Alaiyye, after the Seljuk Sultan Alaettin Keykubat. To the Greeks it was known as Calonoros (The Good Mountain, hence the Italian name of Candeloro), while in classical times it was named Coracesium (Crow's Nest) and was notorious for its pirates.

Alanya lies at the edge of the north-eastern corner of the Mediterranean, which has often felt the influence of powerful rulers of Egypt – the Ptolemies in classical times, the Mamluks in the late Middle Ages and Ibrahim Paşa in the last century. Until recently Alanya also carried on a profitable trade in timber felled in the Taurus mountains and exported to Egypt. It flourished exceedingly under the Seljuks, for whom it was an important port, a frontier stronghold against the Latins and their Armenian allies, and a shipbuilding centre (their cavern-ous shipyards can still be seen at the foot of the hill). Having acquired the city, Alaettin Keykubat had the coastal Red Tower (Kızıl Kule) built by a military architect from Aleppo – another pointer to the proximity of the Arab Near East. This octagonal stronghold guards the narrow isthmus leading to the rock. Past it a road climbs up to the upper walled castle through terraces abounding in cisterns and planted with mulberry trees, for the cultivation of silkworms and the weaving of multi-coloured silk scarves is the main occupation of local women. The strong Seljuk citadel contains surprisingly a gem of a Byzantine church, still preserving traces of its original frescoes. A sheer drop to the sea from the western wall of the citadel is inevitably described as a former execution spot for criminals (*adam atacağı*, man-drop).

Some way east of Alanya, after the large village of Gazipaşa (near the ruins of Trajanopolis), the mountains of Rough Cilicia start in earnest. The modern road follows painfully the contours of the mountain side, dropping now and then to beautiful seaside beaches, to rise again to scrub-covered heights, where nomads are the only people to be seen. Almost exactly half way between Alanya and Silifke, the road descends to the narrow valley of Anamur. The ruins of ancient Anemorium are on a deserted rocky promontory, while the small modern town lies a little inland. But the most splendid monument at this most southerly point of the Anatolian peninsula is the excellently-preserved, unbelievably romantic castle projecting into the sea. Built originally by the Armenians as a point of contact with their allies in Cyprus, it passed to the Seljuks and then to the Ottomans who both looked after it, until the conquest of Cyprus in the sixteenth century removed the threat to this coast.

The road rises immediately after Alanya, which is separated by another 80 miles of mountain corniche from Silifke (Seleucia Trachea) and the delta of the Göksu (Calycadnus), the swift-flowing stream in which Frederick Barbarossa was drowned in 1190. This accident deprived the Third Crusade of its main leader and its chance of success. Silifke, situated some way from the coast, is an undistinguishable town, overlooked by a medieval Latin fortress. It is more easily reached by fast road from Ankara through Konya and then across the Taurus mountains by the pass of Sertavul. The coastal road continues east of Silifke, past two potholes (known as Heaven and Hell, the former presumably deriving its name from a ruined Armenian chapel) to ancient Corycus. In the late Middle Ages the Armenians or Latins built here two castles, one on the mainland, the other on a small island (known to the Turks for the usual reasons as Kızkalesi/Maiden's Castle) which can easily be reached by swimming from the excellent sandy beach. The beach is occupied by a motel which may perhaps soon come under new and better management. This extreme southern coast of Turkey is rich in Roman and mediaeval monuments. Its many castles date back to the struggle, from the twelfth to the sixteenth centuries, when Armenians, Byzantines, Latins and Turks tried to establish themselves in this corner of the Mediterranean. The Roman ruins of Seleucia, Diocaesarea, Olba, Corycus, Pompeiopolis bear witness to the only period of prosperity the coast has known. Another may be dawning as the coast becomes Ankara's southern seaside, but this new role is unlikely to produce great art.

The Cilician plain (Çukurova/Hollow Plain), farther east, is visited more often by businessmen than by tourists. It is sometimes described as a miniature Nile delta, but it is a land not of one river but of three – from west to east, the Tarsus, Seyhan and Ceyhan – and its frontier position has often made it into a neglected battlefield, so that its rich geographical potential has probably never been exploited as fully as it is today. Cilicia has always felt a dual influence – from the plateau in the north and the Semitic plains and beyond them Egypt in the south. Excavations near Mersin have uncovered early pre-historic settlements. The city and name of Adana go back at least to the Hittites who came here into contact with Semitic civilisation. Later the Persians ruled it, until their king Darius was defeated by Alexander at Issus (near Yakacık/Payas in the district of Dörtyol). More stable conditions developed when Alexander's successors established themselves in nearby Antioch. Under the Roman peace, the large increase in overland trade through the Cilician Gates (Gülek Boğazı) led to the growth of Tarsus as the chief city of the province. This busy meeting point between Indo-European and Semite, Europe and Asia, Jew and Gentile, was the birthplace of the Apostle of the Gentiles.

Christianity established itself early, acquiring its very name at Antioch. After its triumph it had to face the threat of Persia, whose Zoroastrian king sacked Antioch and deported most of its inhabitants. No sooner were the Persians repelled than the Arabs surged north, conquering the whole country south of the Taurus. Cilicia was reconquered by the Byzantines in the tenth century only to become a battlefield between Greeks, Turks, Armenians and Latins. The last Christian feudal lords were ejected by the Mamluks of Egypt, whose dominions the Ottomans conquered in the sixteenth century. Modern development dates back to the Egyptian occupation in the nineteenth century when fellahs from the Nile delta were settled in the deserted malarial swamps of Cilicia. When Ottoman government returned, Turcomans and Kurds from the plateau were also moved in. A mixed population of Turks, Arabs and Armenians began to grow again. Adana was now the chief city, and it contained a large Armenian minority which made common cause with the French occupation forces at the end of the Great War. Turkish resistance immediately developed in the fastness of Taurus mountains, and even before the Greeks were swept from Anatolia the French had to withdraw from Cilicia, taking the Armenians with them. Less than twenty years later they completed their withdrawal by ceding Hatay (the sandjak of Alexandretta) to the Republic of Turkey.

Recovery, slow between the two wars, has gathered speed in recent years. It has been based on the cultivation of cotton, supplemented by rice and citrus fruit, on the introduction of tractors, particularly suitable in this flat country, on draining and land reclamation, which has made great progress since the building of the Seyhan dam. Mersin, which was little more than a village at the turn of the century, has become a busy port with a large oil refinery. The much better harbour of Iskenderun has been improved as a supply base for the Turkish Third (Eastern) Army, and to serve traffic with Persia. A pipeline has been built from the Turkish oilfield near Diyarbakır to the Gulf of Iskenderun. It has been followed by a steel mill, while Adana has become an important textile centre. Today the three provinces of İçel/Mersin, Adana and Hatay have a population of some two million, of whom 300,000 live in Adana, Turkey's fourth largest city. In addition, tens of thousands of migrant workers from the plateau come down every year to help in the cotton harvest. But, apart from businessmen and American airmen stationed at the large base near Adana, most foreigners probably go to Cilicia only on their way to Antioch and elsewhere in south-eastern Turkey. As they go through they may wish to see the Hittite remains in the Adana museum, crane their necks to admire the relief of a Hittite king in a cliff above the Ceyhan river (near Misis) and make a detour to visit the castles of Namrun (south of the Cilician Gates), Yılankale (Snake Castle) and Kızlar Kalesi (Maidens' Castle) near Misis, and Toprakkale (Earth Castle) east of the Ceyhan. These castles have a colourful history, usually starting with the Byzantines and going on with Armenians, Latins and Turks. The main Armenian stronghold in Cilicia was at Sis near Kozan (some fifty miles north-east of Adana) and in the castle of Feke, even deeper in the Taurus mountains. Both castles held out until 1375, when they were reduced by the Egyptian Mamluks.

Splendid crusader castles abound in the province of Hatay – the coastal Rock of Roissel, south of Arsuz; the castles of Bağras (near the pass of Belen, between Iskenderun and Antakya/Antioch), of Cursat (Kuseyir), some ten miles south of Antioch; of Trapessac (near Kırıkhan) and Sultankale (Sultan's Castle), both north-east of Antioch. They and the citadel of Antakya itself bear witness to the efforts of the crusaders to safeguard

their principality of Antioch, which they wrested from the
Seljuk Turks in 1098 and finally lost to the Mamluks in 1268.
Of the earlier golden age of the province in Hellenistic and
Roman times very little is left. The main cities, Antakya/
Antioch and Iskenderun/Alexandretta, as well as the new deserted Seleucia Pieria (south of Samandağ, near the mouth of
the Asi/Orontes) were founded by Alexander or his successors.
Antakya, the picturesque capital of the province, has a Roman
bridge on the Orontes, much-restored Hellenistic walls (whose
length of over twenty miles gives an idea of the immense metropolis which they enclosed) and above all the splendid Roman
mosaics in the museum. The Christian past of the city is represented by the Crusaders' church of St Peter, leading to the
cave where the first Christians met, and by the mediaeval
church which has now become the mosque of Habip Neccar.
Of the main pagan sanctuary, the temple of Apollo at Daphne
(Harbiye), nothing is left, but the gardens and waterfalls there
retain an idyllic charm. Seleucia Pieria, the Seleucids' first
capital which later enjoyed great prosperity as the port of
Antioch, has left us little beyond a Roman gate and traces of
a canal cut by the Romans through solid rock to avert the
danger of flooding. The village of Samandağ on the other side
of the Orontes is being developed into a holiday resort on the
strength both of the archaeological interest and the excellent
sandy beaches in the area.

The 700 or so miles of the Black Sea coast of Anatolia, between the Bosphorus and the Soviet border, have until recently
attracted few tourists. Communications were difficult except
by sea, since the parallel ranges of the North Anatolian mountains (Pontic Alps) cut off the region from the interior, and often
press against the sea, subdividing the coastal strip into isolated
segments. There are, it is true, coastal plains – at the mouth of
the main rivers (the Sakarya, Kızılırmak and Yeşilırmak) – but
none of these compares in size with plains on the western and
southern coasts. The climate is less certain: it is everywhere

temperate with mean annual temperatures of 13 to 14°C (as against 20°C in Anamur on the south coast), and a range of 6 to 23°C (while on the other side of the mountains Karaköse has a recorded range of -43 to $+40$°C), but rainfall is heavy as the mountains catch the wet northern winds. Rize, on the eastern Black Sea coast, is Turkey's wettest province with an annual rainfall approaching one hundred inches. True, Samsun in the centre has less than a third of this, but rainfall is everywhere heavier than in Istanbul, and the coast, green with forests, orchards and fields, is often swathed in mists. Since, except at places like Trabzon (Trebizond) and Sinop, history has touched it lightly, the Black Sea coast should be visited rather for its memorable views of sea and mountain, for pleasant temperate summers, for fishing in the sea and the numerous trout streams, and in order to get acquainted with its people – the hard-working proverbially irascible Lazes, some 40,000 of whom retain their original Caucasian tongue.

Most of the cities from Ereğli (Heracleia) to Trabzon and beyond into the Soviet Union, were founded by Greek colonists, and visited by Greek sailors and merchants, archetypally represented by Jason who won the Golden Fleece from Colchis (in the country of the Lazes). In addition to its timber, nuts and fruit (the word cherry is derived from Cerasus, modern Giresun, whence Lucullus is said to have introduced this fruit to Rome), the Black Sea coast traded in the minerals found in abundance in the mountains which line it. Copper, lead and manganese are still being mined: the famous silver mines which gave to Gümüşhane its name meaning 'Silver House' have been exhausted, but coal is an important newcomer with the Ereğli-Zonguldak field supplying the needs of the whole country.

It is from the shores of the Black Sea that civilisation – Greek civilisation in the first place – spread to the barbarians: local Anatolian people, as well as Cimmerians and Indo-European Scythians in the great plain of south Russia. In early historical times the coast was inhabited by Indo-European Thracians in the west, the rather nondescript Paphlagonians in the centre and the Caucasian people of the Pontus, the ancestors of the Lazes, in the east. Pontus traditionally extended from the mouth of the Halys (Kızılırmak) to that of the Phasis (Rion) rivers, and this isolated fertile strip was drawn into world history when the first Persian empire was formed and Pontus found itself on the route between Persia and the barbarians beyond the Black Sea. Persian and Greek influences met in Pontus, as they did, in different proportions, on the Armenian plateau farther south. And when the Romans first established themselves in Anatolia as the defenders of local Greek kingdoms against the Seleucid dynasty in Syria, they had to face a challenge from the separate world of the Pontus. Mithridates, who tried and failed to stem the Roman advance, was typically a descendant of Persian royal satraps, educated in the Greek city of Sinope. Under the Romans and the early Byzantine emperors the resources of Pontus in timber and minerals continued to be used, and contact was maintained through this area with the Caucasus to the east and southern Russia to the north. In the thirteenth century Genoese traders appeared on the coast of the Black Sea, assuming the role earlier played by the Greeks. The castles which they built to protect their factories survive at Amasra, Giresun, Tirebolu and elsewhere.

After 1071, the Seljuks and their attendant Turcomans quickly took possession of the interior, but they only acquired a proper outlet in the Black Sea in 1194 when they occupied Samsun. The much better harbour of Sinop fell to them at the beginning of the thirteenth century. The Seljuk penetration isolated the Greeks of Trebizond, who had in any case broken loose from Constantinople when the Byzantine capital fell to the Latins. The Greek empire of Trebizond was an isolated Christian state where the dynasty of the Comneni, itself of Caucasian origin, ruled over a mixed population of Greeks, Armenians and miscellaneous Caucasians. It survived until 1461 when Mehmet II, the conqueror of Istanbul, finally put an end to its independence and to that of the remaining Geno-ese colonies. Politically, the empire of the Comneni in Trebi-zond behaved like any other small Anatolian state, mainly concerned to keep off the raiding Turcomans. It was uneasily balanced between Constantinople and Konya, between Konya and the Mongols, between the Ottomans and Tamerlane, and later the Ottomans and the Turcoman chieftain Uzun Hasan (Hasan the Tall), while internally it was torn by feuds between the Byzantine party (known as *scholarii*) and local feudal lords. Its main revenue was derived from trade with Persia, a trade which was largely in the hands of Italian merchants.

After its conquest by Mehmet II, Trabzon and the other cities of the Black Sea retained an important Christian popu-lation, which was reinforced in the nineteenth century by migrations from the interior. The Armenians, extremely num-erous in the area, were finally deported in the Great War, while the Greeks, after failing in their design to recreate a State of Pontus, left in the exchange of populations in 1923. The eastern Black Sea coast also suffered severely from the fighting which accompanied the advance of the Czarist armies to Trebizond and beyond. After the Great War recovery was slow: the frontier with the Soviet Union was sealed, traffic with Persia insignificant and thousands of local people sought employment in Istanbul and other cities away from the area. Trabzon was gradually eclipsed by Samsun, a centre of tobacco cultivation, which also benefited from better communications with the interior, particularly after it was linked by rail to Ankara. Today Samsun has a population of 110,000, against Trabzon's 65,000, while the population of the whole Black Sea region has reached 5 million. The cultivation of tea east of Trabzon, of tobacco round Samsun, the growth of the tradi-tional production of hazel nuts, the development of the Ereğli coalfield and the construction of steel works at Karabük and Ereğli, now provide a reasonable livelihood for the local people.

One popular way of visiting this area is by a slow steamer of the Turkish State Maritime Line, calling at all the ports as far as Hopa near the Soviet border. One can also go by rail to Samsun and Zonguldak, or fly to Samsun and Trabzon. Road communications are improving, although the projected coastal road from Istanbul to the Soviet border will take time to complete.

From Istanbul a hard-surface road leads to the popular summer resort of Şile (said to derive its name from Achilles), which has excellent sandy beaches, including a whole island of sand on which an attractive motel has been built. From Şile a tricky but exciting road follows the coast eastwards to Ağva, a small fishing village at the mouth of a stream, overlooked by wooded slopes. Ağva is becoming known to Turkish holidaymakers in search of a cheap holiday. Others, notably civil servants from Ankara, go to two small resorts on either side of the Ereğli coalfield. These are Akçakoca, which has a steep pebbly beach and ugly little hotels, and Amasra with its beautiful Genoese castle. The Paphlagonian coast (province of Kasta-monu) is still most easily reached by sea, as is Sinop, pic-turesquely situated on the long peninsula which shelters from the north wind the only good harbour on the coast.

Sinop's lack of good communications with the interior explains the rise of the more accessible Samsun, which now has a good artificial harbour. The flat country near Samsun has more in common with the Mediterranean than with the rest of the Black Sea coast, where the slopes of hills and mountains are covered with a patchwork of woods and small fields of maize, and are dotted with wooden houses, often built on piles, and usually surrounded by fruit trees. Samsun is the oldest Turkish city on the coast. It was, therefore, appropriate that Mustafa Kemal Atatürk should have landed here on 19 May 1919 at the start of the Turkish War of Independence, and that he should have gone on to an even more Turkish city – Amasya, situated dramatically in a gorge of the Yeşilırmak river, and surrounded by its celebrated apple orchards. Samsun, Amasya, Çorum and Tokat are full of mosques, built by the Seljuks, local feudal lords or Ottoman Sultans. The people of the Black Sea coast and of its hinterland are known for their attachment to Islam, and this feeling was enlisted by Atatürk in the struggle against the Greeks. Later, when he decided to challenge the traditions of Islam, it was in Kastamonu, one of the most conservative towns of the area, that he first appeared wearing a hat in public and ordered the people to follow his example.

The coast between the mouth of the Yeşilırmak and Trabzon is largely devoted to the cultivation of hazel nuts, whose capital is at Giresun. Then at Trabzon the scenery becomes reminiscent of the Mediterranean. There is tobacco once again and olive trees. The sky is often blue. There is also the most important collection of Christian monuments to be found on the coast.

The old city is set on a flat hill (hence Trapezous, the Table), bounded by deep gorges, and defended by well-preserved mediaeval walls which are largely the work of the Comneni. Inside the walls, the Byzantine domed cathedral has been converted into mosque (Ortahisar Camii). Use as a mosque has also saved the most famous monument of Trabzon, the church of St Sophia, lying by the coast, west of the walled city. St Sophia, now administered as a museum, was built by the Comneni in the thirteenth century and the influence of Seljuk art is visible in some of the carvings. Inside, impressive frescoes are gradually coming to light. However, it is the shape of the building which makes the strongest impression, with its compact elegance characteristic of late Byzantine architecture.

There are other churches in Trabzon, but most of them are in ruins except those which are used as mosques (like St Andrew/Nakip Camii and St Eugenius/Yeni Cuma Camii). One abandoned ruin which has lost little of its grandeur is the monastery of Sumela, built, it seems, under Justinian but restored by the Comneni and thereafter kept in good repair until the departure of the Greeks in 1923. Sumela lies inland from Trabzon on the road which goes on to climb the Pontic Alps by a series of hairpin bends until it reaches the pass of Zigana at a height of 6,600 feet. The monastery is built on a narrow mountain ledge, some 800 feet above the bed of a stream. It is accessible only by a narrow staircase. The large complex of buildings of different dates includes a church built in a grotto. There are some wall paintings dating back to the Comneni. Size and site – the magnitude of the buildings and their resemblance to a deserted eyrie – make a strong impression on the romantic imagination.

But on the whole, in spite of its history and its monuments, Trabzon tends to disappoint. The city has turned its back on the sea, which can only be enjoyed from a distance – from the municipal garden inside the old citadel or the high hill surmounted by a rich Greek merchant's fretwork villa, which the citizens of Trabzon generously presented to Atatürk. The harbour is disfigured by a modern cement factory and there are no waterside cafés or restaurants. However, one can eat reasonably well in restaurants in the new city on the hill, and local fish, which is hardly ever to be found in smaller seaside towns, is well cooked in the Istanbul style. Food and drink are the one relaxation, for the atmosphere is thick with provincial boredom, and the new university on the road to the airport, east of the city, keeps severely to itself.

So after a visit to the monuments, the traveller turns to the countryside – to Sumela, particularly if he intends to go on to Erzurum, to the mineral spring of Kisarna (Caesariane) or to the tea country to the west of Trabzon. Rize, the tea capital is easily reached and makes a good stopping place. There is a seaside hotel and good off-shore bathing. A few looms still produce the celebrated Rize cotton cloth. The shops are remarkably well stocked, witnessing to the prosperity brought by tea. But the pride of Rize are its botanical gardens on a hill overlooking the sea on one side, and a valley dotted with villages and their newly built whitewashed mosques on the other. The mosques, as much as the shops, owe their existence to the cultivation of tea, for local peasants invariably express their thanksgiving for their new prosperity by building new mosques or adding minarets to existing oratories.

East of Rize the mountains crowd in on the sea. The road occasionally turns inland, crosses streams, climbs hills, and is almost everywhere surrounded by the terraces of tea plantations. Above them there is a belt of deciduous forest, gradually giving way to conifers. The extreme south-west of Turkey round Marmaris and the extreme north-east in the crook of the Black Sea, different in their ways, the one bright and clear in the Mediterranean heat, the other lush and misty, present the lover of natural contrasts with the most exciting scenery in Turkey. The province of Rize has the added advantage of being rarely visited by tourists.

At Pazar, one begins to hear the ancient Laz tongue and even Turkish is pronounced with a strong accent, where every 'k' turns into 'ch', and strange vowels break the rules of harmony common to all Turkic tongues. East of Pazar there is a turning into the mountains, leading to the village of Çamlı-hemşin, whose Laz inhabitants are said to speak a dialect unintelligible to anyone else. Natural hot springs provide a less academic attraction. Hopa is a small and uninteresting port connected by road with the interior. This road follows the Çoruh valley to Borçka where there are Muslim Georgians who are akin to but neither understand nor are understood by the Lazes. The wild mountain region beyond Borçka – between Artvin and Erzurum – is full of ruined Georgian churches in the valleys of the Çoruh and of its many tributaries. During the Middle Ages this region was known as the principality of Tao and was ruled by autonomous Georgian princes. The churches and monasteries which survive belong to the heyday of these princes before the appearance of the Seljuk Turks (eighth-eleventh centuries). Lake Tortum, with the highest waterfall in Turkey, lies on the road from Hopa to Erzurum.

But to return to the coast. From Hopa a short but difficult road goes on to the village of Sarp, divided by a stream into Turkish and Soviet sectors. No one, not even the local inhabitants, is allowed to cross the frontier, which on the Soviet side is protected by the usual array of fortifications and searchlights with a ploughed-up strip of land to register footprints. On the Turkish side visitors who wish to bathe from the black pebble beach are warned not to photograph or examine with binoculars this distant edge of the Soviet world, lest the Russians trouble the Turks with another protest about suspiciously-behaving foreigners. Turkish villagers from Sarp have not seen their neighbours and relatives on the Soviet side of the frontier for more than fifty years and fear in any case that these have been deported. Facing the Soviet wall of exclusion and isolation, they have built on the banks of the frontier stream a mosque with a tall minaret. 'At least we can make sure,' one of them said to me, 'that our brothers, and the infidels too, hear the call to prayer.'

7. The Plateau

'The best thing about Ankara is leaving it', the Turkish poet Yahya Kemal used to say in days when the capital still approximated its original conception of a neat garden city in the middle of the Anatolian plateau. Atatürk's new city (Yeni-şehir) is built in a shallow depression dominated by two hills – the hill of the old walled city of Ankara with its Seljuk citadel, and Çankaya hill, chosen by Atatürk for his presidential palace. While the new city was small and clean, the crisp air of the Anatolian steppe (*bozkır* – grey country) could permeate it. But today the depression has been built up to the surrounding rim of hills and, as more and more houses have been put up to accommodate the capital's one million inhabitants, trees lovingly tended under Atatürk have been uprooted, small suburban villas have been replaced by large blocks of flats and shanty towns have grown on the periphery. The dense conglomeration which has developed is blanketed by thick smog in the winter, fed constantly by central heating appliances burning low-grade coal, while in the summer the heat of the plateau is made worse by the dust rising from innumerable building sites.

Necessity is the magnet that draws most people to Ankara. Central Anatolian peasants are there because of unemployment in their villages and because the shanty towns in which they now live are preferable to the hovels which they have left behind. Three universities attract a large number of students and teachers. Above all, the fact that Ankara is the seat of government and of a highly centralised civil service necessitates the presence of hordes of civil servants, specialists, journalists and, of course, foreign diplomats – all with their attendant porters, cleaners, drivers and other servants. There is in addition a large floating population of petitioners from distant provinces, civil servants trying to secure transfers, businessmen wheedling Ministers for permits or contracts, foreign advisers and others. To cater for them Ankara has a larger range of good and acceptable hotels than any other Turkish city.

Ankara residents make a virtue of necessity. Their city, they say, is more orderly, better run, easier to get about in than Istanbul, just as it is cheaper both absolutely and through the fact that with its more limited range of attractions it is less conducive to extravagance. All of which is true, although it does not make a pleasure out of the contemplation of a dusty concrete wall. But there are also genuine compensations: a good ballet, a creditable opera and a reasonable symphony orchestra, TV, three broadcasting channels and in some ways a more cosmopolitan intellectual society than in Istanbul, since in Ankara foreign diplomats, lecturers and advisers mingle with westernised Turkish officials, dons, producers and artists. There are good restaurants, but few satisfactory *meyhanes* (pubs), so that drinking outside the interminable round of cocktail parties is done largely in chilling hotel bars.

There are also historical monuments: the castle surrounded by its double wall – partly Byzantine, largely Seljuk, a number of early mosques, and for classicists the famous Monumentum Ancyranum. This temple, dedicated to the cult of Augustus and of Rome, has the longest known Latin inscription (with a Greek translation). The site was originally used for the worship of a Phrygian deity, for Ankara (Ancyra) was at first a Phrygian settlement, before being conquered by the Gauls and becoming the centre of Galatia. The fact that a language akin to their ancestral tongue was at one time spoken in the district tends to excite visiting Welshmen, but the Gauls have left almost no trace of their occupation of this or any other site in Turkey. As usual, the town did well under the Romans when peaceful conditions allowed it to benefit from its position on a trade route across the plateau. In Byzantine and Seljuk times it served as a regional stronghold, but since it is surrounded by agriculturally poor land it did not enjoy much prosperity until the introduction of the long-haired angora goat. In the eighteenth and nineteenth centuries, trade in mohair, which was largely in Armenian hands, allowed Ankara to support a population of some 50,000. However, European competition and the successful acclimatisation of the angora goat in South Africa impoverished Ankara by the beginning of this century. Atatürk chose it as the headquarters of his national resistance movement because it was linked by rail to Istanbul, while lying just beyond the reach of his enemies. He then retained it as a capital partly because he distrusted Istanbul, but largely because he felt that since Turkey was more or less reduced to Anatolia it should be governed from within this vast peninsula. The central position of Ankara has since been reinforced by new roads and railways which radiate from it. These have also made it easier to escape from the city, which particularly in the high summer is deserted by all who can find an excuse to move to the cooler climate of Istanbul. Good communications and the existence of numerous hotels also make Ankara a convenient centre for an exploration of the plateau. There are still comparatively few motor cars in Turkey and those that exist are concentrated in the two main cities. The country roads are therefore all but empty of traffic (with the exception of the murderous Istanbul-Ankara highway), and the visitor with a motor car can see most of the plateau in speed and comfort.

Before setting out, the traveller interested in archaeology will visit the Hittite museum in Ankara. It has a rich and beautifully arranged collection exhibited in a restored early

given 40 martyrs to the Christian faith, Sebaste was in Byzantine times an important Armenian political centre. Turks appeared on the scene some time before the fateful battle of Malazgirt in 1071. After it, Sivas became the capital of the Muslim Danişment Emirs, before coming under the direct rule of the Sultans of Konya. Soon afterwards it was captured by the Mongols, one of whose governors, Eretna, established a local dynasty which held sway until the emergence in 1378 of one Kadı (Judge) Burhanettin. Burhanettin's principality became the paramount power in central Anatolia before falling prey to the nomad Turcomans. Order and prosperity were restored by the Ottomans, but Sivas was in the meantime devastated by Tamerlane. Of the three main architectural monuments, the aptly-named Great Mosque goes back to the Danişment Emirs, the ruined hospital and medical school (Şifaiye Medresesi) bears witness to the enlightenment of thirteenth-century Seljuk Sultans, and the superb front of the Çifte Minare Medresesi, whose sculptured portal is framed by two elegant minarets, is attributed to an early Mongol Governor. However, to most Turks today the most evocative building in Sivas is the hall in which Atatürk assembled his second resistance congress in Anatolia in September 1919. It was this congress which gave him his first political title, that of 'Chairman of the Committee Representing the Congress'. The clumsy wording concealed the reality of the leadership of the nationalist movement, but it served its purpose until the spring of the following year when Atatürk was elected Chairman of the Grand National Assembly in Ankara. Sivas lost its Armenian inhabitants in the Great War, and its population in 1937 was under 40,000. Since then it has quadrupled as a result of Atatürk's railway which linked it with Ankara, Samsun, Malatya and Erzincan, and then of the beginnings of industrialisation.

The railway provides the easiest access to the small town of Divriği to the south-east. A centre of Paulician heretics in Byzantine times, when it was called Tephrike, this town has a lovely Seljuk mosque and hospital, famous for the baroque extravagance of the sculptured main portal. The most important iron mines in the country are situated in the vicinity.

The road east from Sivas crosses the watershed between the Kızılırmak and the Euphrates. Erzincan lies in a narrow and fertile valley of the northern arm of the Euphrates, known as Karasu (Black Water). Under the Seljuks and the Mongols who destroyed Seljuk power in 1243 at nearby Kösedağ, Erzincan was the most populous of all the Armenian cities. However, a series of earthquakes, up to and including the disastrous one of 1939, have left few important monuments standing in the small modern town. From Erzincan the road and railway follow the Karasu valley before climbing to the plateau of Erzurum.

Erzurum, lying at an altitude of some 6,000 feet and surrounded by mountains, has always been an important fortress, held by Armenians, Byzantines (who called it Theodosiopolis), Arabs (who knew it as Kalikala) and of course Turks. Its present name, which became current under the Seljuks, was transferred from a nearby town called Erzan. The Ottomans acquired Erzurum only in 1515 after they had defeated the Persians, or rather the Shiah Turcomans of Persia. In the nineteenth century Erzurum became the main Ottoman fortress against the Russians, who occupied it three times. The last occasion was in the Great War, and when the Russians withdrew after the Revolution, Erzurum became the main centre where Turkish troops regrouped in preparation for the War of Independence. The local commander, a staunch nationalist called Kâzım Karabekir, helped Atatürk to organise his first resistance congress in the town. And while Atatürk was in Ankara directing the fight against the Greeks, Karabekir attacked and defeated the nationalist Armenian Republic, formed after the Russian Revolution, and secured the return to Turkey of the districts of Kars, Ardahan and Artvin, which the Russians had ruled since 1878. Erzurum remains today an important military base, while a new university is trying to inject scientific methods into stock-breeding which provides the live-lihood and could make the fortunes of the inhabitants of the high plateau. In spite of its embattled past, symbolised by its citadel which goes back to the Emperor Theodosius in the fifth century, Erzurum has preserved its Seljuk Great Mosque and Coranic college, as well as an Ottoman mosque attributed to the famous Sinan.

A mountain ridge separates Erzurum from the plain of Pasin-ler and the basin of the Aras (Araxes) river which, after form-ing the frontier between Turkey and Russia and Russia and Persia, flows into the Caspian. At Horasan on the Aras the road divides. The turning north-west leads to Sarıkamış, where in 1914 the Young Turk leader Enver Paşa sacrificed a whole army in an unplanned winter assault on the Russian positions. The road goes on to the frontier city of Kars, famous in the annals both of Armenian dynasties and of Russo-Turkish wars, and still bearing the traces of its occupation by the Russians between 1877 and 1920. The Soviet frontier – and the only recognised crossing between the two countries – is 50 miles away. The frontier is formed here by a tributary of the Aras, called Arpa-çay (Barley River). In a gorge of the Arpaçay, on the Turkish side of the frontier, lie the ruins of the dead city of Ani. In 961 Ani became the capital of the Armenian Bagratid dynasty; in 1045 it fell to the Byzantines, only to pass to the Seljuks some 20 years later. The ruined Armenian churches – and also the Seljuk monuments – of Ani were all built between the tenth century and the fourteenth century, when the city was abandoned by its inhabitants. The site, fortified by nature and strewn with majestic ruins, lying at the edge of an impenetrable frontier, has a strong romantic appeal. It also provides a good illustration of the Armenian contribution to the development of architecture. Armenian influence on Seljuk art – for example on the polygonal or round mausoleum, known as *kümbet* – is obvious, while the resemblance of the Armenian tall blind arch to Gothic forms raises the possibility of the transmission of

Armenian architectural ideas through the Crusader principalities of the Levant.

The southern fork from Horasan, leading to Persia, is of less interest, the ruined palace and mosque of Ishak Paşa (seventeenth century) near Doğubeyazit being the main architectural monument of note. Doğubeyazit is the starting point of mountaineering expeditions to the 17,000-foot high Mount Ararat (Ağrı Dağı). The ascent has often been made in modern times, but no amount of evidence can disprove reports that remains of Noah's Ark lie buried under the mountain snow. To the south of Ararat, the deep valley of the Aras near Iğdır has an unexpectedly tropical climate allowing the cultivation of rice.

Another frequently visited Armenian site in Turkey is the ruined church of the Holy Cross on the island of Ahtamar, near Gevaş on the southern shore of the salt and dead lake of Van, lying at an altitude of over 5,000 feet. The town of Van can be reached by a long train journey from Ankara to Tatvan and thence by ferry, or by a quick flight. It is the centre of an enclosed basin, almost a separate world, which was the home of the civilisation of Urartu (eleventh-sixth centuries B.C.). From its limestone cliff the citadel of Van, rich in Urartic and other inscriptions, dominates the old city, which before its capture by the Seljuks was the capital of the mediaeval Armenian kingdom of Vaspurakan. Van preserved its Armenian connection until 1915, when an uprising in the rear of Turkish troops fighting the Russians led to the deportation of all Armenians from eastern Anatolia.

Van and its surroundings also occupy an important place in Turkish history : Malazgirt, where at one blow the Seljuks won mastery over the Anatolian plateau, lies not far from the northern shores of the lake, from which it is separated by the extinct volcano of Süphan Dağı (over 13,000 feet high). Even before the Seljuks, Malazgirt was a Muslim enclave in Christian Armenia, and its Emirs are credited with the foundation, on the

northern shore of the lake, of the town of Ahlat, famous for
its many early Turkish mausolea.

Today the Armenians have been replaced largely by their
historic enemies, the Muslim Kurds, thought to be descendants
of the Medes. It is impossible to say how many Kurds there are
in Turkey, how many consider themselves Turkish, while speaking their distinct Iranian language, and how many have been
completely assimilated. The 1960 census showed some
2,000,000 Kurdish-speakers in Turkey. This is probably an
underestimate, and some authorities believe that nearly
4,000,000 people in eastern and south-eastern Anatolia –
roughly south of Erzincan and Erzurum, and east of the Kızılırmak and Ceyhan river basins – speak Kurdish dialects. One of
them, Zaza, spoken in the Tunceli (Dersim) mountains, south
of Erzincan, differs substantially from the others.

The Kurds, some of whom are nomadic to this day, have
always been known as country people, if not country bump-
kins, and in the towns of south-eastern Turkey Arabic is spoken
more commonly than Kurdish. However, these town Arabs had
traditionally given their allegiance to the Ottoman State, which
they represented and to whose civil hierarchy they gave many
recruits. Links with the Turkish establishment have survived
under the Republic and have favoured the gradual assimilation
of urban Arabs into Turkish society.

South-eastern Turkey, or upper Mesopotamia – south of the
Eastern Taurus and east of the Amanos mountains – is a region
apart, both geographically and historically. In this border area
Semitic Assyrians met Indo-European Hittites, producing the
later hybrid Hittite culture. Here too Greek and Semite met in
Seleucid Syria. After the triumph of Christianity, the majority
of those who spoke the Semitic Syriac tongue adopted hetero-
dox teachings – those of the Nestorians, Monophysites (Jacobites) and Monotheletes. In the seventh century the Arabs
quickly swept to the Taurus and beyond. In the ninth-tenth
centuries, the resurgence of Byzantine power, often working

through the Armenians, affected only part of the area – roughly the upper Euphrates, and not the upper Tigris.

Diyarbakır (Amida), which had figured largely in the wars between Rome and the Persians, was not saved from the Arab flood by its famous black walls. Captured by the Arabs probably as early as 638, it has stayed in Muslim hands almost continuously ever since, the Arab Caliphs being followed by the local Kurdish Marwanid dynasty, then by the Seljuks, Turcomans, and finally by the Ottomans. The black walls are still the main tourist attraction of the city. Built originally by the Byzantines, they were repaired and reinforced by successive Muslim rulers. The walls extend for some four miles, and with the citadel at their north-eastern corner, their numerous bastions and towers, their monumental gates and tunnels, they are as perfect an example as can be found of mediaeval city fortifications. They enclose a large number of mosques and *medreses*, including the Seljuk Great Mosque. Today Diyarbakır has a population of over 100,000. It has a large air base and a university, named after a local son, Ziya Gökalp, a political thinker of Kurdish or partly Kurdish origin who was the leading theoretician of Turkish nationalism. He thus represents the role of Diyarbakır in spreading Turkish influence through the nationally-mixed area of the south-east.

To the south-east of Diyarbakır, the provincial capital of Mardin was an important Arab frontier centre until its capture by the Seljuks. The main historical buildings in the city (the Great Mosque and two *medreses*) go back to the Seljuks and to the Turcoman Emirs who succeeded them. The spiritual leader of the small surviving community of Arabic-speaking Jacobite (Monophysite) Syrians resides in the nearby monastery of Bey-tülza'feran.

Between Diyarbakır and Siirt to the east, lies Turkey's main oilfield – round Raman, Garzan and Batman. Oil and electric power – from the huge Keban dam on the Euphrates, east of Malatya – may well be the main contribution of the south-east to the welfare of Turkey. Copper is mined at Ergani, between Diyarbakır and Elazig to the north-east, and the richest chrome deposits in Turkey are at nearby Güleman. The ancient tradition of eastern Anatolia is thus being perpetuated, for Assyrian traders first went to Cappadocia, and Assyrian armies occupied Milid (Malatya) to obtain minerals – copper, silver and iron; and it was under the Hittites that the technique of iron-working was first mastered and that the people of Anatolia became renowned for iron-smelting.

The western part of upper Mesopotamia (known to the Arabs as Diyar Mudar) has had a more varied history. After the destruction of the Hittite kingdom of the plateau, it was ruled by independent Hittite princes (the so-called Syro-Hittites), one of whose capitals was at Karkamış (Carchemish) on the Euphrates (near the village of Cerablus, on the Turkish side of the frontier with Syria, south-east of Gaziantep). The highlands overlooking Diyar Mudar and those separating it from the basin of the Ceyhan are particularly rich in late Hittite antiquities. The most interesting remains of this culture, including the famous bilingual inscription in Hittite and in Phoenician, are at Karatepe, overlooking the Ceyhan river. Malatya (near the Hittite Milid and the classical Melitene) has yielded a whole series of Hittite reliefs, and a well-known statue of a lion.

The Hittites were succeeded by Assyrians, Persians and, after Alexander's conquests, by Greek Seleucids. Because of the proximity of the Seleucid capital of Antioch, Greek cultural influence was strong. Possibly the best-preserved group of Hellenistic statues has been found on the top of the 7,000-foot high Nemrut Dağı, north-east of Adıyaman. A 30-foot tall statue represents the local king, Antiochus I of Commagene, surrounded by local gods. A city in Commagene, Samosata (the modern Samsat, on the Euphrates, south-east of Adıyaman) was the birthplace of the satirical writer Lucian (born c. A.D. 125), the author of the *Dialogues of the Gods*, of whom it has been said : 'A Semite by race but not by education, a subject of Rome but not a Roman,

a writer of Greek but not a Greek by birth, he was by circum-
stances singularly freed from every tie, prepossession or pre-
judice which might have stood at all in the way of his deriving
the largest possible amount of amusement out of the world.'

Christianity must also have spread from Antioch. According
to tradition, St Luke, a native of Antioch, painted a likeness of
Christ on a linen cloth, and sent it to Abgar (or Abkar, a dynastic name), king of Edessa (Urfa, Arabic Al-Ruha, the capital of
a province known in classical times as Osrhoene). This was the
famous relic, known as *mandylion*, which was carried in
triumph to Constantinople in 994, may then have found its way
to the West, and bears significant similarities to the famous
Holy Shroud of Turin. The tenth century was a period of
Byzantine revival. Conquered by the Arabs in the seventh century, Maraş (the Hittite Marqasi), Malatya (Melitene) and Urfa
(Edessa) all enjoyed a Christian interlude – under the Byzantines, Armenian lords and the short-lived County of Edessa
(1098-1146). The area reverted to Islam by the exertions of
Turkish and Kurdish commanders, including the great Saladin
(Salâhattin), passing finally to the Ottomans in 1515-16, when
Sultan Selim I defeated the Egyptian Mamluks and their allies,
the Turcoman Dülgadır.

Today the most important and the most purely Turkish city
of the south-east is Gaziantep. Earlier known simply as Antep
(Arabic Ayntab), it received the title Gazi (victorious warrior
for the faith) in recognition of the valiant resistance which it
put up against the French in a ten-month-long siege in 1920.
Under the Republic the city prospered, largely at the expense
of Aleppo (which used to be the commercial capital of the
whole area but was now cut off behind the Syrian frontier), and
partly thanks to the economic potential of its fertile plain,
famous as the centre of the production of pistachios. Its citizens
are known as energetic and lively, and their consumption of a
particularly fiery brand of *rakı* is said to be the highest in the
country. Gaziantep is also bound to benefit from the comple-

tion of the CENTO Highway, on which it lies, and which will provide the main route from the Mediterranean to Persia.

Urfa, farther east, is more notable for its associations than for its sights. The *mandylion* has gone, and so have the Christians, whether local or Latin. But Urfa does retain one memorial of the reign of the Abgars. This is the Fish Pond of Abraham, originally, it seems, a pagan sanctuary where sacred fish were bred, but now incorporated into the Muslim version of the Biblical tradition. The Fish Pond is today appropriately in the grounds of a Muslim *medrese*. Paganism, the Bible and Islam meet also in Harran (between Urfa and the Syrian frontier), now a collection of cone-shaped mud huts near the ruins of Muslim mosques, other public buildings and fortifications, spanning six centuries, from the seventh to the thirteenth, but once the city to which Abraham moved from Ur of the Chaldees (in Iraq), and where he lived until he was 75 (Gen. 11.31; 12.4). In spite of this, Harran remained a stronghold of paganism until after the Muslim conquest.

Thus the struggle between paganism and monotheism was fought in the territory of Turkey both before and after the rise of Christianity, in whose history Turkey also occupies an important place. Our moral consciousness was born of that struggle, just as our modern world was largely fashioned in the subsequent clash between the two great monotheistic religions of Christianity and Islam. The decline of Turkey in late Ottoman times and its isolation in the opening years of the Republic have tended to obscure the country's central place in the history of civilisation – our Graeco-Roman, Judaeo-Christian European civilisation, which is now the one civilisation in the world, as Atatürk realised when he shaped the new Turkish national state. Today, when in pursuance of Atatürk's ideals Turkey is becoming part of the European commonwealth, it is easier to realise that we are witnessing a process not of integration but of re-integration. This realisation, this awareness of the rich patrimony of Turkey, should help its citizens raise

their sights above the immediate objects of economic development and technological growth, whose attainment could otherwise impoverish instead of enriching them. So too, the European traveller whose interest is not limited to prices and facilities will find, as he discovers this new, beautiful and promising
land, that he is also rediscovering his own roots.

Bibliography

There are three recent one-volume introductions to Turkey: Andrew Mango, *Turkey*, 1968; Gwyn Williams, *Turkey*, 1967; and G. L. Lewis, *Turkey*, 3rd ed., 1965. Officials may be able to acquire a free copy of *Facts about Turkey*, published in 1972 by the State Information Organisation, Ankara. G. L. Lewis has written *Teach Yourself Turkish*, 1953, and the more extensive *Turkish Grammar*, 1967. The best one-volume dictionary is the *Concise Oxford Turkish Dictionary* (Turkish–English and English–Turkish), ed. A. D. Alderson and Fahir Iz, 1959.

For the history of modern Turkey consult Bernard Lewis, *The Emergence of Modern Turkey*, 1961, and Lord Kinross, *Atatürk: The Rebirth of a Nation*, 1964. An individual interpretation of recent events, as well as of the character of the country and of the people, will be found in David Hotham's *The Turks*, 1972.

There are several guide books. *Nagel's Encyclopedia-Guide*, 1968, is the most recent. There are simpler guide books recently published in the Fodor and Gateway series. The geography of Turkey is discussed in scientific detail in J. C. Dewdney's *Turkey*, 1971. Rich and cultured readers are directed to *Treasures of Turkey* in the Skira series, 1966. To put flesh on the bare bones of the monuments, recourse should be had to Raphaela Lewis, *Everyday Life in Ottoman Turkey*, 1971. Travellers interested in classical archaeology must acquire George E. Bean's *Aegean Turkey*, 1966, *Turkey's Southern Shore*, 1968, and *Turkey beyond the Maeander*, 1971; and Ekrem Akurgal's *Ancient Civilizations and Ruins of Turkey*, 1970.

Classical sites in Turkey are also the chief subject of Freya Stark in *Ionia: A Quest*, 1954, *The Lycian Shore*, 1956 and *Alexander's Path*, 1958.

Among other post-war travel writers, Lord Kinross has described the Turkish plateau and mountain country in *Within the Taurus*, 3rd impr., 1970, and the coasts in *Europa Minor*, 1956. Michael Pereira has given an account of a journey through southern Turkey in *Mountains and A Shore*, 1966, of travels in the north-east in *East of Trebizond*, 1971, and of his stay in Istanbul in *Istanbul: Aspects of a City*, 1968. There is an earlier impressionistic account in R. Liddell, *Byzantium and Constantinople*, 1956. However, there is no straight factual English guide book to Istanbul. Readers who know French should consult E. Mamboury, *Istanbul touristique*, Istanbul, 1951.

Mountaineers will be interested in Denis Hill, *My Travels in Turkey*, 1964; railway enthusiasts will be fascinated by George Behrend and Vincent Kelly, *Yataklı Vagon: Turkish Steam Travel*, 1968. The Shell Company has recently issued a helpful *Motorist Guide to Turkey* (no date).

There are pleasing accounts of recent journeys in R. P. Lister, *Turkey Observed*, 1967; Stowers Johnson, *Turkish Panorama*, 1968; and Bernard Newman, *Turkey and the Turks*, 1968.

Official booklets on Turkey (such as *Your Holiday in Turkey*, Ankara, 1963) as well as maps, can be obtained from the Turkish Tourist Offices in London and elsewhere. Local associations also sometimes make brave attempts to produce English guide-books, e.g. *Antalya for the Tourist*, prepared by 'The Tourist Society for Introducing Antalya' (no date).

Index